THE VICTORIAN HOUSEHOLD

BY THE SAME AUTHOR

Published by John Murray
John Gibson Lockhart
Their First Ten Years
Young Victorians
Elizabeth Rigby, Lady Eastlake

Published by W. & R. Chambers
The Scots Household in the
Eighteenth Century
Saint Mungo's Bairns. The Story of
Glasgow for Children
On Tintock Tap and other Fairy Tales

MARION LOCHHEAD

The Victorian Household

JOHN MURRAY

ALBEMARLE STREET LONDON

To
OSYTH

© Marion Lochhead 1964

Printed in Great Britain
by Cox & Wyman Ltd London,
Fakenham and Reading

Foreword

The Victorian Household is the almost inevitable sequel to *Young Victorians* which in turn followed *Their First Ten Years*. The spell of the last century is not easily broken, and its domestic history alone provides – to borrow the words of one of its greatest authors – 'a difficult study of no inconsiderable magnitude'. Both the difficulties and the magnitude make selection necessary, which must be my apology to any readers who may again in immortal words – 'vish there was more,' or who demand why some famous or favourite house, room or background is not included. A less selective study would easily have become two volumes of Victorian amplitude which, in our expense-haunted day, would be impractical.

This is an attempt at picturing the Victorians at home, rather than at describing the homes themselves in detail, for their own sake; hence the omission of technical matter. The relation between house and owner or tenant, the life lived within the house, the varied and changing pattern of such living have been the theme, and have, I hope made the shape of the narrative.

I am deeply grateful to Sir John Murray for his constant interest and encouragement, and for his help with the illustrations, and to Mrs Osyth Leeston for her stimulating and constructive, almost her creative criticism, especially in the revision of the book. My debt to Dr. William Beattie and his staff of the National Library of Scotland remains cheerfully acknowledged and unpaid. I would also like to acknowledge the help I have received from the London Library.

Contents

Illustrations

Acknowledgements

For courteous permission to quote from certain books in my bibliography I am indebted to the following:

Messrs. Constable for *Mrs Gatty and Mrs Ewing* by Christabel Maxwell

Messrs. Faber & Faber for *With Dearest Love to All* by Mary Reed Bobbitt, to Mrs Sophie Pryor with Messrs. Faber for *Period Piece* by Gwen Raverat and to the Executor of the late Lady Peck with Messrs. Faber for *Home From the Holidays*

Messrs. Heinemann for *Over The Bridge* by Richard Church

Messrs. Laurence Pollinger and the Estate of the late Mrs Frieda Lawrence *Not I But The Wind* and for a verse from *The Complete Poems of D. H. Lawrence*

Messrs. Macmillan & Co. and Mr. George L. Saintsbury for *Notes On A Cellar Book*

Messrs. Methuen & Co. and Mr. Ernest Shepard for *Drawn From Memory* and *Drawn from Life*

The Oxford University Press for *A London Family* by M. V. Hughes, *Three Houses* by Angela Thirkell, *Unfinished Autobiography* by H. A. L. Fisher

Miss Read and Messrs. Michael Joseph for *Miss Clare Remembers*

The Rt. Hon. Thomas Johnston, P.C., for *A History of the Working Classes in Scotland*

Messrs. Routledge & Kegan Paul Ltd., Mr. Angus McLellan and Mr. John Lorne Campbell for *The Furrow Behind Me*

Messrs. Sheed & Ward and Miss Maisie Ward (Mrs Sheed) for *The Wilfred Wards and the Transition*

Victorian Houses

Domestic history ranges from castle to cottage through all the houses in between, which have never been more varied than in the Victorian era; for then came the expansion of the middle class, the growth of wealth, the development of towns, and all these together meant an intricacy of domestic life. All through the centuries men have built dwellings for shelter or defence, and sooner or later women have begun to decorate them. The need for shelter led to a desire for comfort, the need for defence became a demand for privacy and also for display. When the householder had no longer to maintain his fortifications he continued to keep up appearances. The walls that were stout enough to keep out both elements and enemies were more and more adorned, and the more and finer furniture a man had the more likely he was to be respected.

The fortified castle began to yield to the mansion, the clay-and-wattle hut became the stone cottage, and the country dwelling influenced that in town; the rich town house copied the manor, the surburban villa the cottage. The domestic pattern of the countryside did not greatly change between the seventeenth and the nineteenth century. In the eighteenth century the great house reached its zenith enriched by treasures from the grand tour, by paintings and a library. Beneath that a long scale led from the smaller country house and manor through the rectory or vicarage and comfortable country-town house to farmhouses and the larger cottages, down to the labourer's small cottage. In town there was the same gradation from the hereditary mansions or palaces of the great titled families down through varying degrees of wealth and elegance among the minor gentry, the upper-class and professional groups, the rich merchants to the middle- and lower-middle-class villas, the thin terrace houses, the house above the shop, down, down to the poor quarters, the slums which lay in the depth of squalor.

The nineteenth century may claim to have invented one form of dwelling in London: the flat (as distinct from chambers in the Temple or Inns of Court); the blocks of flats, often called mansions, and usually of a certain gentility; but Edinburgh had known them for generations in those tall 'lands' in the Old Town where poor folk might live in the attics, a douce lawyer on one of the middle floors, a countess on the ground flat; and in the New Town blocks of flats were built, as well as the stately Georgian mansions in squares and places and circuses.

The middle-class house has a particular interest from its variety and from the middle-class habit of copying its betters. There is a continual descent of fashion and grandeur. The mansion has its suite of reception-rooms: drawing-rooms, music-room, picture-gallery, ballroom: the prosperous town house has its front and back drawing-room, the smaller one a best parlour, and every man of any social pretensions has, as Dickens remarked, some little back room or other which he will call his study.

The aristocratic and upper-middle-class house had three provinces: that of the owners and their guests, that of the children with nurse or governess, in nursery or schoolroom, and that of the servants (which in turn had its divisions). Even in the smallest house there was a border-line between parlour and kitchen, for it was a poor house indeed that did not employ at least a scrap of a servant-girl, Charley or the Marchioness. This division or pattern was made possible by low wages, which might range from £18 to £20 or £22 a year for cook or nurse, down through £10 to £12 for a housemaid, to £6 for 'a girl' or 'tweeny' who helped both cook and housemaid. The great house had an army of servants; hierarchy is the better word, for there was a grading as strict as that of the peerage (stricter, indeed, for viscounts and barons might mingle easily with earls and dukes, and even commoners be part of the great world; the laws of precedence could be relaxed in private). From housekeeper and butler, lady's maid and valet, through cook and housemaids, down to tweeny and boot-boy the ladder was exactly ranged. One of the most deeply-felt marks of sudden poverty was to have to reduce one's staff; only in the depths were there no servants at all. In the great house the division between upper and lower servants was precise; they might all dine together in the hall, the lower standing respectfully by their chairs until the upper had seated themselves; but the latter withdrew, in procession, after the joint had been carved and served, to eat their pudding and cheese in the housekeeper's room, sometimes known as Pug's Parlour. Within this upper class too, there were sub-divisions, as in the peerage. The law of precedence was strict. The Duchess's maid sat above that of the baronet's lady.

Snobbery, the most comical of human weaknesses, flourished in the Victorian age. Wealth and gentility were both esteemed, and both must be made evident to the world. Hence the servants, hence, too, the imitation of grandeur, the constant building, the accumulation of furnishings and trimmings (which, of course, made servants more than ever necessary), the insistence on taste. It has been truly said that the Victorians did not lack taste; the trouble was that they had so much of it, and so much of that was bad.

'The building activity of nineteenth-century Britain is almost unbelievable,' John Gloag declares in his *Home Life in History*; finding it 'a period of confusion and vulgarity' with the general taste becoming 'first romantic and then coarse', pretentious rather than magnificent, with elegance giving way to respectability. 'Taste had thickened'; there was a love of effect – that essentially vulgar affection – with a misguided effort towards the romantic; the imitative grew at the expense of the creative spirit. There was a revolt against the simplicity and elegance of Queen Anne and the richer, but still restrained, Georgian and Regency styles; in architecture and furniture, as well as in dress, there must be ornament, the more the better. It was a sign and proof of wealth, and it became a sign also of taste tinged with moral earnestness. Ruskin promulgated the Gothic:

'It is the glory of Gothic architecture that it can do anything' – and so a glorious art was degraded; the Gothic touch added in window arches, doorways, porches and what-have-you to houses already built; Gothic ornament lavished upon the rooms.

'Wherever you can rest, there decorate,' decreed Ruskin.

The authors of *Victorian Furniture* (R. W. Symonds and B. B. Whinneray) quote an ecstatic decription of a Gothic drawing-room from J. C. Loudon's *Encyclopaedia of Cottage, Farm, and Villa Architecture*, and give the illustration:

'Every reader, we think must be pleased with it . . . the Gothic pianoforte and music-stool with the Canterbury on the left hand, and the music-stand on the right; the Gothic couch with its foot-stool; the two beautiful chairs; and, finally, the firescreen.'

The modern reader's attitude is likely to be one of stunned incredulity. 'I don't believe it' – that this soaring piano, this solemn couch were really created, used and cherished; yet the evidence of sight is there.

Gothic had religious undertones which were much appreciated; but it was not the only style to be copied: the Elizabethan was equally popular, equally rich, and equally fantastic. The Warwick-shire school of carving achieved Elizabethan effects; a sideboard, offered by the county to Queen Victoria was declined; bought by Mrs. Lucy of Charlecote Park, and shown by her to Ruskin, who pronounced it 'worthy of Michelangelo'. The carved panels show boys tending the grapes, corn being reaped, mounds of fish and game. In effect, guests saw their dinner. Another achievement was the Kenilworth buffet which depicted scenes from Scott's novel: Queen Elizabeth arriving at Kenilworth, meeting Amy Robsart, talking with Leicester. Not only every picture but every bit of furniture could be made to tell a story.

The Gothic and medieval influence lasted long and was pro-found. For Pugin it was a *mystique*; for Morris something more of this earth – though still inspired by romance, by his vision of the Middle Ages:

'Our furniture should be good citizens' furniture, solid and well-made . . . and should have nothing about it that is not easily defensible, no monstrosities or extravagancies. . . . Also . . . except for very movable things like chairs, it should not be so very light as to be nearly imponderable; it should be made of timber rather than walking-sticks.'

Of him we shall see more. But it is remarkable how literature influenced nearly everything in Victorian social and domestic life; how possessions must somehow indicate culture as well as wealth. This Gothic or medieval or Elizabethan reminiscence, those senti-mental pictures, emotional and descriptive music, sentimental drawing-room ballads all showed a love of ideas and associations, were evidence of a well-stored mind, of high aspirations.

The house became more and more a form of self-expression or self-advertisement, as the motor-car has become today, and the self-expression could be ruthless. There was less danger of spoiling an old house than a new, for the former held the life of many generations, and could receive tolerantly the modern contributions. Both could merge into some sort of harmony. Sometimes the fine old Sheraton might be banished to the attics or to the housekeeper's room, but more often it lived on in the drawing-room with the new over-carved, over-stuffed furniture, and somehow subdued its vulgarity.

Over-carved because of ostentation, but also, more endearingly, from some half-hidden sense of romance, a misguided love of beauty; over-stuffed because this was increasingly the age of comfort. A few old ladies might still sit, as they had been drilled in their girlhood, upright, on a high chair, their back not touching the chair-back; but although lounging was highly unladylike (only men lounged, in the smoking-room) even the most refined sat back on a cushioned seat or lay on a sofa. Indeed the sofa became very important; the lady of the house rested on it, when alone, and had a sofa table for her work and her book; two guests shared it at a party, and from the sofa was evolved that most intriguing form of seat, the *tête-à-tête* or *sociable* – made for two, in S-shape, so that the couple, leaning back could look at each other face to face, gaze discreetly into each other's eyes and exchange confidences.

The Victorians were domestic. They liked to travel, and the grand tour was still made, in one form or other; increasingly *en famille*, too, and for an extended time, an autumn and winter in Pau or Florence or Rome; the summer holiday in lodgings by the sea became more and more part of the family year in modest households. They also enjoyed concerts, theatres and the opera, and they liked parties, in fact they were addicted to parties. That itself is a domestic pleasure. But more and more the common way of life was at home. The educated classes read a great deal, and the Victorian novel and periodical were planned for long, leisurely evenings at home. They liked music of an easy, tuneful kind, and playing and singing were common accomplishments among the well-bred. They liked round games; and the ladies of the house were much given to needlework, plain and fancy, but especially fancy; some of it exquisite, some deplorable, being the transformation of some useful object into an elaborate freak: the crocheted cigar-case, heavily embroidered and trimmed with tassels, the boxes and baskets covered, padded and adorned in every inch. Both social and domestic life, in the professional and upper-middle classes upwards to the high aristocracy, centred in the drawing-room; in humbler homes, in the parlour with its centre table draped with a plush cover, a lamp in the middle, mamma and the girls sitting round with their needlework, papa reading aloud, or all of them playing cards.

The drawing-room is as much part of the Victorian novel as the bedroom is of a French farce. The setting is more commonly in a house of gentlefolk – squires, clergy, professional gentlemen – than in either a great mansion or a cottage or villa. In this kind of house the drawing-room was the centre (in the greater one, it was only one of a suite of splendid rooms). The children came down from the nursery, well washed and brushed, for an hour of play or reading with mamma; callers were received here, tea was served; guests gathered before and after dinner; there was a party with music.

It was preferably a large room, and in town was usually double, L-shaped, which had its points. People who wanted a quiet talk might withdraw into the back part of the room. It must be fully and elegantly furnished, with an array of chairs and sofas and little tables, and on some of the little tables a variety of ornaments, albums and photographs; a piano with music-cabinet, and, if anyone in the family played the violin, a music-stand; pictures large and small; a china-cabinet, one or two *vitrines* or treasure-tables containing miniatures, little boxes, all sorts of *bibelots*.

In many houses, especially those in the country or a country town a conservatory opened off the drawing-room, a delicious place of blossom and greenery and fragrance; in some town houses it was a small greenhouse, perhaps hardly more than a deep bay window, built out on the landing.

The large Victorian house was distinctly functional; there was a room for every purpose or occupation, for every time of the day. The family descended from their bedrooms (the master of the house had his own dressing-room) to the breakfast-parlour or morning-room. Here the lady of the house might sit with her work or her letters, after she had seen cook and given out stores; here, if there were no schoolroom the children might do their lessons, under mamma's supervision. But we prefer a house in which there is a proper schoolroom with a governess in charge, as well as the nursery for the younger ones. Lunch was served in the dining-room, and the children came down to that; it was their dinner. After lunch, the lady received calls in the drawing-room, or paid them in other drawing-rooms; the evening was spent here, as a rule, but in a country house there was also the library, a more masculine apartment, with heavier furniture, more sombre colours, velvet rather than silk, and leather rather than velvet. The dining-room, too, was heavily furnished, in dark colours, crimson or dark green, with a Turkey carpet, and large, strictly functional furniture: sideboard or buffet, side-tables, dining-table and chairs; no ornamentation or superfluity except on the chimney-piece.

In the country house too there was the smoking-room, for gentlemen did not smoke in the drawing-room. In the library it was permissible; a man could enjoy a cigar over the new book or periodical; in the dining-room, after the ladies had withdrawn, there might be cigars as well as port, but the scrupulous wine-lover might hesitate to spoil his palate and insult the vintage. In the smoking-room a man could let himself go; he might retire upstairs, lay off his evening coat in exchange for a smoking-jacket, put on a smoking-cap (made and embroidered by loving hands) so that neither clothes nor hair might smell of the horrid fumes. There was the billiards-room too (accessible to ladies as well), for in the increasing popularity of country-house parties there must be more games than cards, especially on wet days.

Social habits helped to plan the house and its rooms. It grew more complicated as society in general grew more complex. The eighteenth century had been comparatively static, and people stayed more or less in that station to which it had pleased God to call them; but now they tended to move, upwards for preference. The middle class grew immensely, and fell into many groups or sub-divisions. From medieval times through Tudor and Stuart to the Augustan era it had consisted chiefly of merchants in the town, yeoman and farmers in the country. In the nineteenth century the merchant class alone expanded greatly. It included wholesale trade which for some unfathomable reason ranked higher than retail, the warehouse, export office, business, in the City being more genteel than the shop; shipping management or ownership of mines and factories, and being something in the City or the Stock Exchange. To this class belong the Podsnaps and Dombeys of early and mid-Victorian years, the Forsytes of the latest decades; 'warm' men, most of them, but highly susceptible to financial chills, they found a certain ostentation necessary as proof of their stability.

The house itself moved further and further from its own source of wealth, from the City westwards to certain opulent and dignified, if not superbly aristocratic squares. The Podsnaps and Dombeys furnished richly and gloomily, the Forsytes relaxed a little, permitted themselves or their wives more individual preferences, a closer adherence to fashion.

The professions make their own domestic pattern, nearly always interwoven with that of the minor gentry, as in the case of judges and barristers and the upper layer of solicitors. Doctors advance more rapidly than any other professionals; the apothecary of Jane Austen's society was decidedly middle class – though, to be sure, Mr. Perry was greatly respected. Mr. Gibson in Mrs. Gaskell's *Wives and Daughters*, Trollope's Dr. Thorne, Mrs. Oliphant's Dr. Marjoribanks are all men of substance and dignity, of considerable importance in their respective country towns and countrysides, well content with their position. In London, the fashionable physician lives in his own fashionable quarter, may become titled, and is likely to be received in the great houses in a social as well as a professional way.

In and out of this great middle class, with excursions into the higher and occasional retreats into the lower, wander the authors, artists and musicians, and those former rogues and vagabonds, the actors and actresses. These last reached their social zenith in the nineties, but long before that we find them at home among the gentry. Fanny Kemble and her sister Adelaide Sartoris pay long country-house visits. Browning and Thackeray are fashionable diners-out, Tennyson and Leighton are made peers, Landseer is almost *ami de maison* of Royalty. Morris and Burne-Jones make their own lively and artistic world within the large, prosperous, cultivated upper-middle class.

Most fascinating and most influential of all is the advance of the clergy. The parson had been rising steadily in social rank and importance since the seventeenth century; in the eighteenth century and the Regency he was very often a gentleman in the narrowest snob sense of the word: Henry Tilney and Edmund Bertram are younger sons. Throughout the Victorian age he is, more often than not, the cadet of a county family, presented to the family living, possessed of private means; a product of public school and university, not of any seminary or theological college. The pattern is certainly different in Scotland where the minister might be a son of the laird, was often the son of a minister, and often the son of a poor man, educated at the parish school, proceeding to the university on a bursary, living in poverty through his academic years, and receiving an intense theological training after graduating Master of Arts. The manse in Scotland was, in most cases, either a reproduction of the young minister's boyhood home, or something much above it in comfort and dignity. In England it varied; it could be little better than a cottage, austere and bare, the incumbent living on the edge of poverty – like Mr. Crawley. More often it was comfortable and even elegant, with an air of the country house about it, and reminiscence of college rooms. But always it held its place between the great house and the small, the mansion or manor and the cottage, inclining sometimes to one rather than the other, but open to the householders of both; never absorbed, always apart.

The importance of the Thirty-Second Article of the Church of England cannot be over-stated. A married clergy induced or caused, by physical paternity or by mental inspiration, much of the fiction of the nineteenth century, and the parsonage recurs frequently as setting. The Brontës and Mrs. Ewing were daughters of the vicarage, Trollope's most popular novels were scenes from clerical life; clerical memoirs and biographies abound, and give more clearly than any others a picture of social life within and around the parsonage, above it and below, in social rank.

With this clerical life is closely, inextricably interwoven that of the public schools and universities. Most headmasters were in Holy Orders, and the headmaster's house has more than a whiff of the vicarage atmosphere; conversely many a vicarage is tinged with scholastic or academic hues. Seeing the Head in his own drawing-room was rather like seeing the vicar out of church. Tom Brown was surprised and impressed by the cosiness, the homeliness of the formidable Dr. Arnold's drawing-room, the young Moberlys at Winchester knew very little of a barrier between house and school, the Bensons at Wellington received sixth form boys as guests at Sunday breakfast.

The Oxford and Cambridge dons were the last Anglican churchmen to be bound by celibacy, and when that bond was loosed there was a rush into matrimony and the subsequent house-building, housekeeping and hospitality. Dinners were held not only in the Master's or Dean's or Warden's house (for heads of college had always been permitted to marry) but in a family house complete with nursery. Fortunately, memoirs or biographies by college wives provide entertaining documentary evidence.

The Victorian house, large or small, rich or homely, as seen through contemporary journalism, treatises on taste, advice to housewives, and the like, and through some photographs and illustrations can be almost incredibly ugly or comic.

In fiction and memoirs it becomes delightful, for then it is a home, it is alive and warm, filled with real people and all their talk and activities. In fiction, too, description becomes a mirror both of the setting and background and of the author's own mind and taste. We must use all these sources in a balanced retrospect.

Advice about furnishing may indeed startle us. In *The Young Ladies' Treasure Book* treatment is prescribed for the fireplace. Not only should there be mantelshelves loaded with ornaments, there should be drapery; a valance on the mantelshelf, even curtains for the hearth. A particularly elegant valance was suggested in white velvet, painted with orange-blossoms and finished with a green and white fringe. This would make a suitable wedding gift. Above 'this superb hanging' might be placed amber glasses and a 'peculiarly beautiful' centre-piece, of a large conch shell with a sleeping nymph and a cupid. On another shelf appeared a marble clock and a pair of ornaments.

One artist and architect who took himself and his responsibilities as *arbiter elegantiae* most seriously was Charles L. Eastlake, nephew of Sir Charles Eastlake the President of the Royal Academy and husband of Elizabeth Rigby. He published some *Hints on Household Taste*. He deviates, fairly often, into sense in his advocacy of what is useful and functional, his respect for good workmanship, his insistence on comfort. He has, however, his whimsies and one of them is the chimney-piece. A mere shelf with a clock and perhaps a vase or statuette is too trivial. There must be an overmantel of considerable importance. In the library he suggests a strip of looking-glass, and above that an erection of shelves holding china:

'A little museum may thus be formed and remain a source of lasting beauty to its possessors, seeing that "a thing of beauty is a joy for ever".'

Another expert, Robert Edis, in his *Decoration and Furniture of Town Houses* shows an arrangement of four tiers of shelves, also loaded with china (the vogue for collecting porcelain had begun) and topped by an elaborate frieze of figures and carved texts – again the influence of literature and culture. His hearth has curtains. In his library is a very masculine arrangement of shelves and cupboards to hold pipes and guns, with a set of tiles and plaques for adornment. In a bedroom, the mantelshelf is made to serve as dressing-table with a looking-glass above it, and some small cupboards. This is practical enough – and we have seen it in this present age in some French hotels. It is stated firmly that this, of course is not for a lady's bedroom.

Whatever we may think of shelves and valances no lover of literature can decry the looking-glass; for out of this came a masterpiece, *Alice Through the Looking-Glass*. Tenniel's drawing shows a fairly simple arrangement of looking-glass, clock, a pair of ornaments and a valance. If there had been no looking-glass in the drawing-room would there have been this sequel to Alice's first adventures?

Answer comes there none, but we are led gently into rooms in fiction. These may now serve as curtain-raiser.

The Victorian House in Fiction

'She pointed to a wide arch corresponding to the window, and hung, like it, with a Tyrian-dyed curtain now looped up. Mounting to it by two broad steps and looking through, I thought I caught a glimpse of a fairy place, so bright to my novice eyes appeared the view beyond.' Thus Jane Eyre on her first morning at Thornfield discovered its splendours. Coming straight from the austerity of Lowood, it is little wonder that she was captivated by what was 'merely a very pretty drawing-room' with a white carpet 'on which seemed laid garlands of flowers' and furnished with crimson couches and ottomans. On 'the pale, Parian mantelpiece' stood ornaments of red Bohemian glass, and long pier glasses reflected 'the general blending of snow and fire'.

The description is a mirror both of the author's own taste, curbed in her life by poverty, and that of the early Victorians. They had not, in the eighteen forties, when *Jane Eyre* was written, descended to the opulent horrors of the sixties and seventies. This room has the elegance of the Regency. It is one of the famous rooms in fiction, and the party it receives is unforgettable: the ladies sinking gracefully on those crimson couches and ottomans, their ample skirts of silk or muslin billowing around them, almost as in a scene from ballet. Indeed one can see much of this novel expressed in ballet.

There is a quality of enchantment about *Jane Eyre* which partly explains why it has always captivated young readers. The story of the poor heroine's journey in the cold darkness, her arrival at the mansion and welcome by kind Mrs. Fairfax in her warm, bright parlour, her delight in her own pretty bedroom with its papered walls, carpeted floor and blue chintz curtains, so unlike the bare boards and plaster of school, her wide-eyed admiration of this brilliant drawing-room and the splendid dining-room with purple chairs and curtains and stained-glass window – all this reminds us of a fairy tale. The drawing-room is still more brilliant when Jane and Adèle come down to await the guests after dinner, Jane in her pearl-grey silk Adèle in her rose-coloured frock, They find 'a large fire burning silently on the marble hearth, and wax candles shining in bright solitude and amid the exquisite flowers with which the tables were adorned. The crimson curtain hung before the arch'. It would seem to have been a double curtain, purple on the side of the dining-room, crimson on that of the drawing-room.

Charlotte in her Yorkshire parsonage, which was adorned only by the most exquisite cleanliness, dreamed of splendour, of colour, warmth and light. Her dreams may be schoolgirlish – white carpet, ruby glass, snowy marble – but of a schoolgirl endowed with fastidious taste. Girlish too is her delight in the ladies' dresses, in the silks and satins of the matrons, the floating, diaphonous muslin of the girls, but again that delicate austerity in her prefers the black satin and pearls of gentle Mrs. Dent to 'the rainbow splendour of the titled dame' Lady Ingram in shot silk and azure plumes. The austere taste compelled Jane Eyre to choose, for her trousseau, pale grey and black rather than the pink and blue selected by her bridegroom. The latter were indeed wrong for pale little Jane, but one must regret she did not permit herself rich, dark colours: crimson or wine colour, or dark blue.

Thornfield had, no doubt, a conservatory to produce those exquisite flowers, but the conservatory did not open off the drawing-room as it does in a novel by the other Charlotte – Miss Yonge. In *The Heir of Redclyffe* Amy enters from the conservatory carrying a camellia, newly in flower. Philip insists on taking it from her and so mishandles it as to break the delicate blossom: symbol of the wreckage he is to make of her happiness. This drawing-room, the Edmonstones', is not described in detail, but it is very much part of the scene, almost part of the action of the book so full is it of the life of the characters. We are shown more clearly that very Victorian apartment, Mrs. Edmonstone's dressing-room. It is no mere adjunct to her bedroom, but much more of a sitting-room, though not for her private use only. Charles, the crippled son of the house, spends much of his time there on a sofa with his books, and there Mrs. Edmonstone gives Charlotte, the youngest of the family, her lessons. There, too, sooner or later all the family come to discuss domestic and local affairs. The only furniture in the room proper to its name and function is the dressing-table with its looking-glass and some japanned boxes.

Charlotte Yonge rarely indulges in splendour. One of her most vivid pictures is of the shabby, homely schoolroom in *The Daisy Chain*. The Mays are numerous and not wealthy, and there is little money to spend on furniture and adornment. The schoolroom with its wainscoted walls, crowded bookshelves, blue chairs and worn carpet is loved by its occupants and it reflects both their love of learning and their indifference to style, almost even to comfort. When Meta Rivers, the heiress who is to marry Norman May, first visits them she is surprised, almost dismayed by the bareness of the bedroom shared by three of the girls: only a strip of carpet by each bed, no fine furniture. But it is unmistakably a house of gentlefolk and of book-lovers.

Charlotte Yonge could appreciate and depict beauty of a kind unusual in her day. The most entrancing room in all her novels is the cedarwood bedroom in the old city mansion where Honora, in *Hopes and Fears*, brings her young guest Phoebe. There is very little furniture and what there is is unobtrusive; sliding panels in the walls open to reveal shelves and cupboards 'which the old usage of household tradition called awmries', an anticipation of our modern built-in furniture. There is a deep window recess with a seat and a table, and a box of mignonette on the sill. To a Victorian reader it must all have appeared startlingly austere. The whole house is un-Victorian, being 'one of the most perfect remnants of the glories of the merchant princes of ancient London' still in private occupation. The hall is panelled, like the bedroom, in cedarwood, carved, by Gibbons, with festoons of fruit and leaves. The floor and staircase are of white stone, and there is a stained-glass window depicting Solomon and the Queen of Sheba, 'a stumpy Vrouw . . . with golden hair all down her back'. The rooms have oriel windows looking on a grass plot with gravelled walks and laburnum trees, and on the river beyond.

It would be hard to choose between that cedar room and the seagreen cave of a bedroom in which the greater Charlotte made Lucy Snowe awake, after her delirious illness in *Villette*; in the house she discovers to be that of her godmother Mrs. Bretton. This is 'a cabinet with sea-green walls', a dressing-table draped in white muslin over pink, a green and white arm-chair, and green

and white china on the wash-stand. A scarlet satin pincushion
with gold pins adds vividness, and makes up the effect of sea
colours: green and foam-white and coral. It is enchanting. The
parlour downstairs has its own charm and harmony, being all blue
and fawn and gold, with a blue and fawn carpet, blue chairs and
curtains, and a wall-paper patterned with forget-me-nots and gold
leaves. A gilt-framed mirror hangs between the blue-curtained
windows, and on the mantelshelf stand some delicate vases and
the relics of a dolls' tea-service which must have belonged to Mrs.
Bretton in her childhood, for she has no daughters, an endearing
detail and glimpse of that very dignified lady's personality. She
has, undoubtedly, good taste; besides her youth must have been
pre-Victorian, with Georgian standards of elegance.

Lucy, like Jane and like their creator, Charlotte, was starved of
colour and richness, and like Jane, denied herself even of what she
might have had. Jane's dresses are black or grey, Lucy chooses
dun-coloured muslin for the *jour de fête* on which all the other
teachers and the girls at Madame Beck's *pensionnat* are in white,
and she is reluctant to wear the pink silk evening dress given her
by Mrs. Bretton, envying the latter the sober dignity of her brown
velvet. But Lucy, in the rapture of her engagement to Paul
Emmanuel, is entranced by the tiny house he has prepared for her,
in which to await his return from overseas and their marriage. It is
all in miniature; the parlour 'very tiny, but I thought very pretty.
Its delicate walls were tinged like a blush', painted, apparently,
not covered with a patterned paper; the floor was waxed and
polished in the continental manner, with a square of carpet in the
centre. 'There was a little couch, a little *chiffonière*, the half-open
crimson door of which showed porcelain on the shelves. There
was a French clock; a lamp; there were ornaments in biscuit
china'. A stand held flowering plants, and on a *guéridan* stood a
work-box and a vase of violets. The kitchen was almost like one
in a toy house, built for a child's exercise in domesticity, with its
small stove and oven, its cupboard containing a green dinner
service, its 'few but bright brasses'. Upstairs were two 'pretty
cabinets of sleeping-rooms'. The whole house reduced in scale
would make a perfect dolls' house. Was Charlotte perhaps satisfy-
ing a secret and unfulfilled longing of her own studious, mature
childhood which had so many books but so few toys? At the back

of the house was the large schoolroom of the *externat de demoiselles* which Lucy and Paul Emmanuel had planned to conduct together after their marriage. Thus were presented, in visible and tangible form, the two aspects of life to which she looked forward, which Charlotte herself would have chosen.

This is a dream house and we can imagine its creation as Charlotte sat alone in the parlour of the parsonage at Haworth, her father, equally solitary, in his study. The description is poignant in its detail, in the smallness, brightness and delicacy of everything. It is so intimate that we almost hesitate in reading, as Lucy hesitated on the threshold, believing it to be the home of some friend of Paul Emmanuel on whom she feared to intrude.

Charlotte Brontë was none of your cloudy-minded geniuses whose feet scorn this earth. Celtic in blood through her Irish father and Cornish mother, inheriting a double share of poetry, passion and vision, she was by birth and up-bringing a Yorkshire-woman, and a credit to that county of good housewives. We shall see, later, how fastidious she was in her own home, and she endows Jane Eyre with a positive zest for housework. In the days of preparation at Thornfield for Mr. Rochester's return with a house-party, she is 'happy in helping or hindering her [Mrs. Fairfax] and the cook' – but one may omit the 'hindering', for she takes any task in hand cheerfully. In her self-imposed exile from Thornfield and from Rochester, when she has found refuge with the Rivers, she is installed in a cottage as schoolmistress. The work is congenial, the setting adequate. It gives her shelter, it is her own, and she is well pleased with the small room with white-washed walls and sanded floor, four painted chairs, a table, a cupboard and a clock. Upstairs, her bedroom has a bed and a chest-of-drawers. It is all she needs, and she has an almost Franciscan delight in the essentials – Brother Fire and Sister Water – which bring warmth and cleanliness. When, one winter evening St. John Rivers brings her a copy of *Marmion*, she finds herself rich: 'I closed my shutters, laid a mat to the door to prevent the snow from blowing under it, trimmed my fire' and, settling down, in warmth and candlelight, 'soon forgot storm in music'.

When another turn comes in her fortunes, and she finds herself heiress to her uncle's fortune, and cousin to the three Rivers, she insists on sharing her inheritance of £20,000 with them. It is ample for each of them; she, and Diana and Mary can give up their teaching or governessing and live together in the old family house which is also St. John's parsonage. The description of the grand cleaning and re-furbishing conducted by Jane and Hannah the old housekeeper, is a classic of domesticity.

'Happy at Moor House I was, hard I worked. Hannah was charmed to see how jovial I could be amidst the bustle of a house turned topsy-turvy, how I could brush and dust and clean and cook.' The house having emerged in shining cleanliness, is renewed in furnishings, with tact and discretion on the part of Jane. Her inherent love of comfort, comeliness and a quiet richness is fulfilled. She keeps the homely old chairs, tables and beds, dear to their owners, and buys new carpets and curtains, dressing-tables and mirrors for the bedrooms, some 'antique ornaments in porcelain and bronze' for the parlours: everything 'handsome without being glaring'. The best parlour and bedroom are entirely refurnished in mahogany and crimson, which is certainly not glaring but is very comfortable, and no doubt handsome. Finally there is a grand baking of Christmas cakes, puddings and pies, until the house has an aroma of warmth and succulence; it smells of Christmas, and is all Jane claims for it: 'a model of domestic snugness', very proper in a vicarage. It is difficult to forgive St. John his cold and stinted praise, but his sisters make up for it by the warmth of their gratitude and admiration.

G. K. Chesterton has said that Emily Brontë is elemental, like wind and fire, and Charlotte only comparatively domestic – like a house on fire; but with all his insight, he missed an essential part of Charlotte; her love of order and brightness, of security, even of cosiness, her domestic genius. Emily did not crave comfort; the beauty she loved was of the moors and wide skies, and beyond that, of the imagination and soul. She dwelt apart. Had fortune come to Haworth, and with it, renewed health, Emily would have accepted both with little comment, and gone on her way with little change of habit. But Charlotte would have delighted in having everything 'handsome without being glaring'; and it is good that she had at least some measure of that delight in her last years. Her novels show dream-fulfilment not only of her great and hidden passion, but of her little affections and desires, her very feminine and endearing love of prettiness.

Rooms in fiction may reflect the novelist, as they do Charlotte Brontë, or, more objectively, their owners, as in Trollope. He describes nothing so vivid or so exquisite as the drawing-room at Thornfield or the house in *Villette*; but only Archdeacon Grantly could have owned that breakfast-room at Plumstead Episcopi. 'Neither gorgeous nor grand', which would have been unbecoming in a clerical establishment, it was heavily opulent, without much taste or elegance. The 'colours might have been better chosen, and the lights more perfectly diffused', but it was perhaps with a sense of clerical propriety that 'those thick, dark, costly carpets' had been laid down, 'those embossed but sombre papers hung up; those heavy curtains draped so as to half exclude the light of the sun'. The silver was heavy, the breakfast set of 'old, dim, dragon china worth about a pound a piece' – and sounds exquisite, but at that time the vogue may have been for flowery patterns and bright colours.

The breakfast served in that dull and opulent room is one of the famous meals in fiction: with hot dishes on the table and a cold ham and sirloin on the sideboard. The tea is the very best, the coffee the very blackest, the cream the very thickest. 'There was dry toast and buttered toast, muffins and crumpets; hot bread and cold bread, home-made bread, bakers' bread, wheaten bread and oaten bread, and if there be other breads than these, they were there; there were eggs in napkins and crispy bits of bacon under silver covers; and there were little fishes in a little box and devilled kidneys frizzling on a hot-water dish.'

We are expected to find it all very dull, for Trollope is not yet on happy terms with the Archdeacon and Mrs. Grantly. They are to mellow greatly during the Barchester Chronicles, the Archdeacon is to become a ripe character, his wife to reveal a heart susceptible to pity and to pain; but in *The Warden* they are still in the making: the Archdeacon pompous, his wife somewhat colourless although she can assert herself on occasion.

Trollope is, in fact, 'getting at' the Archdeacon through his surroundings and possessions, just as he 'gets at' Mrs. Proudie through his account of her alterations in the Palace. We share the disgust of the Archdeacon and Mr. Harding at the appearance of a sofa 'a horrid chintz affair' in the Bishop's study: 'a most unprelatical and almost irreligious' piece of furniture, and at the new curtains of 'gaudy, buff-coloured trumpery moreen' which replace the old ones, of a pleasantly faded, rich crimson or wine-colour; trumpery by all means, for we know Mrs. Proudie's standards, but gaudy seems hardly the right word for buff colour.

The study itself is a small back-parlour instead of one of the large rooms on the first floor, which had been used by the late Bishop Grantly. These have been annexed by Mrs. Proudie to make a suite of drawing-rooms and boudoir for herself and the Bishop has meekly submitted. The Archdeacon also fulminates against the new round dining-table: a middle-class, low-Church affair, fit for a middle-class parlour rather than an episcopal dining-room, it even hints at high tea. The only seemly kind of table, to his mind, was an oblong length of gleaming mahogany, reflecting the silver of the épergne and fruit-dishes, the glow of port in decanter and glasses.

Trollope paints in broad strokes, never in miniature; he gives only enough detail to indicate the background and atmosphere of a house, the nature of its owners. He can, in this manner, convey the heavy comfort of Plumstead Episcopi, the dignity of the Palace under the old Bishop, its vulgarity under the new, the elegance of Mr. Arabin's Deanery, the poverty of the Crawleys' vicarage, the order and comfort of Framley Parsonage.

His contemporary, Mrs. Oliphant, has something of the same method; there is less detail than we might expect in her domestic novels, but she too can convey expertly the precise degree she chooses to indicate of comfort or poverty, elegance or stuffiness. Her most detailed treatment occurs in one of her most entertaining novels, *Miss Marjoribanks*, where the heroine, Lucilla, is introduced, just home from school, newly grown up, resolved to be a comfort to her recently widowed father. That her father does not wish to be comforted in no way deflects or deters her. The late Mrs. Marjoribanks has been, like poor Mrs. Weir of Hermiston, 'a dwaibly body', though not unhappy; amiable in a shadowy way, and now not greatly missed by either husband or daughter. Dr. Marjoribanks has already arranged his own semi-bachelor way of life. Lucilla must not interfere with that, otherwise he is indulgent to her demands. Her suggestion of re-furnishing the drawing-room in order to banish sad associations is not encouraged; she may re-furnish, but she need not pretend to sentimental notions.

It is, after all, her province, and it will give her something to do. Lucilla, a very managing young woman, with a faint resemblance to that most enchanting of interfering heroines, Jane Austen's Emma, sees her drawing-room as a *salon*, the centre of social and intellectual life in Carlingford, the country town where her father has his excellent practice. She has, besides, ideas about interior decoration which would do credit to any woman's magazine. One is that the colour of a room 'should go well with one's complexion. People think of that for their dresses, but not for their rooms which are of so much more importance'. Rejecting blue, as likely to go tawdry, she chooses green:

'I think that I have enough complexion at present to venture upon a pale spring green.'

A background of red would be most unbecoming to her tawny hair; so a pale green paper is chosen, with a darker green carpet; the chairs are to be red or violet which will harmonize with the green, and we feel sure that Lucilla will take care always to sit in a violet rather than a red chair, or to have a green cushion behind her head. It is all done to her satisfaction, and is still in the forefront of her thoughts, while she is receiving and refusing a proposal from her cousin Tom, who deserves much better treatment, and whom she is glad to marry in the end. At the moment however, she is distracted by a fear that Mr. Holden, the decorator, and his men will hang the pictures wrong. As soon as she has dismissed Tom she runs upstairs, and finds that 'the St. Cecilia which she had meant to have over the piano was hung quite in the other corner of the room, by reason of being just the same size as another picture at the opposite angle, which the workmen, sternly symmetrical, thought it necessary to "match".' In spite of this venial error Lucilla is complacent about her drawing-room and has hardly a thought to spare for her wooer.

The drawing-room becomes the scene of many parties, while Lucilla proceeds with the awakening of Carlingford. It provides much talk, is generally admired as a proper setting for its mistress, a reflection of her personality. It so impresses another suitor, a very dull Mr. Ashburton, that when he has resolved to propose to Lucilla he surveys with misgivings the dismal drawing-room in the large and dismal house left him by his old great-aunts, 'the dusky curtains and faded carpets, and the indescribable fossil air

which everything had . . . the odd little spider-legged stands . . .
the floods of old tapestry-work'. He tries to picture it furnished to
suit Lucilla's complexion and enlivened by her presence but his
imagination is weak, and even if it had been strong it would have
been crushed, for Lucilla will not have him. She has the sense to
take Tom when he comes home from India and offers himself
again. Her father has died suddenly, leaving her with little money,
and this marriage will end all her difficulties; but it is one of true
love as well, and prudence need not diminish romance. In her
happiness she is benevolent to her father's successor, Dr. Ryder,
and his wife. They are to have the house and she insists on leaving
them the carpets which is more than could be expected of her;
but 'they are all fitted, and if they were taken up they would be
spoiled'.

Dr. Marjoribanks's house has always been comfortable and
Lucilla makes her part of it modern and artistic. For sheer grandeur we must go to Disraeli. *Lothair* is the highest, widest and
handsomest of Victorian novels. It opens with a domestic scene
of the purest and most magnificent kind 'in the sitting-room of
Brentham where the Duchess sat surrounded by her daughters,
all occupied with various works. One knitted a purse, another
adorned a slipper, a third embellished a page. Beautiful forms in
counsel leaned over frames glowing with embroidery, while two
fair sisters more remote occasionally burst into melody as they
tried the passages of a new air. . . . It would be difficult to find a
fairer scene than Brentham offered in the lustrous effulgence of a
glorious English summer'. It was a palace in the Italian style, surrounded by 'a gardened domain of considerable extent, bright
with flowers, dim with coverts of rare shrubs'.

The breakfast-room, opening on its own garden, is hung with
modern paintings, sketches and miniatures; breakfast is served to
the house-party on half a dozen round tables 'which vied with
each other in grace and merriment, brilliant as a cluster of Greek
or Roman republics, instead of a great metropolitan table like a
central government'.

In the evening there is music in the drawing-room. 'It was a
musical family without being fanatical on the subject. There was
always music but it was not permitted that guests should be
deprived of other amusements', and the Duke used to take some

of the gentlemen off to the billiards-room. A great garden and croquet party is held, in a setting almost as gorgeous as the mansion itself: 'a marvellous lawn, the Duchess's Turkish tent with its rich hangings', and, for contrast, there is the elegant simplicity of the Duchess's dairy:

'A pretty sight is a first-rate dairy with its flooring of fanciful tiles, and its cool and shrouded chambers, its stained-glass windows and its marble slabs, and porcelain pots of cream and plenteous platters of fantastically formed butter.'

Brentham is only one of the Duke's residences. In London he owns Crecy House, once a royal palace where the vast hall is hung with paintings of the Black Prince, the ceiling 'in panels resplendent with Venetian gold, bright with the forms and portraits of British heroes'. The corridor round the hall contains one of the most celebrated private collections of pictures in England and leads to suites of magnificent rooms. When young Lothair is bidden to dinner with the family, they dine in the Chinese saloon which is of comparatively moderate size. For the coming out of the youngest daughter, Lady Corisande, there is a ball:

'The palace, resonant with fantastic music, blazed amid illumined gardens rich with summer warmth.'

Lothair can match this grandeur in his own chief residence which has the unusual name of Muriel Towers a most Gothic and romantic castle, set on a wooded steep above a wild valley. He drives through a forest, by 'a sinuous lake with green islands and golden gondolas' and up a stately avenue to the steps of the castle where all his household await him. They are grouped hieratically: steward and house-steward, head butler, head gardener, chief of the kitchen, head forester and gamekeeper; a grave and distinguished housekeeper, and behind those dignitaries the minor orders of maids and grooms.

Lothair passes through the hall to the armoury, and on to the mausoleum where stands the tomb of his grandfather, built during the life of its occupant, of alabaster with a gold railing, and an effigy of the deceased in his coronet: 'a fanciful man who lived much in solitude, building castles and making gardens'.

Proceeding, Lothair explores with delight the courts and quadrangles of his domain, each with its own garden; passes through 'ballrooms and baronial halls and long libraries with curiously stained windows, and suites of dazzling saloons' and finding it all so comfortable, so modern in all the magnificence, with no refinement lacking, and all the latest publications laid out on the tables. Beside all this the most gorgeous palaces of legend appear unsubstantial dreams.

Disraeli gives a local habitation and a name to the most soaring Victorian dreams. Yet such magnificence was different in degree not in kind from much contemporary opulence. Descending rapidly the social scale we find a kindred touch of fantasy in Dickens, along with a realism both comfortable and squalid. One can see, feel and almost smell both the comfort and the squalor; and the fantasy can be comic. This particular blend is found in Boffins' Bower in *Our Mutual Friend* where Silas Wegg comes to improve the minds of Mr. and Mrs. Boffin by reading to them from that immortal work: *Decline-and-Fall-Off-The-Rooshian-Empire*. The room has been furnished to suit both husband and wife. 'Mrs. Boffin . . . is a highflyer at fashion' and has made herself a genteel parlour, obviously expensive in furnishing, with a flowery carpet, a sofa, sofa-table and footstool which all stop short of the hearth; for here begins Mr. Boffin's 'luxurious amateur taproom' with sanded floor, and a wooden settle and table on either side of the fire, one table bearing the eight volumes of *The Decline-and-Fall-Off*, the other a genial array of bottles and glasses. In the farther part of the room are to be seen not only such ornaments as stuffed birds and waxed fruit under glass cases, but larder shelves laden with pies and joints of meat. The arrangement may lack harmony but it is distinctly connubial, and infinitely more welcoming than either the dismal opulence of the Podsnaps or the glitter of the Veneerings. The latter are 'bran-new people in a bran-new house in a bran-new quarter of London' and everything is so new and glittering that 'if they had set up a great grandfather, he would have been brought home in matting from the Pantechnicon, without a scratch upon him, polished to the crown of his head'. Mr. Veneering has been granted a crest – a camel, which is reproduced in all his silver: 'A caravan of camels take charge of the fruits and flowers and candles, and kneel down to be loaded with salt.' There are no such whimsies in the Podsnap mansion.

'Mr. Podsnap could tolerate taste in a mushroom man who

stood in need of that sort of thing, but was far above it himself. Hideous solidity was the characteristic of the Podsnap plate. Everything was made to look as heavy as it could, and to take up as much room as possible' which sums up the worst kind of Victorian furnishing. 'Everything said boastfully: "Here you have as much of me in my ugliness as if I were only lead".' The table was dominated by a corpulent épergne surrounded by four silver wine-coolers, 'each furnished with four staring heads, each head obtrusively carrying a big silver ring in each of its ears'.

This is mockery of opulence at its ugliest but the picture of the rich house where Bella Wilfer is brought by her John is drawn for our admiration. They return after their honeymoon to a modest and cosy cottage, with a pink and fluttering maid in attendance, but after a while, when the long, intricate plot has been unwound, they move to the new house which is exquisite in the eyes of its mistress if startling to those of the reader. It contains not only a conservatory but an aviary 'in which a number of tropical birds, more gorgeous than flowers, were flying about; and among those birds were gold and silver fish, and mosses and water-lilies, and a fountain and all manner of wonders'. It must be conceded that this would be a paradise for the baby when he grew into boyhood.

What endears itself most to Dickens and to his readers is cosiness. Bella's fine house is cosy, so we accept its lushness. Boffins' Bower is cosy and fantastic, and so, even more, is the castellated abode of Mr. Wemmick in *Great Expectations*. That grim-faced clerk is transformed when he takes Pip home to his 'little wooden cottage in the midst of plots of garden, and the top of it was cut out and painted like a battery mounted with guns . . . the smallest house I ever saw, with the queerest Gothic windows (by far the greater part of them sham), and a Gothic door almost too small to get in at'. The establishment is reached by a drawbridge or plank over a chasm four feet wide and two deep, has a flag run up on Sundays, and a nine o'clock gun. In the garden is a bower beside an ornamental lake with a fountain worked by a little mill, with a water power enough to make the back of your hand quite wet.

'I am my own engineer and my own carpenter and my own plumber and my own gardener,' Wemmick tells Pip, and his Aged Parent pronounces it 'a pretty pleasure ground, sir. The spot and the beautiful works upon it ought to be kept together by the Nation, after my son's time, for the people's enjoyment.'

Wemmick is the progenitor of all the owners of mock-Tudor Kosy-Kots and Dunroamins full of gadgets and whimsies, with gnomes in the garden. His house is his treasure as well as his home, a museum too, of curious relics: a forger's pen, a razor or two which has done deadly work, besides more agreeable ornaments of glass and china and some trifles of his own carving. He is the perfect example of the Englishman who lives a double life of the most virtuous kind, who sheds his business self with his office coat.

'When I go into the office I leave the castle behind me,' he tells Pip, 'and when I come into the castle I leave the office behind me.'

Dickens loves comfort, neatness and order, but he is indulgent to the haphazard ways of the young and of the amiably eccentric, to the first Copperfield home and that of the Micawbers. Squalor he describes with realism, with pity, in the case of poverty, with satiric force when it is produced by perverted high-mindedness as in Mrs. Jellaby's house. Her thoughts are fixed on Borrioboola-Gha, and the room where she receives Esther Summerson, Ada and Richard is cold, dirty and untidy, the bedrooms are bare and uncomfortable, Esther finds her curtain fastened up with a fork, there is no hot water because the boiler is out of order, and the kettle is, after a long search, found on Richard's dressing-table. The drawing-room fire smokes and they have to sit with open windows. Dinner which would have been good had it 'had any cooking to speak of' is casually dropped on the table by a raw young servant; breakfast, next morning, is served in the uncleared table: 'crumbs, dust and waste-paper were all over the house'. Little wonder that Mr. Jellaby sat in dumb misery and that Caddy wished Africa were dead: 'I hate and detest it. It's a beast.'

When the three young people arrive at Bleak House they find it very unlike its name. It is altogether warm and welcoming:

'It was one of those delightfully irregular houses where you go up and down steps out of one room into another, and where you come upon more rooms when you think you have seen all that there are . . . cottage-rooms in unexpected places, with lattice windows and green growth pressing through them', and many

odd little passages. Esther's room is full of corners, and leads
down by two steps to a sitting-room, up by three steps to Ada's
bedroom. The furniture and ornaments are of the quaintest
diversity. Esther has a set of engravings of the months depicting
'ladies in high-waisted gowns and hats tied under the chin, hay-
making in June, gentlemen pointing with cocked hats to village
steeples in October', some crayon portraits, a needlework picture
of a kettle, some fruit and the alphabet, and a picture of 'four
angels of Queen Anne's reign taking a complacent gentleman to
heaven, in festoons, with some difficulty'. Ada's room is all
flowers, in paper and curtains, chintz and brocade; Richard's is a
comfortable mixture of bedroom, sitting-room and library, while
that of their host, Mr. Jarndyce is bare and austere, with an un-
curtained bed and open windows, a tub for his cold bath standing
in a wash-closet. Altogether, the rooms 'agreed in nothing but
their perfect neatness, their display of the whitest linen, and their
storing-up, wheresoever the existence of a drawer, small or large,
rendered it possible, of quantities of rose-leaves and sweet
lavender'.

The passages have 'mangles in them and three-cornered tables,
and a Native Hindoo chair which was also a sofa, a box and a
bedstead, and looked in every form something between a bamboo
skeleton and a great birdcage'. It is altogether a perfect specimen
of the most delightful kind of Victorian house, full of oddities,
unexpected in shape and contents, full of warmth, fragrance and
comfort.

Esther and Ada are dragooned by Mrs. Pardiggle into visiting
the hovels beside a brickfield, with pigsties close to the windows
and a tub put out to catch the water dripping from the roof. In
one, they find a poor mother nursing her dying baby; her husband lies smoking on the floor, the eldest daughter is doing some
kind of a washing in dirty water. The husband lets fly at Mrs.
Pardiggle:

'I wants an end of these liberties took with my place. I wants an
end of being drawed like a badger. Now you're going to poll-pry
and question according to custom. . . . I'll save you the trouble. . . .
Is my daughter a-washin'? Yes, she's a-washin'. Look at the water
Smell it. That's wot we drinks. . . . How do you like it, and wot do
you think of gin instead? Ain't my place dirty? Yes, it's dirty – it's

nat'rally dirty and it's nat'rally onwholesome; and we've had five dirty and onwholesome children as is all dead infants, and so much the better for them and for us besides.'

It may seem the depth of poverty but there is a deeper level in Tom-All-Alone's where Jo the crossing-sweeper lives, 'that is to say – Jo has not yet died'. These dens are inhabited by squatters in 'a crowd of foul existence that crawls in and out of gaps in walls and boards; and coils itself to sleep in maggot numbers . . . and comes and goes, fetching and carrying fever, and sowing more evil in its every footprint than . . . all the fine gentlemen in office . . . shall set right in five hundred years'.

Above this destitution and dereliction is the pinching ugliness of the Smallweeds in 'a rather ill-favoured and ill-savoured neighbourhood'. They inhabit a grim basement parlour where Judy dispenses tea to her repulsive grandparents from an iron tray with iron bread basket and pewter butter plate. When they have finished, the little maid Charley in her rough apron and large bonnet is summoned, given a basin 'of various tributary streams of tea from the bottom of cups and saucers and from the bottom of the teapot', with the fragments of 'a Druidical ruin of bread and butter' and expected to be grateful. Judy is very sister to Miss Sally Brass who feeds the Marchioness on a mound, a positive Stonehenge of cold potatoes with a scrap of cold meat. But the Marchioness has a rescuer in Dick Swiveller.

From mean discomfort we pass to comfort with dreariness at the Snagsbys' above the law-stationer's shop in Chancery Lane. Guster, the little maid-of-all-work, comes from the workhouse, at a wage of 50s. a year, cheap, because she takes fits; but 'except when she is found with her head in the pail or the sink or the copper, or anything else that happens to be near her at the time of her seizure, she is always at work. She is a satisfaction to the parents and guardians of the 'prentice who feel that there is little danger of her inspiring tender emotions in the breast of youth; she is a satisfaction to Mrs. Snagsby who can always find fault with her; she is a satisfaction to Mr. Snagsby who thinks it a charity to keep her'. Guster is not altogether miserable; she regards the establishment as 'a Temple of plenty and splendour. She believes the little drawing-room upstairs, always kept, as one might say with its hair in papers and its pinafore on, to be the most elegant apartment in Christendom'. Having cleaned and polished this apartment, Guster helps to set out the best tea-service with 'excellent provision made of dainty new bread, crusty twists, cool, fresh butter, thin slices of ham, tongue and German sausage, and delicate little rows of anchovies nestling in parsley; not to mention new-laid eggs to be brought up warm in a napkin, and hot, buttered toast'.

A delectable meal, but the presence of the Snagsbys and their guests the Chadbands might spoil our appetite. For comfort with dignity and benignity, we must go to Minor Canon Row in the Cathedral Close at Cloisterham, to breakfast, dine or sup with the Reverend Septimus Crisparkle and his mother. Their dining-room is the most charming of all the rooms in Dickens, and might be chosen for the ideal house, with Archdeacon Grantly's dim old dragon china on the table, and, for the rest, Lucy Snowe's pink-washed parlour and sea-cave of a bedroom, Mrs. Bretton's blue, fawn and gold drawing-room, and Charlotte Yonge's cedarwood hall and bedroom.

This dining-room has 'a most wonderful closet, worthy of Cloisterham and of Minor Canon Corner. Above it, a portrait of Handel in a flowing wig beamed down at the spectator, with a knowing air of being up to the contents of the closet, and a musical air of intending to combine all its harmonies in one delicious fugue'. This cupboard had no common, hinged door, but two slides, pushing up or falling down from the middle. In the upper half were shelves of jams, spices, pickles and all manner of preserves. 'Every inhabitant of this retreat had his name inscribed upon his stomach. The pickles, in a uniform of rich brown double-breasted buttoned coat and yellow or sombre drab continuations, announced their portly form in printed capitals as Walnut, Gherkin, Onion, Cabbage, Cauliflower, Mixed, and other members of that noble family. The jams, as being of a less masculine temperament and as wearing curl-papers, announced themselves in feminine caligraphy like a soft whisper, to be Raspberry, Gooseberry, Apricot, Plum, Apple and Peach.' On the lower shelves were oranges 'attended by a mighty japanned sugar-box to temper their acerbity if unripe. Home-made biscuits waited at the Court of these powers, attended by a goodly fragment of plum-cake, and various slender ladies' fingers to be dipped into sweet wine and kissed'. And the sweet wine, with a host of cordials – orange and lemon, almond and carraway seed, lived in 'a compact leaden vault. . . . There was a crowning air upon this closet of closets of having been for ages hummed through by the Cathedral bell and organ, until those venerable bees had made sublimated honey of everything in store'.

Towards the end of the century, in 1892, the enduring validity of the Dickens world, at the Wemmick level, was proved by the emergence of Mr. Pooter from George and Weedon Grossmith's *Diary of a Nobody*. He would have enjoyed an evening with Wemmick and his Aged Parent, and perhaps brought home some ideas. His own taste was less fantastic. This amiable, conscientious and woofly clerk writes proudly of his six-roomed residence, The Laurels, Brickfield Terrace, Holloway. It has a front garden and a back garden, the latter close to the railway but the landlord takes £2 off the rent because of the noise of the trains. There are ten steps up to the front door but intimate friends use the side entrance to save the girl the trouble of coming up from the basement. It is a genteel house with a breakfast-room, and a double drawing-room upstairs which has a piano by W. Bilkson (in small letters) from COLLARD & COLLARD (in large letters).

The Pooters give a party. Carrie – Mrs. Pooter – has ideas; she hangs muslin curtains over the folding doors, has the back drawing-room door taken off its hinges and curtains hung up, and puts bows of Liberty silk on the frames of the enlarged and tinted photographs on the walls. By this time the aesthetic movement had reached even the humbler suburbs. When Mr. Pooter is rewarded by his firm with a well-deserved rise in salary, Carrie suggests and he agrees that they can now afford a long-coveted chimney glass for the back drawing-room. And so we leave them in elegant felicity.

3

Mistress and Servants

Servants were a status-symbol, necessary not only to good house-keeping but to self-respect and social dignity. To lack a servant was to pass from genteel poverty, where a light still dimly glowed, into the darkness of vulgarity, among the unknown and unknowable. Poverty might be no disgrace but the loss of gentility was degradation. The Micawbers at their most impoverished had the Orfling, but their gentility was unimpeachable; Miss Sally Brass, though neither poor nor genteel, could not have attempted to manage without the Marchioness, but was content to harry and starve her, even Miss Judy Smallweed employed Charley. Dickens's novels are full of little maids-of-all-work, some miserable, some cheerful; and there is a very pleasant mistress-and-maid companionship between Miss Betsy Trotwood and her Janet, an almost motherly tenderness in Peggotty for poor little Mrs. Copperfield.

Dickens portrays real domestic life, even when he caricatures it. Domestic service was exactly ordered and arranged from the mansion with its hall to the cottage or villa with its 'general'.

A pre-Victorian handbook, *The Complete Servant*, by Samuel and Sarah Adams, remains valid, though with modifications, for much of the century. It gives a scale of wages relative not only to the rank of each servant but to the income of the employer. The authors had themselves been upper servants, steward and house-keeper respectively, and claimed to have written their manual with the help and supervision of a lady of quality.

They suggest spending a quarter of the income on wages except at the lowest rate of income; a widow or spinster with £100 a year would not spend £25; she would have a girl at five to ten guineas a year. Above that, and for families of husband and wife with children, a scale of wages, with the appropriate number of servants is given. At the £5,000 height there should, for efficiency and dignity, be a staff of twenty-four: eleven females, and thirteen males, the latter including the outdoor staff. They would

nge in dignity from housekeeper down to scullery-maid, from
utler to outdoor labourer.

Mrs. Beeton elaborates the scheme, giving details of wages and
uties. The table in the 1861 edition of her noble *Book of Household
Management* is headed, on the masculine side, by the house steward,
ho rises from £50 to £100 a year, followed by the butler – who
. less than ducal household might replace him – with from £40 to
60. The gardener could outpass them at his zenith of £120. The
west orders of all, the page and the stableboy earned, respec-
vely £8 to £18, and £6 to £12; but if sober, industrious and
ainstaking they might each become in time a footman or even a
utler (for that stately functionary must have begun some time
nd somewhere; he did not emerge full-grown and habited in
olemn black) or a coachman. On the feminine side the house-
eeper could earn as much as £50, the lady's maid £25, the cook
45. The head nurse and head housemaid ranked with the lady's
naid, financially; their juniors and inferiors earned from £8 or
10 to £14 or £18. A deduction might be made if beer, tea and
ugar were supplied.

Mrs. Beeton's relation of staff to income gives the £1,000 a year
amily a cook, upper- and under-housemaids, and a man; at £750;
cook, one maid and a boy; at £500 cook and maid. To employ
nything masculine, however diminutive, was the first sign of
ffluence.

At £300 and less, down to £150 there could be only a maid-of-
ll-work, perhaps only a girl for 'the rough'; the poor widow or
pinster with £100 a year must do her own work.

Only the grand house, of course, had a head nurse with a nurse-
maid under her; the moderate household employed only one;
nd if there were a grown-up or nearly grown-up daughter she
night look after the children. But whether she were head nurse
vith underlings, or nurse-maid-of-all-work, she was a very
mportant person, whose habits, manners and morals must be
arefully scrutinized.

'Patience and good temper are indispensable qualities; truthful-
ness, purity of manners, minute cleanliness, and docility and
obedience almost equally so.'

The nurse must know something about childish ailments, must
be a good needlewoman, something of a laundress. In a great

house the under-nurse or nursery-maid cleaned the nurseries, in smaller one she might, if she were sole nurse, be helped by the housemaid; but one of the problems of such households was the of nursery service. The unhappy mistress had often to arbitrate between the nurse who expected to have trays and coal brought up and the housemaid who considered that to be none of her duties. After studying the latter's time-table, one can sympathize. She must rise early, never later than six o'clock, open the shutters in the rooms downstairs, clear and lay the fires, sweep and dust the rooms, lay breakfast; after breakfast, deal with the bedrooms which included emptying baths and wash-basins and chamber pots. Hot water had to be carried up to the bedrooms before breakfast.

The family might, at various times, employ three types of nurse – not including the sick-nurse. The monthly nurse attended the mistress at her lying-in, looking after her and the baby until she was well enough to be up and about. This person ought to be of discreet age, between thirty and forty, must be clean in person and habits, and the latter must not include 'snuff-taking and spirit-drinking'. Sairey Gamp did exist, but only a mythical Mrs Harris would willingly send for her! If the mother were unable or unwilling to suckle her baby, a wet-nurse was employed: preferably a healthy young woman between twenty and thirty, of sound morals and good appetite not given to dram-drinking, avoiding fried food, pickles and other strong or pungent viands. Regular, nourishing meals must be given her; and never, never must she dose the baby with syrups and cordials as a sedative. The implication is horrifying. How much of the infant mortality – among the well-to-do families – was due to drugs heedlessly or deliberately given by an impatient or lazy nurse to a fretful child can only be guessed – with pity. This admonition and warning recurs frequently in books on nursery management and children's health. Tiny Paul Dombey was well cherished by Polly, and left longer in her care he might have grown more sturdily; he might have served as an argument for the French way of putting children out to nurse in the country. Each grade of nurse brought her particular problems.

The cook was given special admonitions:

'Cleanliness is the most essential ingredient in the art of cook ing; a dirty kitchen being a disgrace to both mistress and maid,' one all too easily incurred in a dim basement, with beetles. In cooking, clear as you go and do not accumulate piles of greasy pans and dishes, of scraps and vegetable peelings. Forethought and method were admirable:

'Think of all you require, and acquaint your mistress in the morning when she is with you, so that she can give out any necessary stores.'

For cleanliness and efficiency the cook should wear short skirts, not the fashionable trailing length:

'We say this in the kindest possible manner, for we do not object to servants dressing as they please, or following their fancies in fashion, at proper times and in proper place. We are sure cooks would study their own pockets and convenience, and obtain the good will and approbation of their mistresses, by abolishing the use of senseless encumbrances in their kitchens.'

They ought to be well supplied with aprons; twelve made a proper outfit.

In a small household the cook's duties included cleaning the hall, but in a large establishment that was the work of one of the housemaids.

Proceeding upwards, Mrs. Beeton comes to the housekeeper's room which was not only her private parlour and the drawing-room of the upper servants after dinner; but office and dispensary, and, if not still-room and store-room, at least the repository of the finest preserves and delicacies. The housekeeper was the direct representative of her mistress; vicereine as the butler or the steward was viceroy. She had no female equal, although the lady's maid came very near, in her own distinctive function. Her duties were manifold, her qualifications had need to be high and varied; for she must know a good deal about cooking (the making of preserves and sweetmeats was very often in her hands) and of book-keeping and household accounts, must be a good needle-woman having the care of the household linen. She did not, of course have to soil her fingers – in the domestic phrase – with anything approaching heavy or dirty work; was waited on, usually by the still-room maid, breakfast and tea brought to her in her room; but her day was full of duties, of constant supervision, seeing to every detail of housework, giving out stores, looking to the condition of the furniture and hangings, organizing all the arrangements. Her evenings could be well spent in doing accounts, making inventories, and after that no reasonable mistress would grudge her an hour or so of leisure to gossip with lady's maid or butler over a cup of tea or glass of wine.

The housekeeper (or, in a less-than-grand house, the mistress) had to organize the great spring cleaning, when every place, from attic to cellar was thoroughly cleansed and polished; beginning with the chimney-sweeping, ending with the taking down of heavy winter curtains and putting up fresh ones of chintz or muslin; perhaps covering the velvet or brocade chairs and sofas with bright chintz. In autumn the reverse change was made. In many houses, fires went off after the spring-cleaning, or at least from May till October, and the hearths were filled with plants, or screened off, or otherwise put out of commission. Summer, when the daily round was easier, was the time for repairs, for mending linen, for making jam and bottling fruit; this continued in autumn, with preparations for the cold days ahead. In December came the delectable business of Christmas cookery.

As for the mistress – she of a moderate establishment of cook and one or two or three maids, who did her own housekeeping though not the actual housework, ought to rise early, like the virtuous woman of the Proverbs, and see well to the ways of her house; example was more effective than precept. The ethos of the home was created by her.

'As with the commander of an army or the leader of an enterprise, so it is with the mistress of a house. Her spirit will be seen through the whole establishment. . . .'

'Of all those acquirements which particularly belong to the feminine character, there are none which take a higher rank, in our estimation, than such as enter into a knowledge of household duties.' At the same time, Mrs. Beeton assures her readers, 'to be a good housewife does not necessarily imply an abandonment of proper pleasures or amusing recreations.'

But the housekeeping comes first. The lady's day begins with a bath – cleanliness is emphasized at every stage; then she sees to her children, the exact scope of her duties depending on whether or not she employs a nurse. After breakfast, she visits the kitchen, discusses the day's meals with the cook, gives out stores, arranges duties. Then she may perhaps 'devote herself to the instruction' of the young children (assuming a governess for the older ones), and thereafter feel blamelessly free to 'keep the latter portion of the morning for reading or for some amusing recreation'. There were serious-minded ladies who would never read a novel in the morning, only an improving volume of history or biography. Our lady might prefer needlework; perhaps making a new frock for one of the children, by hand or on her new sewing-machine, which in the sixties had still the fascination of a toy. 'These duties and pleasures being performed and enjoyed' it was time for luncheon, which was the children's dinner and which they ought to have with their mother and any guests who might be present.

'Many little vulgar habits and faults of speech and manners are avoided by this companionship. . . . Children, too, who are accustomed to the society of ladies at their meals will show no awkwardness or shyness at the entrance of a stranger or when they are from home.'

After lunch, the children returned to their nursery or school-room, for lessons or play, and presently to be taken for their daily walk, and mamma paid morning calls; the word 'morning' being applied to visits, functions and dress, up to the evening. Calls might be a pleasure but were always a duty; links in the chain of society:

'The choice of acquaintances is very important to the happiness of a mistress and her family. A gossiping acquaintance who indulges in scandal and the ridicule of her neighbours should be avoided as a pestilence.' The rules of convention could, however, be a protection as well as a discipline. The discreet lady, while observing the courtesies, could keep less desirable acquaintances outside the circle of friendship, in an outer zone of formal recognition.

These morning calls might be of ceremony, friendship or condolence. For the second, no rules need be made; one simply went to see a friend. For those of ceremony there was a ritual: formal calls must be paid after a dinner or a ball or any party and should be paid on new-comers to the neighbourhood, on a bride. The caller might remove her fur, but not her shawl or mantle, and certainly not her hat or bonnet. Conversation should be light and cheerful, avoiding argument, scandal, and (this is most bracing advice) small moans and miseries, trivial talk about trivial troubles. These were boring to the listener, or, if heard with interest, brought 'a load of advice . . . too often of a kind neither useful nor agreeable'. Servant difficulties and worries about the children were best left at home. As for major events and emotions 'whether joy or sorrow', these should be 'communicated to friends' not to mere acquaintances. And never, to anyone, must a wife utter any complaint or criticism of her husband. Loyalty, decency and reserve regulated conversation, which was an accomplishment, a social art:

'We should store our memory with short anecdotes and entertaining pieces of history' with which to entertain hostess and fellow-guests.

These visits were preferably brief; should other callers arrive, the first comer must linger only until they were settled, avoid giving any impression of hastening or being hastened away, and after 'taking a kind leave of your hostess' bow to the new-comers and so gracefully depart.

Children taken out by mamma, for a treat, should never accompany her into the drawing-room, but remain in the carriage – with one hopes a doll or a book for company. Sound advice – and sounder still the admonition: 'It is not advisable at any time to take a favourite dog into another lady's drawing-room, for many persons have an absolute dislike to such animals, and besides this, there is always a chance of a breakage of some article occurring through their leaping and bounding here and there, sometimes very much to the fear and annoyance of the hostess.' In the Victorian drawing-room this chance of breakage might be called a certainty; little tables laden with china and silver, low footstools, frilled chair-covers, table-covers, curtains easy for catching in claws, all made a potential circus ground for any dog.

For her calls, the lady must be correctly dressed, with under rather than over-statement of fashion and elegance. On calls of condolence black should be worn, or at least a plain, dark-coloured gown, bonnet and mantle. The conversation on these visits must be subdued, 'in harmony with the character' of the call; for 'sympathy with the affliction of the family is thus expressed, and these attentions are pleasing and soothing'. These visits, too, were properly paid within a week 'after the event which occasions them', or, if the acquaintance were slight, 'immediately after the family has appeared at public worship'. One was not expected to be in church on the first Sunday after a bereavement. What happened if the bereaved did not attend the same church as the would-be caller is not clearly indicated; in the country, they would, in town they might; but in the sixties, people still tended to go to the parish church, and were probably not so prone, as they were later, to go sermon-tasting or ritual-seeking; to wander from low St. Thomas's to high St. Simon's or the reverse. Non-churchgoers if any were probably not called on at all.

The lady at home, receiving morning calls, must lay aside 'the occupations of drawing, reading or music' but might continue her light needlework – 'and none other is appropriate in the drawing-room' – while she conversed, and 'particularly if the visit be protracted or if the visitors be gentlemen'. Why? Because gentlemen were likely to linger, or in order to impress them with her feminine accomplishments, or to ward off such flirtatious advances as might be encouraged by a negligent attitude. Plain needlework, the flannel or calico garments for the poor, the mending of children's or husband's clothes, and of household linen, was (if not done by a nurse or housemaid) presumably to be kept for another time and place, for the morning, in the breakfast-room or back parlour. The mending might well be assigned to a maid, but working for the poor, or for a good cause was among the duties of a lady:

'Charity and benevolence are duties which a mistress owes to herself as well as to her fellow-creatures; and there is scarcely any income so small but something may be spared from it'; and leisure was rarely small.

Morning calls included the leaving of cards; if left by the lady herself, not handed in by a footman, the bottom right hand corner was turned up. A married woman left cards on behalf of her husband as well as herself. Some cards had printed on the back, in each corner, a word to indicate the nature or purpose of the call: *Félicitations*; *Adieu*; *Affaires*; *Visite*; a useful refinement, though not without some risk of error and confusion.

Parties could be gay, but a dinner-party was a serious matter. The casual invitation by telephone for the day after tomorrow would have been shocking had it been imaginable. Dinner invitations should be sent at least a fortnight, preferably a month before the date, and care should be taken to suit the guests to each other. Twelve made a convenient number for pairing down each side of the table. The meal itself was long and elaborate. The first half-hour in the drawing-room was the worst; with no thought of sherry before dinner, conversation must fill the time until all the guests were assembled and dinner announced, when they walked downstairs in procession, led by the host with the lady highest in rank.

In Mrs. Beeton's day the hostess served soup from the great tureen in front of her; fish followed, and to ask for a second helping of either was inconsiderate. It held up further proceedings. Many houses still kept the old way of having several dishes on the table at once: the soup and fish, the removes (those which replaced the fish which was taken away), entrées, roast beef or mutton, chicken, turkey or game, pies and made dishes. The host and hostess carved, sometimes assisted by one or two of the guests; to carve well was a part of social training. When everyone appeared to have had enough of that course the second was brought on. [Or the third, if we count soup and fish as first, and the 'removes', joints and other solids as second.] This was a variety of dishes, sweet and savoury; some lighter meals and vegetables kept company with puddings and pastries. You saw your dinner, and chose what you fancied. Then came dessert: fruit fresh and preserved, ices, sweetmeats in delicious variety; and with dessert, finger-bowls in which to wet the finger-tips. The French habit of gargling was 'a custom which no English gentlewoman would, in the slightest degree, imitate'. Having partaken of dessert and a glass of sweet wine, the hostess 'collected eyes' – signalling discreetly to the lady on her husband's right, and to the others, rose and took her ladies to the drawing-room. The men remained to circulate the port.

Some hostesses had introduced *service à la Russe*, the new way of serving each course separately, the meat carved at a side-table and handed round, followed by the appropriate vegetables and sauces. Old-fashioned folk thought this a fuss, and complained that the meat was cold before its accompaniments arrived; but the new way was rapidly ousting the old.

torian greater magnificence, Eaton Hall

torian lesser monotony

A typical mid-Victorian residence, 1850

A study at Oxford about 1856

In all but the grand houses, the usual family dinner was simple enough: with three or at most four courses of soup, fish, meat and vegetables, and pudding – perhaps not with both fish and meat – a dessert from the garden or orchard in the country; of almonds and raisins, dates, ginger and the like in town; perhaps a sponge cake or sponge fingers. Left-overs were served next day at lunch.

Dinner was followed by conversation and music, and family dinner ought to be followed by an agreeable evening at home, with pleasant recreation; for home 'should possess all the attractions of healthful amusement, comfort and happiness' for its young people. 'To imbue them with the delicious home-feeling is one of the choicest gifts a parent can bestow.' Musical evenings were specially commended, and where mother and daughters could provide music 'husbands and brothers are usually found at home in the evenings'. When not at the piano, the ladies of the house were ideally employed with light needlework while one of the men read aloud.

'A knowledge of polite literature may thus be obtained by the whole family.'

This pattern of cultivated domesticity influenced literature. The Victorian novel is perfect for reading aloud, being ample and leisurely, full of incident and dialogue. It is often allusive, in a very skilled manner, so that the innocent young may hear only of some regrettable but unspecified sin, while papa and mamma knew precisely what it was. It was *polite* literature; and it was often as domestic as the setting in which it was read. Family chronicles were appreciated, the reappearance of characters in one novel after another was meritorious. Trollope understood this; so, in her own sphere, did Charlotte Yonge. The stream-of-consciousness novel had not yet occurred and would not have been approved. Then there were the solid periodicals: *The Quarterly Review* with its long and scholarly articles, these rather beyond the young female mind perhaps; *Blackwood*'s, with a serial by Mrs. Oliphant; *The Cornhill* with delightful serials and agreeable articles or causeries.

Over this scene, as over the busier one of the morning, the mistress of the house presided, 'the Alpha and Omega in the government of her establishment . . . a person of far more importance in a community than she usually thinks she is'.

As *mère de famille* she was greater than as hostess, though the greater included the less:

'Hospitality is an excellent virtue, but care must be taken that the love of company for its own sake does not become a prevailing passion, for then the habit is no longer hospitality but dissipation.'

This way of life did not pass with the sixties or with Mrs. Beeton's own day. Twenty and thirty years later we find the same pattern, the same domestic discipline and economy commended by women writing in the new magazines and pamphlets of the eighties and nineties. Publishers had begun to issue booklets, some at a penny, and editors to publish articles on domestic affairs. *The Economical Housewife*, published by Ward, Lock in 1882, gives a list of duties and of virtues very much in the Beeton tradition:

'Education does much for the servant class nowadays. Some say more than it ought to, but education such as they get, albeit it is what is termed good English, writing and a glimmering [good word] of arithmetic, does not give them one iota of refinement – their daily, hourly associations prevent this, and although a maid may spell more correctly than her mistress, there is a very wide gulf between these two. . . . We must not expect to find our kind where our kind is not.' With this difference in kind, there was need of tolerance, though not of pampering. 'You are mistress absolutely' and must be 'kind, just and equable with them, hold firm the reins in your own hands'. Duties must be clearly defined, and there should be no promises or concessions of 'a day out'. Maids ought to go to church once on Sunday; that was their right; an hour or two off on Sunday evening was desirable if it could be arranged.

The mistress should insist on a neat appearance and on good manners, though she might have to relax her demands upon the cook; who might be 'bluff, fat and coarse' but then 'a good cook is not only a veritable household treasure but often times the pivot whereon turns much of the master's and mistress's connubial felicity'. She deserved good wages, but should have no perquisites: no selling or giving away of dripping, cold meat and other unconsidered trifles. A good cook did not waste anything; she used stale bread for puddings and was adept with left-overs.

The order and cleanliness of the house depended on the housemaids. A daily charwoman was not recommenced. She charged a shilling a day, drank gin and gossiped. Each maid had her duties, and the head housemaid was very important.

'Her path lies very much among her superiors, more with the "upstairs" people than with the kitchen'; so she must be pleasant even refined in looks, voice, and manner and she ought to be tall. In houses that lacked a butler the linen, silver and glass were in her care.

The lady's maid looked after her lady's bedroom and dressing-room as well as her clothes and her person; she must be expert in hair-dressing feather-curling and fine laundry-work, and, of course, needlework; should understand packing. This was indeed an elaborate process, when skirts were long, often draped, or with an over-skirt, or a bustle; bodices were stiff and lavishly trimmed, underclothes worn in layers. Everything had to be laid in folds of tissue paper and stowed carefully in a domed trunk. Like the head housemaid the lady's maid must be well-mannered, 'neat, stylish and refined'.

Another pamphlet, stressing the value of method, order and cleanliness, gives directions for the daily routine of housework, the weekly turning out of rooms, the great spring and autumn campaign, and the getting rid of fleas, flies and bugs – and this in a good middle-class house!

'The smaller the house is, the less excuse there should be for allowing anything like neglect or slovenliness to find a footing.' Where only one maid was kept, with the cook, the mistress must do a good deal herself, and it was a silly, false pride to pretend to know nothing about housework and cooking, and pose as being engrossed by 'higher cares, more enobling occupations'.

In such a house, lunch or midday dinner should be simple, the main meal being a late high tea which made supper unnecessary. Luncheon was still a variable meal, ranging (according to the time and scope of breakfast and dinner) from sherry and a biscuit, or bread and cheese and beer – a nuncheon, in fact, between a substantial breakfast and still more substantial dinner – to a solid if plain dinner. The medium, however, was now common – of a two-course meal of lighter dishes than would appear in the evening; soup, perhaps in winter, salad in summer, with cold meat of left-overs heated up and possibly made more savoury; cheese, fruit, a light wine or more often cider, herb beer or lemonade. Breakfast, in the small house, consisted of one hot dish, which should not be invariably bacon and eggs; in great mansions there were not only many hot dishes, but cold meat or game on the sideboard. The most important meal – except in the high-tea range of homes – was dinner; the hour of which became later and later as the century advanced. The order of courses was now *à la Russe*: soup, fish, entrée, joint, poultry or game; pudding, cheese or savoury, dessert. For the last two dishes of fresh fruit and two of preserved were suggested, with two each of nuts and of biscuits. Ices might also be served.

Domestic journalism, in full tide by the nineties, continued to take the service of maids for granted; but an article in *Longmans' Magazine*, in 1893 suggests more consideration and self-help on the part of the mistress, than formerly; at least in the smaller house:

'The practice of ringing the bell should be restricted. Before a servant answers the bell she has to take off her rough apron, wash her hands, and turn down her sleeves' – and all because a would-be fine lady cannot or will not 'open the door or shut the window herself, or put on a lump of coal'. If this task is too heavy or too menial for her, the maid ought to be told in advance when to come in and make up the fire.

'It is for the parlour to set the example of work' and not only should the mistress help, but the children be set their tasks; the girls could very well make their own beds, dust the drawing-room ornaments, wash china, shell peas, prepare the fruit for tarts and cakes, even learn to bake and to make jam.' 'They will find these occupations more to the purpose than reading *Tit-Bits* and "shilling Dreadfuls" or even trying to write them.' We do not appear to be in very cultivated society.

The standard of comfort had risen, and with it the amount of work; there were daily baths – but not in the bathroom. Even in the first decade of the next century, bathrooms were in small proportion to the number of bedrooms, and in country house-parties it was simply not done for ladies to have their bath anywhere but in their own room, by the fire; luxurious for the bather, but a toil for the maid carrying up cans of hot water, and carrying down slop-pails. Nursery baths too were set before the fire, with towels and garments warming on the tall fire-guard.

This article in *Longmans'*, apart from its suggestions about helping the maid in a small household, deals chiefly with the rich and
great; with a hierarchy of staff and a ritual of duties. Before breakfast, the drawing-room and the master's and mistress's own
sitting-rooms were swept – with tea leaves – and dusted by the
head housemaid; dining-room, library and smoking-room by the
second; while the third dealt with the schoolroom, hall and steps
and all the grates except that in the drawing-room which was left
to the second. The head housemaid then took hot water to her
master and mistress and their guests, and attended to their bedroom fires; the second did the same for the governess and 'the
young ladies', who probably did not have fires. Finally, the head
looked round to make sure that her subordinates had done their
work properly, and went to breakfast. In this house the family
breakfast would be the charge of the butler and footman, or, in an
entirely female staff, of the parlour-maid.

After breakfast the head housemaid (it becomes almost Chinese
in formality) 'did' the family bedrooms and guest-rooms, and
those of the ladies' maids; the second emptied the slops; the third
'did' the rooms of housekeeper, butler and footmen, saw to all the
fires and coal-boxes; and the second 'did' the backstairs.

At one o'clock the head took up hot water, returning during
luncheon to empty the wash-basins, while the second made up
the fires downstairs; at five o'clock she lit the fires in bedrooms
and dressing-rooms, and two hours later, the head again took up
hot water, and lit the gas. During the dressing hour they tidied
together the drawing-room and 'oak-room' and during dinner
tidied the bedrooms; at ten o'clock took up the last hot-water cans,
and made up the bedroom fires for the night.

The men servants as a rule cleaned the dining-room table and
all the mirrors and chandeliers in the rooms downstairs, and the
windows. The maids did the rest. They rose at half-past five,
except on cleaning days' when they rose an hour earlier. Cleaning
days out-numbered the ordinary. On Wednesday came the
thorough cleaning of the ladies' maids' rooms, the smoking-room,
the grates, baths and crockery; on Thursday, the dining-room
and the young ladies' and governess's rooms; on Friday the
drawing-room, the principal bedrooms, the oak-room and schoolroom, the gallery, passages, kitchen stairs and sinks – a nice

medley. The guest-rooms not in use were 'looked through'. On Saturday came the master's and mistress's sitting-rooms, the library, hall, servants' bedrooms, pantries and stairs.

Every hour had its task; order and method were necessary. Aids to work were recommended: lifts, hatches, sliding trays, new and easier ways of heating, lighting, cooking; and, in the small house, more simplicity:

'In large houses, with money to pay many servants, it does not matter how many steel grates have to be kept bright, how much silver polished, how many boots and shoes be to cleaned, but the one or two maids in the small house must not be over-burdened. Consideration and forethought made work easy. The mistress should be kind and tactful, not a scolder but pointing out faults gently, showing a kindly interest in her maids. They, on their part, should count their blessings: ample food and warmth, 'the comfortable life in a lady's house' contrasted with 'the rough ways of their own homes, and the infallibly rough work they will have to do if they marry'.

Three especially wise counsels were given the mistress: to ignore servants' quarrels; to provide good meals: 'It is a very wholesome thing to fast or abstain oneself, but not to impose fasting and abstinence on our dependents'; and to furnish their bedrooms comfortably. It was better to spend money on this than on 'drawing-room gimcracks' – an admonition perhaps aimed at the pseudo-genteel.

Some girls may have muttered a word or two of thanksgiving for a good home, before falling plummet-deep into slumber, some time after ten o'clock, after their sixteen-to-seventeen-hour day. Yet at its best, and in the main, this was a human and often a kind relationship: with consideration and care on one side, loyal service on the other. There was a certain security; a good servant would not be dismissed or neglected in old age.

How much of the comfort and civilization of Victorian life depended on its servants can hardly be over-estimated.

4

Happy Visits.
Country House and College

'I love the country for itself; and the species of life which combines, as these people lead it, the pleasure of the highest civilization with the wholesome enjoyments which nature abounds in, seems to me the perfection of existence.' So Fanny Kemble, now Mrs. Butler, reflected in her diary for 1841, during a visit to Lord and Lady Dacre at The Hoo. Was this the beginning of such country-house visiting? It was already the zenith of its charm, a zenith quickly reached and long held, for this country-house life, shared with many guests, is one of the finest achievements of Victorian domesticity; one should add, recalling the history of servants, of Victorian domestics of the world these numerous servants helped to create and maintain. The sweetness of life which, according to Talleyrand, was never fully savoured after the French Revolution, was still found in England. For dignity with ease, elegance with homeliness, sociability with a free privacy this 'species of life' has never been matched.

For Fanny it had the savour of novelty, the thrill of the newly discovered, She had lately returned from America where she had met and married her husband, a Southerner, lived with him on his plantation, seen and loathed the slave-system. Disagreement on this matter had been, indeed, one of the causes which broke her marriage. Now she was home in England, and with her sister, Adelaide Sartoris the singer, and their children, on a round of visits. They were both of them gifted women, their heredity was distinguished. As Kembles they belonged to the aristocracy of the stage, they had breeding and worldly sense; but the world of the old landed gentry was still new to them and entrancing; they were, however, quickly and happily at home.

The Hoo was an old house, not very grand but with 'an air of ancient stability and dignity, without pretension or ostentation'. It was an outdoor life. The guests were taken to a cricket match at

Hitchin, a village full of Quakers: 'And I rather think the game was played by them, for such a silent meeting I never saw out of a Friends' place of worship.'

They walked a good deal: on Sunday a mile each way to church and back, then another walk before dinner, for the church walk did not count as exercise, only as part of the rite. It was a feudal congregation, all standing respectfully about the church door until the Family had gone in. One day Fanny was mounted, but was a nervous horsewoman, fearing to be 'chucked off'? Was this an Americanism or the entrance of the new slang?

There were other visits, one to the Lansdownes at Bowood: 'Outside, a charming English landscape, educated, with consummate taste into the very perfection of apparently natural beauty. The company were amiable, good, pleasant, and every way distinguished.' Fanny loved it, but her children's American nurse found the protocol of the servants' hall oppressive. As an upper servant she dined in the housekeeper's room and declared: 'I cannot bear to have men in livery and maid servants standing up behind my chair and waiting on me.'

Among the guests were Lord and Lady Francis Egerton, the latter 'made of whalebone and rubber in equal proportions, very neatly and elegantly fastened together with the finest steel springs.' Lord Francis, discussing education, said that for a boy like his nephew, the Marquis of Stafford there was 'but one thing worse than being educated at Eton, that was being educated at home'.

The country-house progress continued to Belvoir where she found the very ethos and essence of this life 'stately and comfortable, very easy and free from stiffness'. There was, at the same time, a certain ceremonial. The Duke's band played before breakfast and before dinner, and at dinner, singers came in with the dessert. There was more music afterwards, in the drawing-room, and one evening Adelaide Sartoris sang so exquisitely that the servants gathered in the hall to listen. There was a ball, too, with guests and servants partnering each other in country dances. But the most notable event was a quiet innovation, the first appearance of a custom that would soon become familiar and almost universal:

'My first introduction to afternoon tea took place during this visit to Belvoir, when I received on several occasions, private and rather mysterious invitations to the Duchess of Bedford's room, and found her with a "small and select" circle of female guests, busily employed in brewing and drinking tea, with her grace's own private tea-kettle. I do not believe that now universally honoured and observed institution of "five o'clock tea" dates farther back in the annals of English civilization than this very private, I think rather shame-faced practice of it.' The Duchess of Bedford was one of the house-party.

Tea had long been an established breakfast drink, and the alternative to coffee in the evening. We find Jane and Elizabeth Bennett presiding, the one over the tea- the other over the coffee-table at a party; but dinner in their day, and for some time after-wards, occurred early in the evening; the tea and coffee equipage came in later, towards the end of the party. As the hour of dining was postponed, there came an increasing gap between that and luncheon. There was time, a place, a need for afternoon tea. At first it was simply tea, as in the Duchess's sitting-room, a refreshing drink with little or nothing to eat; in fact it was like cocktails. Then food crept in – a little bread and butter, a dry biscuit, a morsel of cake, but gradually more and more until the refined opulence of the late Victorian tea-table was reached with its muffins or toasted tea-cake, sandwiches, scones, bread and butter, cakes large and small; a meal for which ladies changed as they did for dinner, though not into full evening dress; the tea-gown being evolved, an elaborate and frothy garment, to replace the tweeds and tailor-mades of the active day.

Fanny Kemble's marriage was one of the early Anglo-American alliances. A later and much happier one was that between Ellen Dwight of Boston, and the Honourable Edward Twisleton, brother of Lord Saye and Sele. It was a match unequal in years, she being twenty-one to his forty-two, but it was love at first sight on both sides, and a love which endured. Their happiness was broken only by Ellen's early death, in 1862. She belonged to the best Boston society; well-bred, serious, cultivated, a niece of George Ticknor, the author of a classic *History of Spanish Literature*. Edward was of the same mental cast, with tastes and habits to suit those of his young wife. He was a friend of the Carlyles, of Wordsworth, of Manning. The aristocracy to which he intro-duced Ellen in England was not of the raffish kind, but of high principles and culture, a society open to authors and scholars.

This bride brought an ample trousseau, of sixteen trunks, but on her first family visit in England, took only her 'large dress box and bonnet box'. The newly married couple were staying at the family mansion in Upper Grosvenor Street, which was typically Victorian in its medley of furniture.

'I should like to have the sorting and arranging of all this variety of possessions,' Ellen wrote to her sisters. 'In my room, for instance, there are twenty-six engravings of one sort or another, some very beautiful proofs, a great curtained bed forty times as wide as I have ever seen before, proving to my mind conclusively that the unseen chambermaids belong to a race of giants.' (She uses the Americanism 'chambermaids' instead of housemaids.)

From London they went on a round of visits:

'Here we are at Banbury Cross, but much to my disappointment we didn't come "on a cock horse" and there is no Cross whatever visible, nor were the musical entertainments on the way anything rich or remarkable.' Banbury was, none the less, 'the most picturesque place in the world', except, perhaps, Salisbury where they had spent a night. They went on to another Saye and Sele place, Broughton Castle, and then to Adlestrop, to stay with Edward's kinswoman, the Dowager Lady Leigh. The Dowager had 'about £4,000 a year at her disposal, and a most beautiful place, with a delightful family around her, and all that a woman need have after her husband's death'. There were thirty servants, indoors and outdoors, with four to wait at table, and everything of the utmost elegance: 'a complete silver service, with dish-covers and all, and silver handles to the knives. The house is beautifully and tastefully furnished, and altogether nothing can be, or certainly need be more luxuriously comfortable.'

The new parson and his wife – she born a Leigh – were staying in the house, before settling into their own. It was a family living, and he was 'one of those aristocratic, clerical younger sons who are so numerous here . . . very amiable, gentlemanly, well-bred, but . . . much more gentlemen at large than clergymen'. Prayers were read, morning and evening, 'in a little room set apart for the purpose', and this bland cleric read the petition 'Have mercy upon us, miserable sinners' as if he would rather have said: 'Thou seest, O Lord, what well-dressed, well-connected people we are.'

Ellen's New-England puritan spirit silently rebelled; she could not agree with her hostess that it was desirable that the clergy should be of the best families; but prejudice put aside, she found this clergyman, Mr. Cholmondeley, very agreeable: 'we discovered three points of intense sympathy – green tea, *The Pickwick Papers,* and *The Arabian Nights.*'

Comfortable though it was, this was 'without exception, the most unpunctual place I ever was at in my life. If dinner was ordered at six, you were not likely to get it until seven', and one day when it was arranged for three o'clock (the hour appears to have been extremely flexible), Ellen ate no luncheon; dinner was not announced until five o'clock, when she, Mr. Cholmondeley and one of the Leigh girls ran a race to the dining-room. Luncheon was usually a substantial meal with a joint of hot meat as well as various left-overs, and plenty of beer, porter and wine.

'Somehow or other you do contrive to eat enormously in this climate.' Luncheon in London had been simple and informal: 'cold chicken, bread and butter, etc, served in the dining-room at two, which everyone goes to and takes when they are ready.'

From Adlestrop they went to the Leigh family seat, Stoneleigh in Warwickshire. House and gardens were large and beautiful, the stables built round three sides of a square equally so in their way, and there was a riding school, linked with the house by a covered gallery 'so that in rainy weather you can ride or walk without the least chance of being wet'.

This American bride did not equably accept the English system of primogeniture:

'Whether such a superb place as this brings most happiness or unhappiness I should not care to decide – I should think it more than doubtful, except in the positions of the holder and the eldest son. They are sure to continue in it during their lives, but the wife and younger children may have to leave it at any moment, and that may be a heartbreaking business. I think everyone of the Leighs are homesick for it.' Her own husband was, who had spent much of his boyhood there. The present owners were most kind and hospitable but their own family came first:

'So you can understand how I look on Beautiful Stoneleigh with a divided satisfaction, can you not? And how, among all the luxury and splendour of England our American simplicity of life loses nothing in my estimation?'

A foreign tour followed these visits, then a while in London. In August 1853 the Twisletons were again country-house guests, at Sir Frankland Lewis's place, Harpton-Kington in Radnorshire:

'A regular English country house' with an avenue of lime trees, a park and a flower garden under the windows. 'The principal room is a large library, filled with low bookcases and comfortable furniture, and a very large window, opening to the ground, at one end, with the flower garden a perpetual bouquet before it.' Opening out of this perfect library were, in succession a small room with a piano, a large breakfast-room, and a study. Upstairs were 'any number of chambers and dressing-rooms, with immense four-posters and immense wardrobes and immense wash-stands, and the invariable toilette and writing tables, with chintz curtains to the bed and windows, and a small sofa covered with the same. This was my room at Adlestrop and at Hams and here, one just like the other, and all the perfection of comfort'.

And this was the pattern of the country-house bedroom for more than fifty years to come; the comfort maintained by fires in winter, by hot water brought to the immense wash-stands in brass or copper cans, with a bath set before the fire and towels warming on a screen. Here the visitor could retire to write letters or to rest on the sofa before changing for dinner. Incidentally one notes here, as in *Jane Eyre* and other novels, the use of 'chambers' for bedrooms, *chambres* not *salons*.

The company was one of 'very intelligent, clever people, very pleasant to be with, and not so fashionable as to think books and pictures humbug'.

Edward was a Wykehamist, and during one round of visits took his wife to Winchester; they went out to Hills as all Wykehamists did, walking to St. Catherine's Hill, 'the appointed playground of the Winchester boys'; to Saint Cross with its almshouses for thirteen poor men, and to the Cathedral for Evensong. They went to church also in Keble's neighbouring parish, Hursley. This was Charlotte Yonge's country, and her parish, so it is likely that she and her parents were in the congregation. At this time she was a young woman, about thirty-one, dark-haired, handsome in her grave way, devout, shy and serious, ruled by parental standards willingly accepted, and by the guidance of her beloved and revered parish priest. She was now the author of a best-seller, *The Heir of*

Redclyffe and of other domestic and some historical tales, besides being editor of the new magazine for girls, *The Monthly Packet*. This year (1854) would see the publication of her new novel *Heartsease*, while its successor *The Daisy Chain* was doubtless in progress.

Keble, whose Tractarian teaching was renewing the Church of England in doctrine and practice, had settled humbly and happily in the apparent obscurity of a country parish. Like George Herbert, two centuries earlier, he was an ideal parish priest. His was 'an ideal church, Gothic of course' always open, with none of the old-fashioned square pews that were still common in many churches. 'If you were to devise with unlimited freedom a home and church for Keble, I do not think you could do better than these.' The Rectory was close to the church.

The Twisletons found themselves seated on opposite sides of the aisle, according to the old fashion of separating the men from the women of the congregation. Between the side aisles and the walls, however, families might sit together.

'It was a regular country congregation', chiefly of farmers in white smocks, with the families, and only a few of the gentry. It was all very reverent and seemly. The clergy faced the altar, the service was chanted by a choir in the chancel, it was all perfectly done – but Ellen did not altogether approve, finding it 'more Romish than English as well as various forms and genuflexions, not usual', and not, in her opinion, desirable. 'There is such a very strong feeling in England that Puseyism leads to Rome.'

The preacher was Dr. Moberly, Headmaster of Winchester and an old schoolfellow of Edward. His large family 'they Mulberries' as an old woman called them, were probably present. They spent their summers in a farmhouse they owned in the neighbourhood.

From Winchester the Twisletons drove to Woodlands, just in time for dinner, too late to change: 'So I washed my face and hands, changed collar and sleeves for nice ones, smoothed my hair and went down as I was, among the full-dressed ladies.' During this visit Ellen was taken to call on a Mr. and Mrs. Bracebridge, 'elderly people who seemed such nice ones – I wished I could just stay with such a dear old lady as Mrs. Bracebridge, kind and tranquil instead of fussy and conscious'. Did this refer to her hostess at Woodlands? And was there a further reference in a later entry made at Hams Hall? This was a most hospitable place:

'The liberal housekeeping here is attractive after —— where neither Edward nor I ever have enough to eat. My appetite is not enormous, but it is completely spoiled by seeing tea, wine and sugar doled out and locked up before my eyes, seeing the butter disappear and knowing that no more can be had, and having cold chicken and tart, etc. elaborately offered at lunch when the disappointment would be extreme and spoil the calculated dinner if you accepted. You have no idea how wearing these little peculiarities become in the course of a week's stay.' [They had stayed at Woodlands from the 10th to the 16th of August.] 'You begin to wonder to yourself how much you are costing them and to wish you could pay at the end of the week.'

From Woodlands they went to a ball at Stoneleigh, which was delightful, and to an archery meeting, that most fashionable amusement of the period, but 'a moral torture to Edward'; then to the hospitable Hams Hall where again they met the Bracebridges, finding them more charming than ever: she 'a very clever and agreeable person, real English cleverness founded on the most accurate information, expressing itself in the most accurate and elegant language . . . with nothing pretentious about it'; cleverer than her husband who was good-natured and had ideas 'but rather muddled ones'.

There were further visits to Stoneleigh and to Adlestrop. At the former, Ellen was taken to a tea-party, five o'clock tea, 'which, coming between luncheon at two and dinner at seven, makes one of the most superfluous entertainments imaginable'. It had become a much more elaborate affair than that known by Fanny Butler. Lady Leigh collected china, 'so that we have a new set for breakfast about every other day, with a little sugar-bowl and cream-jug for each person'. At a dinner for sixteen everything was of silver 'which I never saw in the country before, though often in great houses in London'.

At Adlestrop there was churchgoing, and tea in a cottage with an old nurse; there were picnics, luncheons, and 'the Worcester music-meeting' or Three Choirs Festival. They heard *Elijah* sung in the Cathedral. Ellen was by this time a little tired of country-house visiting, however agreeable it might be; she longed to settle down in her own house, but an outbreak of cholera kept them away from London. This result of bad sanitation was not infrequent, and for those who had to live in London was just one of their tribulations. Later on the Twisletons took a house in Rutland Gate.

Another Bostonian was to supplement and confirm this picture of the sweetness of country life, some twenty years later. He was Richard Henry Dana, a graduate of Harvard, who came to England on a long visit, from 1875 to 1876, with ample funds and impressive introductions. He was well-bred and well-connected, the son of Richard Henry Dana the elder, author of the classic *Two Years Before the Mast*, who had lived in England, at a high social level, and knew his world:

'My father told me', the young man noted, 'in meeting distinguished Englishmen to treat them in the same way that I would treat Mr. Lowell, Mr. Longfellow, Dr. Holmes, and others, with courtesy due from a younger man to an elder', and with as little use of titles as possible. He proved the soundness of this advice on his first country-house visit when, in talking to a lady he over-emphasized her title: 'I saw she fairly cringed, so I learned my lesson.'

His Journal begins in London and the first word in it is 'Rain'. Sunshine, however, both literally and metaphorically, returned to flood the scene. On arriving at his first house, Althorp, he was received by the butler, his hosts, Lord and Lady Spencer having gone to the cricket ground, and taken to his room. Clothes had been something of a problem but he found his 'rough Scottish suit of mixed colour' exactly right. Here he was introduced to afternoon tea, 'now fashionable all over England', and found it 'very refreshing'; the tea very hot, the bread and butter very thin, with a few cakes. 'It helps amazingly till eight o'clock, yet without spoiling the appetite for dinner.' He enjoyed being waited on: hot water brought to his room, his evening clothes laid out, the others put away; in the morning he was expected to take a cold bath. There were oddities of service; next morning he and a fellow-guest had to mark the tennis court, for that was not the duty of either the gardener or the footman. The odd-job man might have done it, but he was employed elsewhere.

Breakfast was ample and informal; people helped themselves and each other from the array of hot dishes on the sideboard. His host departed to his duties as magistrate in the county court at

Northampton, which impressed Dana; this voluntary service was a new idea to him. He was impressed, too, by the courtesy of the table talk: always light and agreeable, never too intimate, never excluding the stranger: 'If they did speak of friends at all, they spoke in such a way that I was able to understand to whom they referred. Considerate good manners are here second nature.'

From Althorp he went on to York, where he spent most of Sunday in the Minster, then over the border to Scotland, and to Edinburgh. In the warm August evening the streets were full of cheerful people and children playing. 'There was a general air of neatness, cheerfulness and goodwill.' Dana called on the Lord Advocate, Lord Young, was kindly received, and bidden to dinner at his country house, five miles outside Edinburgh. This was easy and informal; his host brought him hot water, before dinner they walked six miles along the shores of the Firth of Forth, and afterwards, the guest walked back to Edinburgh by moonlight.

'The sight could hardly be surpassed in any city anywhere, unless at Athens.'

After that he stayed with the Kinnairds at Rossie Priory, and was impressed by their serious and devout way of life. They were Episcopalians, and had their own chaplain and private chapel, with daily prayers and 'a full service' – presumably the Eucharist – on St. Bartholomew's Day. Among their many interests were a Reform School and a school in the village for children who worked in the linen mills. These children's hours were, as a result of the Factory Act, comparatively easy: no longer twelve to fourteen hours a day, but four and half and six, in alternate weeks, and for part of the day they must attend school.

'They said the children were no more troublesome than those of a better class' – which is a distillation of aristocratic Victorian philanthropy.

From Rossie Priory Dana ascended to Inveraray Castle which came very close to Royal state, both through the power and splendour of the Duke of Argyll and through the presence of his royal daughter-in-law the Princess Louise, Marchioness of Lorne. Dana described her as 'good-sized, well-developed, with a German cast of face and a slight German accent'; but not with German table-manners, and with considerable charm and graciousness.

tress and maid about 1860

cheon party about 1890

A jungle of furniture. The drawing-room, Eaton Hall about 1871.
Victoria & Albert Museum, Crown Copyright

A drawing-room of 1893

Her presence imposed a degree of court etiquette, kept, however, at the minimum; on the Princess's first appearance in the morning all the ladies, including her mother-in-law, made a curtsy – 'the short bend of the knee, not the long, backward, graceful movement', but that ended the formality. Breakfast was informal; the ladies came down dressed in the country clothes they would wear all day, until the bagpipes – not, as in mere Sassanach establishments, the bell or the gong – announced the hour of dressing for dinner. The day was spent out of doors; people went walking, fishing or shooting, and lunch was taken at a farmhouse. The weather was 'a wee bit soft' which in cruder terms meant raining all day in a steady drizzle. On Sunday the whole party went to the parish church, except the Princess and one or two other Episcopalians; in the evening prayers were read, the staff of eighteen women and ten men standing, while the family and guests sat.

The Duchess was kind to the young American, even finding him a book to read – *Westward Ho!* – which he regarded as a marked condescension. The family manners though kind were 'a little stiff and quiet', but that might be merely 'a Scottish trait'.

From Argyll to Devon is a far cry, and there he went next, as guest of Lord and Lady Coleridge, arriving at their place so late that he could only be taken at once to his room and go to bed. He fell quickly asleep, but awoke in the small hours, aware of a presence in the room. Rising, he struck a light, but could see nothing, and the door was locked on the inside; but an armchair had been moved from where he had seen it on his arrival. Asked at breakfast next morning how he had slept, he replied discreetly: 'Fairly well'; neither he nor his hosts said anything about a possible haunting.

Apart from this episode, which, in retrospect had its own charm, the visit was a happy one; the party was, no doubt, organized, but so unobtrusively that the effect was one of a freedom utterly unknown in any American house-party. There, one was over-entertained; neither hosts nor guests were left alone for a moment, or given any leisure or quietness, so that 'a three days' visit is a burden, and a week's a torture'. Here, on the other hand, the English have carried hospitality to a fine art' and to the point where art conceals art.

After a continental tour, which was necessary to any cultured

American, young Dana returned to England to enjoy another and kindred way of hospitality; that of Oxford colleges; Oxford in that golden age of English life when it seemed always afternoon, and an afternoon of high midsummer pomps; a world of lawns and sunshine, river and meadows, and in the evening, 'the line of festal lights in Christ's Church Hall'; with fun and good talk, rich learning in the background, and a tradition as smooth and dense as the turf. Dana watched college boat races, heard a debate in the Union on the enduring topic of The House of Lords, was invited to breakfasts, luncheons, and dinners. The average undergraduate, Dana decided, was quite unlike the American picture of one, and when he saw that picture come to life it proved to be an American Waldo Story, the son of the sculptor.

Breakfast in one man's rooms at Balliol was an ordinary or 'cold' breakfast: tea and toast with eggs scrambled on his host's fire, nothing extra brought in from the buttery. 'We were as cosy as cottagers and as happy as kings.' Another breakfast, with the boat crew, was more substantial, consisting of steaks, chops and dropped eggs as well as toast and marmalade.

One day he lunched with Richard Arnold, son of Matthew, a pleasant, friendly fellow and very musical, like his cousin Mary (later Mrs. Humphry Ward) who was also present and who played the piano to them. At dinner in Hall the great three-handled cup of claret was circulated.

Lunch with the Cowley Fathers was more ascetic and less genial, with too much shop talk – only Father Benson's being good – and badly cooked food. Dana was happier dining in Magdalen after chapel, drinking beer from a silver tankard made in 1649. Dessert was served in a Fellow's room with the windows open to the soft air of May, the singing of nightingales, the chiming of bells. Within, there was college gossip from which he 'learned much of the inner life of Oxford, on the whole rather creditable'. In the Bodleian he was shown rare manuscripts and told the story of a former librarian who had made a catalogue of all the books but one – the one on which he was sitting.

Oxford had captured her American guest: 'Like the Niagara Falls it grows on one slowly.' The hospitality was immense yet easy. He liked the freedom, the happy-go-lucky atmosphere, 'more blithe and jovial than Harvard where men took both work an play more seriously'. And Oxford in May was enchanting, full of flowers, of hawthorn and chestnut blossom, green with lawns and meadows, lovely with river and spires. It was a perfect setting for youth and pleasure and for kindness; for Oxford made this young American feel at home, almost an Oxford man. Cambridge in comparison was dull. He found the men there less well-bred; they would even sit on a fence to stare at passing ladies, a thing he had never seen at Oxford or at Harvard.

The Backs were lovelier than any one thing in Oxford, Trinity finer than any one Oxford college, and one chapel – no doubt, Kings – was incomparable; yet, as a whole, Oxford was by far the lovelier.

Cambridge, however, improved on acquaintance. Here too Dana found a pleasant and easy hospitality. He liked the men's habit of breakfasting in each other's rooms instead of in Hall. He began to feel at home; after dinner in Trinity he sang American songs to the guitar, and was much applauded. The day of college education for women was dawning and he saw Girton in building, and lunched with two of the sponsors, Professor and Mrs. Henry Sidgwick – she a Balfour – 'quiet, pale, very agreeable in conversation, and extremely ladylike in her appearance. I wonder whether her genius interferes with her housekeeping'.

It was all another aspect of the country-house life he had already enjoyed; the same in kind, not another world, not even another province of that world. This college hospitality was a reflection of 'the freedom of hospitality which is so remarkable in English society; that is, hospitality among themselves and to anyone who is properly introduced' – which precisely conveys the tone, the ethos at once free and exclusive, generous and selective, of that elusive thing, Victorian society. Wealth might be present and be taken for granted, but degrees of wealth were not estimated; poverty was inconvenient but not disgraceful. Birth and breeding mattered more than rank. A duke, of course, took precedence over an untitled country gentleman; this was accepted and it made things easy to arrange. But the duke did not condescend to the gentleman nor was the latter overwhelmed by the honour of knowing the duke. He might himself be of more ancient lineage.

There were frontiers to this realm of country houses and the colleges to which their sons proceeded. Those of unknown family and background were rarely admitted to intimacy unless 'properly introduced'. Once admitted, they were completely accepted; and marked talent and personality could also admit them. Once within that realm, few were extruded; only a major scandal could bring that sentence. To be of good family, however modest and with however little fortune, made a man a free citizen of one of the most delightful kingdoms in social history.

5

The Professor's House

I

he English love of adjustment, of leaving in every work some
ose ends to be tied up or woven in later, appears in that sole
ntinuance of clerical celibacy after the Reformation, which was
id upon the Dons and Fellows of Oxford and Cambridge, who
ere nearly all in Holy Orders. It did not mean lifelong celibacy,
ily that if they married they resigned their Fellowship, very often
 walk into a college living. Heads of Houses were permitted to
arry, and a married cleric might be elected Dean or Provost,
[aster or Warden of a college. Among these was Dean Liddell of
hrist Church, father of Alice who went into Wonderland, and
en Through the Looking-Glass in an Oxford drawing-room. A
iend and colleague of his was the Very Reverend Francis Jeune,
ean of Jersey, who in 1844 came to Oxford as the Master of
embroke. Mrs. Jeune kept a diary. It leaps across the months,
id its record of sixteen years is more frugal than we should
esire, but for what we are given we are thankful.

The Jeunes found the Master's house dirty and neglected, but
 was roomy and convenient and they settled down comfortably
ith their three children, a boy who went to school, and two girls
ith their governess. The outside world was changing fast, with
ie coming of the railway, the new speed of travel, the new sense
f speed and bustle. Oxford did not change. Its society was static,
ven 'ponderous and wanting in ease' in Mrs. Jeune's eyes, and
iost of the people older than herself. She resigned herself and
oped she would grow accustomed to the dullness but the
riticism recurs.

A dinner at Balliol during the circuit was pleasant because of the
ompany of the barristers. They brought a change of atmosphere
id of conversation from the tedious gossip of the dons. Another
inner, given by the Jeunes for Nassau Senior was 'a more than
sually, for Oxford, lively and agreeable party'. Distinguished

guests, however, were not always enlivening. The luncheon given at Balliol for Mr. Gladstone was impressive rather than amusing. He made an oration:

'I have hardly ever heard a really good speaker, and therefore his presence of mind and fluency struck me as good, but the matter of it was not remarkable, except – which no doubt he intended – for its conveying but little meaning or declaration of his opinions.'

A dinner-party during the same visit was excessively dull because all the men, even the most agreeable of them who usually made light conversation, were too absorbed in listening to the great man to pay any attention to their ladies. Mrs. Gladstone did not help; Mrs. Jeune found her a fine, fashionable woman but with less pleasing manners. When the ladies left the table she disappeared, and did not return to the drawing-room until the men came upstairs. Mrs. Jeune's criticism may have come from suppressed desire to do the same. After their own dinner to the Fellows of Pembroke she recorded:

'It was cheerful and pleasant enough – much more so than when women are of the party.'

At one of those Fellows' dinners they introduced their new round dining-table which the guests, unlike Archdeacon Grantly, approved. It made grouping and general talk easy, with an agreeable touch of informality which did not fall from dignity.

Hospitality between the Heads of colleges was very formal with an implicit rule of cutlet for cutlet. On looking through her visiting-book Mrs. Jeune discovered that 'in the case of the Blisses and Corpus it is *we* not *they* who have appeared to drop the acquaintance by not inviting them in turn, and now it is too late to mend the matter. Mrs. Bliss, I know, is extremely punctilious about returning dinner for dinner, so I suppose we may consider them quite struck off our visiting-list. The loss is certainly not great'. The pussy claws come out at times!

The Blisses proved magnanimous and the Jeunes, to their surprise but not delight, were invited again to Corpus Christi. It was a very dull party except for a little joking from Dr. Jeune which did not go down well, and a very bad dinner.

Much livelier was their own party for some fifteen undergraduates who were not unduly constrained and were duly grateful:

'We were amused by our servant telling us after their departure that they had expressed themselves highly pleased with their entertainment.'

For this she gave the credit to her husband:

'Dear F. is very happy in his manner to young people, and I am sure has none of the chilling formality of a don.'

A fellow-hostess and 'Headess' whom Mrs. Jeune liked and admired was Mrs. Liddell. It is much to be regretted that Alice does not appear, for a glimpse of that immortal child in her real nursery would have been golden-bright. Mrs. Liddell was a lady of strong character and of considerable popularity among the undergraduates in The House. They gave a ball for her. The Vice-Chancellor did not approve, but 'little, I fancy, does she care for V.-C. or any other authority'. Dr. Jeune did not, perhaps, disapprove, but he refused leave for his own Pembroke men to stay out after midnight, and in reprisal some of them pulled up the railings round a grass plot in the quad, and took down several staircase lamps.

Mrs. Liddell was a fellow-guest at a particularly cheerful party at Balliol, given, on New Year's Eve, by a Scot, Mr. Hosier, and full of the spirit of Hogmanay; all that a party ought to be, with children as well as grown-ups, with dancing, a magic lantern, a Christmas tree. The Master forbade it to go on beyond midnight which would have spoiled the fun of passing from the old year into the new; but the ingenious host pulled time by the forelock, put his clock forward one hour, and at the new, fictitious hour of midnight served a grace cup for his guests to 'drink to the year that's awa'' and the one that was coming in. They then sang 'Auld Lang Syne' and 'He's a Jolly Good Fellow' led by Mrs. Liddell, and 'God Save the Queen'. The Jeunes were home by half-past eleven, real time.

Indeed there was much to be said for masculine parties. A very pleasant one was given by Mr. Sewell at Exeter, with singing by boys from Radley, the new school he had helped to build on a Tractarian foundation. A summer party at Wadham was large, brilliantly lit, but frugal in refreshments, only tea and coffee provided, not the usual elegant collation of fruit, wine and ices. Mrs.

Jeune could be critical; of herself as well as of others. 'Ponderous and dull and things went very ill' she noted about one of her own parties; but next night it was 'pleasant and things all right', which is the way with parties. She could be generous in appreciation: 'Everything was in great style' at a party at Christ Church. 'Some very nice music in the New Gallery, and the whole thing very well managed by Mrs. Liddell whom thoughts of her position never trouble, and consequently she is lively and jolly as she chooses to be.'

There were formal calls to be paid, some of them boring, and even disagreeable. One cold January day Mrs. Jeune visited an old lady who could not go out; a 'detestable person' though pitiful, and civil enough to Mrs. Jeune; who was ill rewarded by finding her hostess 'as usual full of hatred, malice and all un-charitableness'.

This winter, of 1854, was one of the coldest of the century, and with coal at 2s. 9d. a hundredweight, heating was costly. Prices rose everywhere; a pair of woollen stockings, bought for a poor old woman, cost 1s. 2d. instead of the former 10d.

Another call was paid on the Misses Pusey, nieces of the widowed Dr. Pusey:

'Found a handsomer and more cheerful drawing-room than one would have expected in his house', for since the death of his wife and of his adored little daughter, he had lived a shadowed life. In due course the Misses Pusey returned the call: 'They are pleasing girls, but they whine shockingly.'

Oxford had its grandeurs and gaieties, especially at Commemoration and at Graduations. In 1855 the Comte de Montalembert came to receive a doctorate, and was the guest of the Jeunes. They gave a breakfast-party for him, and for Gladstone, Monckton Milens, and the Bishop of Lincoln, who was the College Visitor; it went off very well, and after the ceremony came luncheon at All Souls, and in the evening, a huge party at Magdalen: 'a crush, and not at all agreeable'. Commemoration on the whole, however, *was* very agreeable, and 'made me acquainted with some of the most remarkable men in and out of the country'.

In 1858 Dr. Jeune was made Vice-Chancellor, and the range of hospitality widened:

'I mean to make Friday a day for receiving callers. The V.-C.'s lady seems to be expected to see callers, and this, consequently, is as good a way as any of showing willingness to receive those who like to come.'

One Friday she received a hundred guests. 'The rooms looked extremely well lighted, and the effect pleases people. We do not, however, feel sure how evening parties are regarded in Oxford. We shall wait to see how the next is attended before determining on any future ones.'

The V.-C. and his lady were invited, *ex officio*, to Blenheim. It meant a long, cold drive; they went well wrapped in furs and rugs and provided with hot-water bottles. The dinner was very grand, but for Mrs. Jeune very dull. The Duke's end of the table, where her husband sat, was lively, 'but the same could not be said for ours' at the Duchess's. 'Lord Shaftesbury who sat between the Duchess and myself talked very little, and the Dean [Liddell] who sat opposite, as little, and the Duchess sat evidently racking her brains for some subject for conversation, but was unsuccessful'.

The summer of 1859 was gay with balls and parties to one of which Mrs. Jeune chaperoned 'a string of young ladies'. In the autumn of that year the Prince of Wales came up to Christ Church, though not to live in college. A house, Frewen Hall, was taken for him and his suite, with the watchful Colonel Bruce at their head. The Prince called at Pembroke Lodge to matriculate in the presence of the Vice-Chancellor; a specially bound Book of Matriculations was laid ready in the drawing-room, and Mrs. Jeune afterwards took possession of the pen with which he had signed. His Royal Highness made a very good impression on everyone by his courtesy, shown not only in conventional politeness but in his willingness to keep the rules of college and university. He attended a reading by Dickens, and appeared to be amused, and a concert given by Christ Church men; went, indeed, 'to every little amusement which offers itself' very simply and graciously. On Sunday he called on Mrs. Jeune after chapel, and was very amiable. Asked by his hostess where he would sit he chose 'one of the toe-toasters' as she called the small, fireside chairs.

Even allowing for a touch of snobbery, the Prince appears very well in this account of his Oxford days, and the reader wonders, as, no doubt, did many contemporary observers, whether the Queen and the Prince Consort at all appreciated the natural gifts of their son and heir. He never put a foot wrong, on small occasions or on great. There were some large and formal dinners and receptions; Mrs. Jeune and Mrs. Liddell agreed to invite different guests to their respective parties. Mrs. Liddell's was the larger and 'a very pretty, brilliant looking one'; Mrs. Jeune, was complimented 'on having preserved the formalities of the place, combined with as much ease and informality as possible'.

Dr. Jeune had to give up a dinner at All Souls in order to dine with the Prince at Frewen Hall, much to his wife's envy, for the All Souls was 'like all the other dinners' while that at Frewen Hall was small and intimate, with only her husband and Dean Liddell besides the household. The Prince talked a great deal about his recent visit to Rome, speaking 'with the greatest contempt of the absurdities of the Roman Church'. This went down very well, and Dr. Jeune declared that 'if he were to report all the things H.R.H. said, the latter would be the most popular man in England'.

The Duke and Duchess of Marlborough gave a dinner and ball, the latter being described as an evening party, because the Duke had a distinct position and reputation in the evangelical religious world; the name and notion of a ball would be frivolous and unseemly. A nice bit of Victorian euphemism!

Again came the long, cold drive. At Blenheim, wraps were left in the hall, the company gathered in one of the drawing-rooms whence the procession of eighteen couples, headed by the Prince and the Duchess, paced solemnly through room after room, to the Grand Saloon where they dined. A band played 'God Save the Queen' and continued to provide music during dinner. There was not much talk, but there was much to look at: the great room itself, sixty to seventy feet high, lit by gas and candlelight; the table set with plate, alabaster statuettes, exotic fruit; the ladies blazing with jewels.

At ten o'clock the ball guests arrived, and dancing began in the two Tapestry Rooms, The Duchess received the first arrivals, then drifted off, much to the disappointment of late-comers. Mrs. Jeune found her not altogether agreeable, but this may have been due to her deafness. As a ball it was grand rather than gay; there was a lack of space and of partners:

'Some of the Oxford people certainly roamed around looking somewhat disconsolate, but it was nobody's fault precisely.'

The Jeunes' daughters, Margaret and Lydia, now grown up and come out, after being finished in Paris, fared very well. They were warmly welcomed by the Duchess, and Margaret danced with the Prince. At four o'clock mamma and daughters departed, papa having preceded them. They reached home by five o'clock, exhausted but triumphant. It had been gloriously worth while; but they had no energy left for another ball at Woodstock.

Commemoration in the following summer was, naturally, of a special brilliance with large balls and parties, a magnificent luncheon at All Souls, a fête in St. John's Gardens. This was marred by a sudden downfall of rain. Mrs. Jeune, running to cover under a tree, found herself with the Prince, sheltering under an umbrella and looking uncomfortable; and in that exalted and shared discomfort we may leave this Oxford lady.

II

Cambridge from the seventies onward may be seen through female American eyes. In 1870, Caroline Skimmer, the young widow of an American naval officer came to England on a round of visits to relations. One of them was her cousin Jeannette, who was married to Robert Potts, a mathematical scholar and a well-known coach at Cambridge. Caroline stayed with them for the winter of 1870-1, and wrote long letters home, to her sister in Philadelphia.

Her opinion of donnish society was not, at first, high. Among the Fellows was Mr. Clifford of Trinity: 'a perfectly delightful companion, sometimes writes poetry, was senior wrangler and is considered a perfect genius in Natural Science, but like so many geniuses has no nose to speak of, and is weak in character, I feel sure'.

This flaw was apparent to her in all academic society: 'All these people here seem to me to lack something, backbone, perhaps, which a business life gives. They despise business and money, apparently.' They were 'cultivated but not robust, very intellectual but lacking power somehow. They all know a great deal more than I do, but I always feel as if I can tell them what to do.'

Whether or not she did, she captivated masculine Cambridge, even her host whom she considered selfish and unreasonable, by no means an ideal husband to her cousin. Mr. Potts would run to fulfil Caroline's slightest wish; one night he even went down to the cellar to fetch her a bottle of that precious and potent liquor, Trinity Ale. Among other admirers were an agreeable young Arnold Morley, and an older but less agreeable Vernon Harcourt, who came to deliver a course of lectures. He was known as the most disagreeable man in England, and once when six men had arranged a dinner to which each was to bring the most disagreeable man he knew, only one guest appeared; they had all invited William Vernon Harcourt.

The most serious and determined of them all was Richard Jebb, Fellow of Trinity and a brilliant classicist. He proposed and was rejected, and Cara (as she was called in her family) returned to join her widowed mother and younger sister in Philadelphia. Jebb was forbidden to write to her of love; but he wrote of other things, and by luck or by love's guile, of entertaining things. His letters were full of Cambridge gossip, about parties, about the celebrities he met – Tennyson, Browning, George Eliot; and one very charming lady, Anne Thackeray, about whom he wrote with astute ardour:

'You cannot think how charming Miss Thackeray is; it is the charm of a perfectly good heart and a great wit enshrined in a lady.'

His letters made her a little homesick for the England she had discovered and loved, and so, at last, he won. Cara came back to England in 1874, and in August of that year she and her Dick were married. Her decision was prompted by a dream in which her guardian angel bade her accept him. He continued to lecture, and he was appointed Public Orator; and besides his academic work was writing leaders for *The Times*. They rented a furnished house, Peterfield House, and there Cara began her English academic life:

'Fortunately Dick is very easy to please about his eating,' she told her sister. 'In fact, I wish he cared more about it and less about sherry, as I am sure he needs nourishment and not stimulant, but one can't make an Englishman see this subject with *my* eyes. I suppose I have an undue horror of wine.'

Sherry, she thought, gave him indigestion and rheumatism; claret would be more wholesome. Dick laughed, and continued to drink his pint of sherry with dinner.

The bride was at home to callers every afternoon for a week, and her drawing-room was crowded:

'I don't at all mind callers when I have got myself into the proper state of mind by preparation, and when I am dressed and ready.' The callers were chiefly 'Professors and Professorinns, Masters and Mistresses of Colleges' with whom she found favour. Dick said he had never seen 'the stiff old gentlemen and their stiffer wives' unbend so far as they did to his Cara. At a formal party the Vice-Chancellor took her in to dinner and was most genial.

Housekeeping was not formidable, with three servants and a gardener, and all the laundry sent out. The cook had twenty pounds a year, the housemaid eighteen, and Martin the boy or 'waiter', seventeen, with beer money and tea. Dick was hopeless about money, never remembering whether or not he had paid a bill, and his wife longed to take everything into her own capable hands, to 'give him whatever money he wanted, and at the end of the year to show him how comfortably we had got on without anxiety and trouble.'

This problem and his drinking habits continued to worry her. There was a Puritan as well as a managing streak in her, and at last she won, after threatening to leave him if he did not diminish his drinking. Only when her trunks were packed did he yield and persuade her to stay. It was not an easy marriage. 'She had to work to keep him' is the comment of her niece, Mary Hobbitt, who has edited her letters. This was no indulgent American husband; but they made a happy marriage of it for all that.

'Dick is very mortified at his past extravagance,' she wrote, at their first Christmas together; 'and promises always to consult me hereafter.' He gave her a butter-dish for Christmas, and a large black fan, very modish at the moment, for her birthday; he had wanted to give her a sealskin jacket, but 'I would not permit the extravagance'. They had spent fifty pounds on the hire of a piano, the same on cigars and a hundred on books.

Presently they moved to a larger house in St. Peter's Terrace, and Dick was sent to relations in Ireland while Cara dealt with the removal. Her American energy drove her to do jobs for herself; the upholsterer found her cutting lengths of carpet, and was deeply shocked: 'He will never think well of me again.'

A month later she gave her first dinner in the new house. She had an excellent cook, Mrs. Bird, and a girl to help, 'paying her fifty cents, and I will tell you what Mrs. Bird had to do'.

Mrs. Bird had baked the dinner rolls, made white soup and fried twelve fillets of sole. The entrées, *timballes de foie gras* and sweetbreads with truffles and mushrooms, came from the college kitchen; then Mrs. Bird took over 'the main dinner' of roast mutton, boiled turkey with oyster sauce, and roast duck and vegetables. 'Then her labours were ended' for the rest came from the college kitchen: plum pudding, Charlotte Russe, cheese and dessert.

The hostess herself arranged the table, filling the centre of the épergne with artificial flowers so cleverly mixed with laurel and spruce that no one could guess they were not real – fresh flowers were still too dear. Up and down the table were dessert dishes filled with fruit, each place had its wine glasses, and at each corner stood a decanter of sherry.

'Entertaining here is a great pleasure and no trouble to the hostess.' After dinner they played games, and there was 'to crown it all, a row among the cabmen outside who got tired waiting for the guests to go away'; a proof though an awkward one, of its success.

'Dick never shows to such advantage as when acting the host in his own house, and he says I am a good hostess.' Family tradition confirms this; she brought an infectious zest and gaiety into the academic atmosphere. Guests came from London, Leslie Stephen among them, but even in Cambridge by itself, society would seem to have been more exhilarating for Cara than for Mrs. Jeune at Oxford, twenty or thirty years earlier. Or was there a lack of geniality in the Oxford lady?

'I do like Cambridge very much and my house here is quite pretty and satisfactory. Dick grows more and more fond of me as the months go by, and I am getting used to the tremendous change in country habits and associations.'

She liked her assured position, the stir she caused, her obvious popularity. Then came another change. Dick was asked to stand for the Chair of Greek at Glasgow, in succession to Professor Lushington. It would mean giving up his Cambridge appointments, and his leader-writing. Work in Glasgow during the six-

months session from October to March, would be heavy, although
there would also be the six months vacation. After much reflection
he decided to stand:

'I am very desirous now that we should succeed,' wrote his
wife. 'The writing for *The Times* is ruinous to other writing, and
hurried work always, and yet without that resource we should not
be able to live here. Glasgow is near the prettiest scenery in
Britain' – and their house would be out of the smoke and dirt of
the city, up at the new University on Gilmorehill, not long since
removed from its medieval site in the High Street. Cara liked her
new house, but they both felt homesick for Cambridge, and hoped
the present post would be temporary; that Dick would, before
very long, return to Cambridge to succeed old Dr. Kennedy as
Professor of Greek there. Meanwhile he published his *Attic
Orators*, prepared his lectures, and enjoyed with Cara the hospitality of Glasgow. Cara purred. 'Dick has a great deal of social
success. . . . We receive a good deal more attention from the
country (or county) people than would come to our share simply
from the position as Professor.' Dick came of Irish gentlefolk on
his father's side, Scottish on his mother's. 'We and the Ramsays
[the Professor of Humanity and a cadet of the ancient family of
Ramsay of Bamff] and the Thomsons (he later to be Lord Kelvin)
are the aristocratic part of this hard-working University.' Cara was
soon 'considered rather a help in entertaining' and invited to
animate 'slow parties at houses where they do not owe us a
dinner'. She took happily to her new life, enjoyed gardening in
summer and chess in winter, and was successful at a spelling-bee
having had Dick try her on difficult words beforehand.

In the summer, after a holiday in Italy, they returned to Cambridge for the rest of the vacation, and this pattern of life continued for the next thirteen years, until, in 1889, Dr. Kennedy died
and Jebb was appointed to the long desired Chair of Greek at
Cambridge. Meanwhile, Cara's letters continued, with a flood of
gossip. There was a Bachelors' Ball in Glasgow with plenty of
elderly partners who, however, were shy of young ladies; most of
them preferred square dances to waltzes, and when they did waltz
it was with caution, 'stopping for breath when the space becomes
slightly crowded'. Then came the wedding of Charlotte Tennant,
daughter of the wealthy Sir Charles and sister of the future Mrs.

Asquith, to Lord Ribblesdale. Having heard of her beauty, Cara was critical and disappointed: 'Prominent, pale blue eyes, sallow complexion slightly reddening at the nose, hair much like the complexion' did not add up to beauty even when 'lifted about five feet seven inches from the ground', but the English appeared to value slender height more than any other grace.

The Jebbs visited Edinburgh, staying with the Sellars, the Professor of Humanity and his wife. Here they met, among other notables, Mrs. Ferrier, widow of the philosopher, and daughter of Professor John Wilson, 'Christopher North' of *Blackwood's Magazine* in its early and stormy days, friend of Lockhart and of The Ettrick Shepherd, who had known Scott himself and his generation. Here was a living link with a golden age in Scottish literature, herself a personality of vigour – cheerful, explosive, good-humoured. Her daughter was wife of the Principal of Edinburgh University. This was the cream of academic society. In Scotland, Cara noted with approval, 'age is properly respected' and was no bar to matrimony. The famous and brilliant Mrs. Norton was about to marry, at sixty-nine, Sir William Stirling-Maxwell, ten years her junior, who had long been her devoted admirer. They were only now free to marry:

'I think it the end of a long romance, and he wishes to have her called by his name at last.'

Back in Cambridge for the vacation Cara enjoyed garden-parties, with croquet and tennis – the latter much played and 'the nicest game of all'. The men played very well, practising every day. Cara advised her American nieces to learn. One of the brilliant young men was Gerald Balfour, who came to stay with the Jebbs in Glasgow, in the following winter, and was, though welcome, a difficult guest:

'If only he played chess or cards and was not so intellectually above all such drawing-room amusements!' He and his Cambridge set played outdoor games with zest but despised dancing and were not much interested in girls.

'They only ask from you an admiring silence or occasional echo being put out by interruption but resentful of inattention.'

Cara had her own way of social selfishness. On another visit to the Sellars she was happy, at dinner, between two law lords – 'much more interesting than lords by birth', one of them, Lord

Deas, the oldest judge in Scotland; he had known Christopher North and Sydney Smith and reminisced delightfully. When the ladies returned to the drawing-room Cara avoided the 'nooks by the fireside', and when introduced to another lady 'held my ground, cordially but firmly keeping up the conversation *standing*'. When released, she chose a seat accessible to the returning men: 'I'm not going to talk to old tabbies this evening, with a lot of clever men to listen to.' The comments of the tabbies (and Edinburgh tabbies lack neither wit nor claws) may dimly be imagined. Her foresight was rewarded. First came Professor Masson 'and with him I had a nice little talk about women's rights', with which he sympathized, then Professor Geikie the geologist, then her two law lords.

'Indeed, sooner or later every man in the room was presented, showing the great advantage it is to have a good position in the drawing-room' – whatever the other women might think of such buccaneering methods.

Glasgow had many diversions, the Gaelic Ball among them, from which Cara, not being much of a dancer, retired early, thus missing an incident. A certain Captain Cameron, an explorer and the first to cross equatorial Africa – 'I thought him a little jolly myself when talking to him' – kissed his partner; she screamed, and her husband knocked the Captain down. 'There was a great commotion generally.' Next day the Captain apologized, declaring it had been a mistake; he had accidentally stumbled against the lady. All the same, Cara looked forward to hearing an eye-witness account.

The Calico Ball was more decorous. She wore blue velveteen with an Elizabethan ruff and strings of mock pearls; Dick went in the uniform of the Cambridge Volunteers grey breeches, red stockings, silver buckles. One family, the Blackburns, were despondent. A brother-in-law had inconsiderately died and convention forbade their going to a ball; and their costumes were so effective. Mrs. Blackburn's was of calico painted to look like a mummy-case, her daughter's was a peasant costume.

'But they rose superior to custom and went and danced and enjoyed themselves.' In any case, it was not a relation they greatly cared for. This had happened to them before; a niece had died on the eve of another ball. These things are sent to try us and should

F

71

be surmounted; only 'I suppose, if any of her own children died, she would have to stay in a little'.

Glasgow in 1878 was darkened by the failure of the City of Glasgow Bank in which all the shareholders were involved. The Jebbs were safe, but Cara wrote sympathetically of a family of eight daughters, 'brought up with every luxury' and now 'behaving beautifully' in their ruin. Four of them were going out as governesses – 'people are glad to get accomplished ladies' – four as telegraph clerks, for new employments like that were now open to women. It made a sad winter, but with the spring came sunshine and lawn tennis, 'really the best game I ever played, and with thorough amusement and exercise three afternoons a week, life takes on a different hue'. Dick would not play. 'He has the unfortunate Cambridge habit of wishing to do everything he does extraordinarily well, and he can't bear to be beaten.'

He was made an LL.D. of Glasgow, and would henceforth be known as 'Dr. Jebb' except in his own Cambridge which recognized no degrees but of its own conferring. Glasgow had plenty of parties and other gaieties all winter, but not at Christmas which was a Popish festival, any observance of which 'would be to these Presbyterians an encouragement of popery and prelacy'; so shops were open as usual, and churches closed. On New Year's Day, citizens 'could get drunk without reproach, and bow to nothing except the pavement'. The Jebbs bade their servants have a party, inviting two guests each, and themselves dined early, to set the staff free.

Cara did not share her fellow-countrywomen's passion for lectures. Mrs. Caird called one day 'and sat on and on' until Cara bought a ticket for a course of lectures on singing to be given by a lady of limited means. She attended only the first, which was long solemn and boring, with an audience of middle-aged women most of them in black. 'Really some of these charitable people ought to be put into confinement.'

Another visit to the Sellars provoked caustic comment on those Edinburgh young ladies who appeared 'year after year . . . after dinner for the evening part of the entertainment, each a year older and less blooming' and perhaps aware of the amused, unkind glances from the vivacious American lady who so easily attracted men. The Sellars' drawing-room was very pretty, in the new fashion, influenced by the pre-Raphaelites, with Morris wall-paper, prints or photographs of Burne-Jones paintings, old china, Indian silks. None of the daughters was yet married, 'much to their mother's surprise'. Edinburgh did not seem to be a good matrimonial centre.

At Cambridge in these summers tennis parties were the most popular form of hospitality; hostesses did not have to offer much food, only tea, thin bread and butter and cake. Women were by this time (1879) coming up to Cambridge, to their new colleges at Girton and Newnham. Cara approved of this, and desired some of her nieces to come over: 'They would enjoy the life here immensely, and would be capable of the study.' Already there were some American girls among the English. At Newnham, a girl would need an allowance of £100–£150 a year, more at Girton which cost almost as much as Trinity. There was a great change in the feminine outlook; college and other careers, nursing among them, were deflecting many girls from husband hunting.

Cara hoped for an attachment between Gerald Balfour and her guest, Eleanor Butcher, daughter of the Bishop of Meath. She was lovely and he was attracted, but continued to be metaphysical, 'full of earnest thoughts, working hard on philosophy and discoursing on Hegel', which was not conducive to romance. Eleanor had another admirer in F. W. H. Myers:

'A goose and we can't help all looking upon his affair as a sort of comedy. He is very companionable and with an insidious nature.' Eleanor's mother disliked him, and whether through her discouragement or Eleanor's or from change of heart, Mr. Myers married another, and Cara was resentfully critical. She wrote on one occasion of Eleanor's looking 'lovelier than ever, in an exquisite high-bred way which throws such a barmaid beauty as Mrs. Fred Myers completely in the shade'.

Eleanor's beauty did not make her happy in love. Gerald Balfour's fancy for her lasted for days, hers for him lasted for years, making her refuse two other suitors, Walter Leaf the banker and Grecian, and George Darwin, son of Charles.

'These English girls are awfully susceptible. If a man speaks to hem almost, they instantly imagine he is desperately in love with hem.'

But Cara herself found Gerald irresistible. He had been voted the most beautiful youth in England, and at Trinity was nick-named The B.V.M. for the purity of his beauty. When Cara explained the initials he was amused. His brother Arthur was less handsome but was sweeter in manner – 'a young prince in his way' – though under the sweetness lay a certain coldness. He was indifferent, easily bored, and after one unhappy venture in love risked no more.

Cambridge was deserted in the vacation but to go away was to miss much of its charm; it was so quiet, the gardens were so peace-ful. And not everyone had gone away. There was a party at the Sidgwicks' to meet George Eliot and her husband, Mr. Cross, twenty years her junior. Cara pitied her, not without sympathy but not without condescension, for being so much the oldest of the party.

'She adores her husband, and it seemed to me to hurt her a little to have him talk so much to me.'

Yet the great woman 'old as she is and ugly' had charm, and she was becomingly dressed in dark satin and lace. She was said to have gone to all the best dressmakers and milliners in London for her trousseau. Neither the hurt nor the happiness were to last long; by the end of that year George Eliot was dead.

Back in Glasgow the Jebbs entertained – with some reluctance and embarrassment – Bret Harte, whose speech and manners 'made Dick's hair stand on end through most of dinner. He may be a genius, but he is certainly no gentleman'. Cara dreaded his effect on academic society, which was probably less sensitive than she imagined, and sitting between him and Principal Caird she dreaded in particular his saying anything unfit for clerical, as well as feminine ears. He insisted on smoking which no gentleman should do in the presence of ladies. Bret Harte did not, after all, say anything outrageous but he flirted with a lady of a certain reputation, and 'Glasgow does not approve of that sort of frivolity'.

Glasgow dinners on the whole bored Cara. She did not care enough about food and wine to enjoy their gastronomic merits, and preferred a musical party where the hostess offered her sixty guests, some fine music, but sparse refreshments; only ices, cakes and sherry. This was enough for Cara but she realized that it might not satisfy others, and found it 'a little absurd to march everyone down to the dining-room where the long table looked like an expanse of ocean dotted with tiny islands of cakes and ices'.

She was making benevolent plans for her nieces, one of whom, Nellie Dupuy, came over in the spring of 1862, not startlingly pretty but sufficiently good-looking, 'and what is worth a great deal more than mere beauty she has gentleness and self-possession without a shade of pertness'. A dinner for young people was arranged and Cara made over a green cashmere dress, made in the aesthetic Greek style, to her niece, with a blue plush jacket (but that she had better not wear in Glasgow where it was known), and had a ball dress made for her of white tulle over silk, trimmed with flowers. In this Nellie looked charming and she danced every dance.

That summer they went to a new house in Cambridge, Springfield, a large house close to the college gardens and looking on The Backs. It had its own big garden and tennis court, and was altogether like a country house. Rent and taxes came to £200 and the Jebbs had to keep a gardener, but they could afford it. Between Glasgow and Cambridge there had been an interlude in Florence. Gerald Balfour had been there, and been very attentive to Nellie: 'I have never known anyone quite his equal . . . the most superior man I have ever met . . . can call cousin with half the nobility of England' and with an income of £1,000 a year was as exalted in position as in intellect and morals. Yet Nellie would not respond: 'It is as hard to love up as to love down.'

In Cambridge, now that the measure permitting Fellows to marry had been passed there was 'a great matrimonial rush' that summer of 1882. 'I only hope it won't quite spoil the charm of the place by filling it with semi-paupers.' It was all very gay for Cara and Nellie, with young men coming to play tennis, all 'very civil and nice' though without showing any ardent interest. Nellie made a good impression; she did not chatter as much as her fellow-countrywomen were supposed to do, and was often taken for an English girl; intended as a compliment but not so regarded by her.

Her aunt had one criticism to make of her:

'She has never been taught to be unselfish, apparently. You can be as selfish as you like in essentials, but society will not permit the exercise of that quality in minor things.' One must sit on at table, even when one had finished, and one must not slip out of the drawing-room with a book. 'I tell Nellie that nothing is so foolish as to show selfishness in small matters.'

Nellie herself wrote home in raptures about the new house: very pretty, especially the drawing-room' with its Chippendale urniture and yellow carpet and curtains though these proved ..nbecoming, and were taken down, its blue-green woodwork and *portière*.

Among the young men who came about was J. K. Stephen, Leslie's nephew, one of the aristocracy of intellect.

'I believe nobody ever heard of a Stephen who was stupid or a failure,' Cara wrote; and of another Balfour, Frank: 'More than difficult, he is impossible' in his absorption in his chosen work of biology and natural science. 'I don't think in all the thirty years of his life he has ever been in love with anyone.' This was confirmed by his sister, Lady Rayleigh. Frank had said that if a Burne-Jones lady would step out of her canvas he might fall in love with her. If he should ever fall in love and marry, his wife would be enviable, for he was 'the sweetest human soul the earth has ever held'. There was no sign of his falling in love with Nellie and Gerald was being put off by her indifference; then there was George Darwin, but here, Cara thought, there was nothing beyond friendliness on both sides.

Then the summer brightness was darkened. Frank Balfour was killed, climbing in the Alps. Nellie wrote to her mother:

'I never knew anyone who was so loved by everyone, and who was so perfect. We are both so glad we had seen so much of him the very night before he went away' when the two brothers had come to dinner and afterwards had sat by the piano, singing hymns; Frank dreadfully out of tune, but happy. Cara wrote that Cambridge would never be the same again: 'The thought of seeing him again has always been one of the pleasant things in coming back.'

George Darwin came to talk about him; the elder Darwins were taking Springfield for the six months of the Jebbs' session in Glasgow. Nellie wrote mischievously home about George as 'the Constant One', and J. K. Stephen as 'the Willing One' among her Cambridge young men; George was beginning to show her particular attention; he was now one of the most popular men in

Trinity, 'the kind of man the more you see of him, the more you like him'. But when he proposed, he was rejected. Nellie sailed for home before the Jebbs returned to Glasgow; she was still unengaged, and she never married.

Another niece, Maud, succeeded her. Aunt Cara asked her to bring a box of American delicacies: tins of tomatoes, of oysters, muffin rings and a waffle iron, and would she please learn to make waffles in order to pass on the instruction. Also would she please bring a root of the Madeira vine to plant in the greenhouse at Springfield.

The amiable matchmaking was resumed. Cara reviewed her list of eligible young men. Maud was quieter than Nellie, 'not a girl to surprise anyone into matrimony', not likely to attract Gerald Balfour. But she had her own charm. There was a Mr. Cartmell, handsome, accomplished and good; Cara herself had once had a fondness for him, but 'his being a clergyman put him out of the running for me'. He was, however, too old for Maud, being nearly forty. Then there was Mr. Goodhart of Trinity, much liked by the undergraduates, but Cara was not sure: 'Mr. Goodhart may be *her* Mr. Cartmell', she wrote to Nellie. 'Even when I had a fancy for that being . . . I knew he would never do, and that I should become bored to death with him.' She preferred, for Maud, Henry Taylor, a Fellow and lecturer, and barrister as well, who had an ample fortune and could settle £10,000 on his wife. And there was always George Darwin. Cara would have liked to consult him about Maud.

Eleanor Butcher was still unmarried, and becoming a problem. Maud wrote to Nellie that it was painful and embarrassing to see her run after Gerald Balfour, even so far as coming, uninvited, to a tennis-party where he was a guest.

'I was so amused, and Aunt Cara angry and without being rude, was not very gracious.' Eleanor still had her admirers; George Darwin among them, and Walter Leaf who was 'as good as gold, of which he has such plenty' but unfortunately very plain, short and bandy-legged.

Henry Taylor proposed to Maud by letter and was refused, also by letter. He wrote again – 'Can't a man understand a "No" unless it is shouted at him?', demanded an exasperated Cara – and a second, more forthright refusal had to be written.

It was George Darwin after all. In the following spring he followed Maud to Italy where she was touring with another aunt, offered himself, and was accepted, to the joy of Aunt Cara.

'He must call me Cara not Aunt. I can't stand that from a man so near my own age.' He was thirty-eight.

To Maud she wrote:

'Unless you *are* engaged, do not go out with him at all without a chaperone. You can sit and talk to him in the hotel drawing-room.' A girl must not give the faintest impression of being fast, or cause any comment.

'I feel so happy for you . . . You will grow very fond of him, and in things where you need improvement, you will improve each other.' Maud must be careful of her speech and spelling; not write 'staid' for 'stayed' or say 'in the blues' when she meant 'in low spirits'; 'Spelling and punctuation are often the indication people get of the education you have received, and language shows the class of society in which you have been placed.'

The marriage proved a very happy one. Maud liked her new setting as much as Cara had done, and according to Cara 'likes the best things, and she likes to feel herself among bright, clever people'.

They set up house in Springfield while the Jebbs were in Glasgow, until a house of their own should be ready. Maud's sister Carrie came over, and her cousin Ella. Cara continued to dream of marriages. Gerald Balfour might, she thought, marry Laura Tennant; instead, he married Lady Betty Lytton and Cara approved. In 1889, as we have seen, she and Dick returned to Cambridge for good: 'A great relief not to have to make the usual move to Scotland in October.' Jebb had left a brilliant name, but they had, on the whole been in but not of Glasgow. Cara never perceived, let alone absorbed the ethos of a Scots university. One notes especially the lack of any reference in her letters to Glasgow students. The Jebbs would not appear to have entertained the professor's classes – as did some kindly professorial homes. There was, of course, no college life; the men came up for classes and lectures many of them from very poor homes, most of them to work desperately hard, for a degree meant a career, a profession. There was no communal life; they lived in lodgings, those who did not have their homes in Glasgow, of a degree of comfort or frugality that depended on their means. Few if any of them could call cousin to the nobility or gentry, and so, for all their qualities of mind and character, had little to commend them to their Professor and his wife who, with all their charm and distinction were so eminently snobs. Cara would have found it difficult to be a kind hostess to a party of honest, hard-working but uncouth young men; but we should like her much better if she had tried.

III

The story of Cambridge is continued in the next generation; told entrancingly in her *Period Piece* by Gwen Raverat, daughter of George and Maud Darwin. In her childhood in the nineties her father was Fellow of Trinity and Professor of Astronomy. Her mother, even more than Aunt Cara, was enchanted by Cambridge:

'A Utopia of tea-parties, dinner-parties, boat-races, tennis parties, antique shops, picnics, new bonnets, charming young men, delicious food and perfect servants'; a golden age, an earthly Paradise.

They lived in a house called Newnham Grange which had once belonged to a family of grain and coal merchants. On one side it looked on The Backs, on the other on a stretch of the Cam between two mills, and there was a water-gate under one of the granaries. The river smelt, the site was damp but they loved it. They laid out a tennis court in the cobbled yard, made one of the granaries into a gallery, pulled down the others, built a bridge across the river to an islet. In the house itself they installed a bathroom and indoor speaking tubes between the rooms; but these were rarely used. It was easier to shout. 'Anyhow our house was never the sort of place where you ring the bell for the maid to put coal on the fire.'

The bedrooms, nursery and passages were lit by 'hissing, unshaded gas burners', the dining-room by candles, the drawing-room by an oil-lamp, but soon the new electric light was put in, and after that the telephone. The nursery windows looked on the river, and there was always the sound of water; there were other sounds too, of horses' hooves and of wheels, from farmers' traps, carriers' hooded carts, 'the slow four-wheelers', and sometimes 'even slower, even heavier . . . the plop, plop, plop of the oldest horses in the world . . . pulling the funereal Girton cabs out to Girton, with four melancholy Girton students in each'. The Newnham students went to lectures on foot, dons and under-graduates walked, workmen rode on penny-farthing bicycles. The organ-grinder brought a gay sound and at night came the lamp-lighter.

'Nearly all the life of Cambridge flowed backward and forward over our bridge and before our house.'

Cambridge was still domestic and exclusive. The young Dar-wins belonged to 'the first hatching of Fellows' children'. Socially, the town did not exist, only the gown. It was a world supported by servants. Mrs. Darwin had many interests and activities: 'In a sense, the maids ran the house.' It was very much *her* house, but 'that was the way she ran it'. The foundation of domestic govern-ment was 'the Inviolability of the Locked Cupboard'. Everything must be given out by the mistress. The servants were trustworthy, the cook, Mrs. Phillips, was in every way excellent, but even she had to ask for everything down to a box of matches. The maids had their method; they asked for more than they needed; but the rule was observed.

It was a world of Ladies, and 'Ladies were ladies in those days. They did not do things for themselves, they told other people what to do and how to do it', a perfect description of Victorian housekeeping at its best. The game was played by both sides. Mrs. Darwin disliked lard, her cook used it but under another name, and both were satisfied. 'The cook knew well enough that part of her job was to listen to her mistress talking, after which she did exactly what she had always intended to do.'

Cook was a personage for dinners were important, still formal and elaborate, with anything from eight to ten courses. A dinner without entrées was not to be thought of. At Newnham Grange everything was done by the cook, nothing sent in from the college kitchen. One very grand dinner for Lord Kelvin consisted of clear soup, brill with lobster sauce, chicken cutlets with rice balls, oyster patties, mutton with vegetables, partridge with salad, cara-mel pudding, pears and cream, cheese straws and ramequins, fruit and ices. A simple dinner for four was of soup, smelts, mushrooms on toast, roast beef, apple charlotte, toasted cheese and dessert

And of course the appropriate wine went with each course. The children had their share of the treat when they came down for dessert – when their parents were alone – and were regaled with fruit, fresh or crystallized, almonds and raisins, chocolates or ginger. A kind butler or parlour-maid could be trusted to keep some delicacies from a dinner-party for the nursery.

The Darwins kept a modest establishment of three servants; their next-door neighbour, a rich widow, kept eight, besides a coachman and footman for her carriage and pair. Carriages were not common in Cambridge, where distances were not long. Doctors, of course, drove on their rounds, usually in a brougham; most people hired a cab when they wanted one, until the safety bicycle came in and then everyone cycled, even the ladies going to dinner-parties with their skirts tucked up.

We see Aunt Cara through the eyes of her grand-niece: with her auburn hair and 'charming Rubenesque countenance and a deep, rich voice like red velvet'. She was careful of her complexion and used to play tennis wearing a little black velvet nosebag fastened with elastic to prevent sunburn. Her grand-niece found her entrancing; very practical, very managing, perhaps not altogether lovable, not really warm-hearted, but so intelligently interested in people, so anxious to win their affection that she gave the impression of warmth:

'Of course her worldliness shocked me . . . I was abominably serious and high-minded.'

Aunt Cara kept a carriage and used to take her niece out driving, sometimes with a reluctant grand-niece perched on the narrow back seat of the victoria.

Life was by no means entirely frivolous. Ladies had engagements on charitable committees to which Mrs. Darwin took easily and kindly. There was also a very intellectual Ladies' Discussion Society. And among purely social duties that of chaperone was important for no unmarried girl could go unattended to a party where she might be exposed to the dangerous male. A Darwin uncle, Francis, already widowed, was engaged to one of the lady lecturers at Newnham; he was thirty-five, she twenty-seven, but he must not call on her unless the Principal, Miss Clough, was present. 'One sometimes wonders how anyone was ever able to get engaged at all.' Fortunately these two had managed it and their subsequent marriage, for they became the parents of a poet – Frances Darwin, later Frances Cornford.

The link between country house and college life was strong in this family. Charles Darwin had lived at Down House in Kent and there his widow spent the summer (the winter always in Cambridge); there came all the aunts, uncles and cousins. Maud found it dull, with too many relations, too little social life, too much scientific talk. The children loved it, partly because they were Darwins and to them the place was beyond criticism. 'At Down House there were more things to worship than anywhere else in the world.' It was enchantment, from their arrival at the station four miles away, the drive in a wagonette through narrow lanes to the house with 'the unmistakable, cool, empty country smell' and its 'big, underfurnished rooms' – an early, not a mid-Victorian house.

Grandmamma and the great-aunts had breakfast in bed and the children used to pay a round of morning calls. Aunt Kitty read aloud to them: *The Little Duke; The Children of the New Forest; The Princess and the Goblin.* Aunt Kitty was a Perfect Lady, boasting that she had never in her life made a pot of tea, been out alone in the dark, or travelled without a maid. She had always been delicate, although thriving at eighty-six, and delicacy is conducive to gentility.

The new Darwin house in Cambridge, set up when Uncle Frank married Miss Ellen Crofts of Newnham, was full of lovely things, for he was the artistic member of the family. He and his wife followed the aesthetic cult of the nineties, with prints of approved pictures, some Japanese fans and a touch of 'greenery-yallery'.

Prints and reproductions were among the most approved wedding-presents in Cambridge of the period: Fred Walker's 'The Harvest Moon' was a favourite, as were Watts's 'Love and Death' and 'Hope'; and always 'The Sistine Madonna'.

For brief postscript, there are accounts of this academic world in two memoirs by academic ladies. Florence Keynes, in her *Gathering Up the Threads* recalls her own coming to Cambridge, in 1882, among the first of the Fellows' brides; as the wife of John Neville Keynes of Pembroke. She remembers Mrs. Jebb in her elegant victoria, the horse-trams which children could easily race, and all the 'gracious society and happy sheltered life' of that golden age and secluded world, more sheltered even than that of the country house – which, after all, was the centre of a rural community, and had many responsibilities and cares. Mrs. Keynes knew the dinner-parties and the formal calls. Dinner-table talk could be brilliant and it could be formidable; so could the silences. The most silent man in Cambridge was said to be the great mathematician Professor Stokes; but one lady charmed him into speech, and she was a niece of Mrs. Jebb – whether Nellie or Maud is not stated. When asked how she had done it, she replied:

'I asked him which he liked best, Euclid or Algebra.'

Mary Paley Marshall's memories begin in her father's rectory, in the 1860's; a large, rambling house in a country parish near Stamford; with three maids kept and a gardener-groom. The cook had from £10 to £12 a year, the nurse-maid £5. Daily help was easily found, the farmers' daughters coming in to work all day for a shilling.

Life was cold in winter, with no bedroom fires, not even hot water bottles in bed. Summer was delightful, with croquet and archery parties in the garden, and long visits, rarely less than a month, from friends. The girls were taught at home, chiefly by a German governess, and from their father learned Euclid, Latin and even a little Hebrew. They read Moral Tales, gulping down the sermon, and in the evening their father read aloud the English classics and Greek plays in translation.

In 1871 Mary went up to Newnham as one of Miss Clough's first five students, and later she became a lecturer:

'This was the pre-Raphaelite period, and we papered our rooms with Morris paper, bought Burne-Jones photographs and dressed accordingly.'

In 1876 she became engaged to her tutor, Alfred Marshall. For him, marriage meant giving up his Fellowship and they had very little money. Presently, however, he was appointed Principal of Bristol University, with a salary of £700. Mary's own small capital bought their house, for £1,200; they kept two maids, paying the elder £20 the younger £12. They had to entertain officially, and at dinner-parties 'the greengrocer round the corner came to wait'. Somehow they contrived to save about £200 a year and have a two-months' holiday abroad.

After five years in Bristol they went to Oxford, both of them to lecture on Economics, and to take a house in Woodstock Road. In 1885 they returned to Cambridge, and built their own house, Balliol Croft, in the Madingley Road; for some time the only house there, and surrounded by trees.

Mary joined a Ladies' Dining Society of ten to twelve members, who dined with each other once or twice a term, sending their husbands to dine in college, or sending them a tray in the study. The ladies expected a good dinner with good wine and good talk. Among them were the Darwin wives; Mrs. Creighton, wife of the future Bishop; Mrs. Sidgwick, Principal of Newnham; the Baroness von Hügel; and Mrs., now Lady Jebb, for Dick had become Sir Richard. There is a final glimpse of that all-permeating lady:

'She took the place by storm, and don after don fell before her. . . . She was always full of life and fun and smart sayings'; and she discovered and announced that if the topic of sex were introduced, everyone became animated. In those days it had the charm of freshness, even of daring. When asked whether she would rather be beautiful or good, Cara replied:

'Why, beautiful of course. You can make yourself good, but you can't make yourself beautiful.'

6

A Scholar's Miscellany

I

It is a little surprising and to Mrs. Jebb would have been disconcerting to find no mention of her in the recollecions of her hostess in Edinburgh, Mrs. Sellar. That lady's academic life began in 1852 when she, Eleanor Dennistoun, daughter of a wealthy Glasgow family who gave their name to a district of the city, married William Sellar, who was assistant to Professor Ramsay of the Chair of Humanity in the University. Their life in Glasgow was brief, for young Sellar was presently appointed assistant and successor to the Professor of Greek in St. Andrews. This meant a happy period of academic life in a small city which was more like Oxford and Cambridge in its academic essence than either Glasgow or Edinburgh could be. It was not yet 'the city of the scarlet gown' for the students' distinctive garb had fallen out of use. Mrs. Sellar wore a red cloak because she liked the colour, and provoked some comment:

'Folk canna help their taste. See Mrs. Sellar in yon scarlet cloak,' said one old woman in kindly pity.

As in Oxford and Cambridge there was an interchange of dinners. Society was enlivened by the coming of a new Principal, Dr. Tulloch, and his wife. There were no colleges, in the English way, and hence no college kitchens as resource for the academic hostess; but there was Bell. Today, an accomplished cook, is always called in for important dinner-parties. Professor Sellar was said to have declared: 'The only people I care for here are Bell Tulloch and Principal Today.'

The year was divided into two parts; from October till March, the academic term, the Sellars lived in St. Andrews; the rest of the year might be spent in travel or in a country house, The Sellars had a Highland home, Ardtornish, on the Sound of Mull, and, when that was given up, one in Yarrow; in their latter years they lived in Galloway.

In the eighteen-sixties Professor Sellar was appointed to the Chair of Humanity in Edinburgh, and they came to a house in Buckingham Terrace, There was no Professors' Court or Quadrangle in Edinburgh, as there was in Glasgow, but they had colleagues among their neighbours and there was always the University circle as one of the interesting circles which made up Edinburgh society – the legal and the clerical being equally important. A near neighbour was Professor Crum Brown with whom Sellar used to drive every morning from the West End of the New Town over to the University in the heart of the Old. Crum Brown was a polymath, and a Sellar daughter, newly grown up and come out, when going to dine at his house was told:

'You will have an excellent dinner and some unusual conversation.' She enjoyed both. 'Chinese folk-stories and the history of the Anti-burgher Secession' were among the topics.

The Sellars were kindly hosts to the students. Six or seven of them were always invited to breakfast on Saturday when there were no classes. Among their private and intimate friends were the Stevensons, parents of Robert Louis. The young Eleanor Dennistoun had been bridesmaid to Miss Balfour when she married the engineer and lighthouse-builder, Thomas Stevenson. Then there were the Fleeming Jenkins, the Professor of Engineering and his vivid, charming wife who, on her first formal call on Mrs. Stevenson had met and been captivated by her long-legged, brilliant, erratic son whom she knew at once to be a poet.

Edinburgh was legal in pattern, though the Church was of high dignity and importance; but society tended to converge on the Law Courts and Parliament House as a small English city upon its Cathedral Close. Mrs. Sellar recalled a question of precedence. One of the Lords of Session, Lord Moncrieff, arrived early for a dinner; his hostess welcomed the chance of settling a problem: in strict protocol should he or the Bishop of Edinburgh take her down to dinner?

'Most assuredly I do. The Bishop here is only the head of a dissenting body, not a Lord Spiritual.'

Jowett visited them from Oxford; he had been a friend since Sellar's Balliol days. A welcome but a difficult guest, he was not at his best on formal occasions, being shy, silent and reserved. At one party he sat next to the indomitable woman doctor. Sophia Jex

Blake to whom none of these adjectives could be applied. Asked, afterwards, about his experience, Jowett replied:

'*Lex* is the Latin for law, and I suppose *Jex* for jaw.'

One wonders what he would have made of Mrs. Jebb and she of him; and wonders still more what would have come of her encounter with another redoubtable matriarch in Glasgow, Mrs. Story. The Jebbs' final departure to Cambridge prevented this, much to our loss, though perhaps for the better peace of Glasgow. The Storys came from manse to college house. The Reverend Robert Herbert Story was minister of Rosneath on the Gareloch when he met the vivacious Miss Janet Maughan at a General Assembly party in Edinburgh in 1863. She was a mature thirty-five and had enjoyed a full and gay girlhood and young womanhood in mid-Victorian Edinburgh; as unlike the imagined mid-Victorian girl as possible. Her preference was for the military over the clergy, and when the Lady Provost, an intimate friend of hers, asked her to help at this reception for the ministers attending the Assembly she agreed reluctantly: 'Parsons were not much in my line.' Driving up to the house she saw a very handsome cleric alight from a cab and enter.

'I'll begin with that one who arrived just before me,' she told her hostess, who retorted: 'Oh! I see you know very well how to take care of yourself.'

The handsome cleric stayed by her side all evening; and in the following October they were married as she had intended they should. Mrs. Story was charmed with her new life; with the manse itself, 'a nice, old-fashioned house in a pretty garden', with the parish, its people and their neighbours. Like Mrs. Elton she roused much interest in the congregation on her first Sunday, wearing, with sober elegance, a dark brown silk dress with a shepherd's plaid shawl and a straw bonnet trimmed with violets and a cluster of rosebuds under the brim:

'I thought I looked very well, and my husband said I did.'

Unlike Mrs. Elton she had tact and good manners, and made many friends in the village and among the farmers as well as at the neighbouring country houses. There was at the same time, an awareness of social distinctions.

'The members of the dining society of Rosneath were only seventeen. There were many more residents but they did not give dinners, restricting their hospitality to less formal functions' – but not less enjoyable. The farms were as hospitable as 'the better class houses and villas' offering country teas of home-baked scones, home-made jam, honey and thick cream. There were evening parties too, which began with tea, continued with music and cards and ended with supper. One hearty hostess thus addressed the company:

'Ladies and Gentlemen, I am sure we have all spent a very pleasant evening and we are very much obliged to those who have so kindly played and sung to us, and now, I think, we shall all be the better for a little rest and refreshment. Them that's dry, folly me.'

Miss Maughan's marriage at thirty-five and to a country parson, had surprised her friends, some of whom predicted that she would be bored by domesticity and rural life; but she took very kindly to both, and on the few evenings they were left by themselves sat contentedly mending and darning while her husband read aloud to her. She took over all the duties of the lady of the manse, inherited from her mother-in-law. (Her husband had succeeded his father as minister.) She taught in Sunday School, looked after various parish organizations, visited and entertained the congregation, received many guests; among them was Mrs. Oliphant, an old friend of the family, now an established and almost best-selling novelist. Her industry and versatility were immense, but unobtrusive. No woman was ever less of the professional writer in manner; she had the capacity for living two separate lives. But the housemaid reported her asking for extra candles; she wrote late into the night, or into the morning, then appeared at breakfast ready to be leisurely and companionable. though not always ready (according to her critical hostess).

'When she pleased she could be very agreeable, but she did no always please, and when indifferent to her company, she was very silent.'

It was not indifference; it was a depth of shyness and reserv which Mrs. Story could never comprehend; and with it, no doub something of the novelist's instinctive withdrawal, to observe an to absorb.

Visiting ministers came – Principal Tulloch among them, wit his wife; and there was a dinner, twice a year on Sacramer

Sunday, for the Kirk Session. Social life in Edinburgh had been a good training, and Mrs. Story was an imperturbable hostess; when six guests proposed themselves just after she and her husband had come home from a holiday, she continued 'more than usual calm', and arranged a late and lavish breakfast instead of a more formal luncheon. It could happen that her 'unfortunate love of hospitality was answerable for an occasional breeze', as when, in her Episcopalian ignorance she arranged a lunch party for a Fast Day – that solemn day of prayer which used to precede the Presbyterian Communion or Sacrament Sunday; the nearest approach in the Kirk of that time to Good Friday. The party had to be cancelled.

In 1887 the minister was appointed to the Chair of Church History in Glasgow University, and the Storys, with their two daughters left the country manse for No. 8 The College. They found old friends among the Professors – the two Cairds, John the Principal, and Edward the Professor of Moral Philosophy, and their wives; and made new ones: the Ramsays, the Gairdners, the Dicksons. The latter lived next door, and with them Mrs. Story found not only formal but homely hospitality:

'It was a real enjoyment to sit round their comfortable tea-table, and get a cup of Maggie Dickson's own special brewing. She always made the tea herself, in an ordinary kettle on the drawing-room fire, and a very fine cup of tea was the result, seasoned with a racy gossip over our own and our neighbours' affairs.'

Gown entertained gown, sometimes including the scarlet gown of the undergraduate. The students, for their part, gave dances to which the professors' wives came as chaperones, sitting in state. They were bidden to parties in the College houses; once to a play written and produced by Mrs. Story, sometimes to lunch. This was rather an ordeal, and the young men used to wait for each other on the doorstep, entering in a bashful bunch.

The Town also entertained, and sumptuously:

'We . . . assisted to bridge over the gulf that had long existed between Town and Gown', and 'cultivated friendly relations both with those within the walls of the College and with numbers of people outside, more especially with the members of the City Corporation who were mostly people of importance and wealth.'

Mrs. Story is at times, of an almost endearing snobbery, so open and naïve is her liking for the high and grand. Town dinners were luxurious: 'Lucullan banquets', with half a dozen entrées and a flow of the famous Glasgow punch 'that insinuating if deleterious combination which had too often far-reaching consequences'. With the rich food and wine went an equal wealth of talk. The company was 'a mixture of money and brains' – the brains having made the money, and included distinguished guests. Mrs. Story met, at one dinner, Lord Coleridge 'with his highbred English tones' and Lord Young with his 'caustic, telling Doric', both of them highly entertaining.

Among their own guests were the Bishop of Peterborough who was duly impressed by finding himself in a room with sixteen professors, and Boyd Carpenter of Ripon who shared with his wife a power of thought-transference. Once, in church, he communicated to her the fact that he had left his sermon at home; she replied – also by thought – that she would fetch it, but was told not to go herself but send their son who was with her in the pew.

Glasgow balls were even better than the dinners, with charming rooms, a good band and 'a gorgeous supper with oysters and champagne'. Mrs. Story was more appreciative of such pleasures than Mrs. Jebb.

In 1898 the Professor was made Principal, and they moved to 13 The College. The flow of guests increased; most notably at the ninth Jubilee celebrations of the foundation of the university. The Principal and his lady were left limp after shaking hands with some three thousand guests: 'though I had been prescient and had removed my rings, knowing by frequent experience the effects of a good, hearty Glasgow squeeze.'

Principal Story's reign saw the turn of the century, the death of the Queen, the coming of women students – they had, indeed, begun to come up during his professorship. His wife who now saw her fourth reign, who could recall a pre-Victorian childhood and a Victorian girlhood, now watched those learned and decorous girls in their long skirts and high-necked blouses, cross the quadrangle to their classrooms, and, in due time, approach the Principal on his rostrum in the Bute Hall to receive their degrees in arts, science or medicine.

II

Victorian Edinburgh honoured character as well as learning; character in the full sense of the word, which was individual, strong and colourful. A touch of eccentricity was esteemed. Whatever may be argued about the depressing effects of Calvinism and of Victorian propriety, Edinburgh gave her citizens a wide liberty and her citizens, if they chose, could live well and at ease. These were ample days when one need not have ample means to furnish a library and a cellar, these kindred repositories of learning and good living. Both were possessed by George Saintsbury who came to Edinburgh in 1895 to succeed Masson in the Chair of English and Rhetoric. His scholarship informs many books of literary history and criticism, but his full personality is expressed in his Notebooks and his Cellar Book which is by way of being autobiography: *Vita in Vino*.

'For twenty years of the time [when he was making his Cellar] I was a journalist and in other ways a working man of letters . . . while for full another twenty, I occupied a position in which, as one received much hospitality, it was not merely a pleasure but a duty to show some.' This duty he nobly and memorably performed.

When he came to Edinburgh he was fifty; he had been a schoolmaster for eight years, Assistant Editor of *The Saturday Review* for eleven. His cellar was first laid down in the eighties, when he moved into 'one of the new regions west of Kensington', into a new house with builders of generous mind.

'They let me choose my papers; they furnished me with a bath of extraordinary elaborateness, where you could float on an upward douche like a cork in one of the shop fountains; subject yourself to what was called a "wave" (it was more ingenious than exhilarating) and, by turning various cocks and levers in the hood, administer showers of most interesting variety. But what was even more to my taste was that they let me have . . . an apartment in the basement "suitable to the purposes not of eating but of drinking": a perfect cellar with no stoves or pipes near it, and "its greatest length backed on solid earth".'

In Edinburgh he lived, at first, in a large eighteenth-century house with ample cellars. One had been used for coal, the other was infested by rats. Bounce the Scotch terrier tried to deal with them, but in the chase knocked over and broke two magnums of champagne. 'If he had got the rat it would have been some consolation for a rather expensive kind of sport.'

Soon, in 'that most hospitable of places, Edinburgh' he established his reputation as host and scholar, as man of letters and as *gourmet*. His Cellar Book is unique: part memoir, part essay, part household book, part history of the wines he knew. It is spiced and laced with anecdotes, as, his brief dialogue with the shopman in Fortnum and Mason's who, when he was buying some Schabzüger cheese, asked anxiously: 'Excuse me, sir, but are you acquainted with this cheese?' On being assured that there was an old acquaintance between cheese and consumer, he was relieved. A lady had recently come back to complain of its pungency; she had eaten it like Cheddar. It must be grated, mixed with butter and spread thinly on toast.

Saintsbury kept a list or pageant of dinners in London and in Edinburgh, in town and country; simple meals of six courses: soup, fish (fried trout) fillets of beef, roast duckling, apricots, and 'sardines *Dieu-sait-comment*; a prescription of my wife's, named by me', accompanied by sherry, champagne, port, and green Chartreuse with the coffee. Champagne in those days was very much a dinner drink, almost an all-purpose one. Another simple meal omitted champagne, offering merely sherry (always with the soup) *Château Yquem*, *Château Margaux*, and port; with the oysters, *consommé*, red mullet, cutlets, grouse, macaroni pudding and shrimp toast.

An ampler meal consisted of:

Consommé aux Pointes d'Asperges; John Dory with *Sauce Livornaise* and *Filets de Saumon â la Gelée; Côtelettes à la Joncourt;* Plovers' Eggs; *Aspic de Volaille à la Reine;* Haunch of Mutton; *Mayonaise de Homard; Soufflé Glacé au Marasquin; Canapés de Crevettes.* With this marched a noble procession of wines: *Montilla; Johannesberg Claus Auslese; Château Grillet; Champagne (Dagonet) in Jeroboam;* [He used to wreath the jeroboams as centre-pieces]. *Romanée Conti; Château Margaux;* port, and a sweet sherry, *Padre Ximeno.*

Dinners varied according to place, season and number of guests. A 'June-eating' for a French guest very properly offered nothing

French but the wines and the savoury – which consisted of olives; the meal began with oxtail soup, and continued with whitebait, mutton, chicken and iced gooseberry fool. A country dinner offered among other good things, boiled salmon, forequarter of lamb, and cherry tart. The ideal company was 'the sonnet form or "fourteener"'; twelve guests with host and hostess, giving the proper arrangement of six a side, lady and gentleman alternating, the lady of highest rank on her host's right. At one dinner, this lady declined the *soufflé*, as did her neighbour on the other side; their example was followed right round the table until the *soufflé* reached the host.

'I am sorry to keep you all waiting' – but this was a favourite of his. 'It looks very good. May I change my mind?' murmured the first lady. Her neighbour also changed his; and so back round the table went the *soufflé*, every guest partaking, only Mrs. Saintsbury consistently declining. The host murmured 'sheep' to himself, as he watched the chain of acceptance.

III

A modern scholar in his mid-Victorian childhood knew a living link with the Georgians. H. A. L. Fisher was born in 'a little white slip of a house' in Onslow Square; it still survived when, in 1939 he began his *Unfinished Autobiography*. The children used to look out for their neighbour, Mr. Justice Byles, riding past every morning on his white horse, to the Law Courts; and sometimes they saw, walking together, old Mr. Carlyle and Mr. Froude, celebrities remote from the small boy who was himself to be so great an historian. He had glimpses, hardly retained, of 'the most august babies in the land' in the most exalted nursery – in Marlborough House, for his father was private secretary to the Prince of Wales; hence a royal godfather for the boy and the name of Albert.

His father was, in the son's fond recollection, 'a beautiful scholar in the old Oxford sense of the term'; with no modern learning, little knowledge of the minor authors but a profound love and knowledge of the great poets of antiquity. The family was one of many generations of clerics, scholars and soldiers, 'a race of quiet, retiring men, well content with a modest station in life, scholars, bird lovers, landscape painters and sportsmen, Anglicans all of them and orthodox in an old-fashioned way, and English to the core'. Through his grandmother he could claim kinship with Wordsworth, and his Aunt Emmeline had a certain fragile talent which might have brought her fame. 'But she was married as a girl to a poor Wiltshire clergyman, and a few years later succumbed to the burdens of a family and a parish.' She had published the almost inevitable slender volume of verse, strongly opposed by Wordsworth, who was not, however, above making use of her talent. Once, while staying with the family he received a command from the Queen to re-write the National Anthem on a less bellicose note; he funked it, and handed the task to Emmeline whose version won her not only a compliment but a silver inkstand from the Queen.

On his mother's side there was French blood from a young Chevalier, Antoine de l'Etang, page, and some said would-be lover to Marie Antoinette. On the maternal side, too, were two distinguished grand-aunts, Mrs. Cameron, 'the creator of artistic photography', and Mrs. Thoby Prinsep, hostess of Little Holland House, and friend of a host of mid-Victorian celebrities, G. F. Watts, for whom, indeed, she made a home at Little Holland House, Burne-Jones, George Eliot, Gladstone, Herbert Spencer. So there were the two streams of heredity; on his father's, one of quiet scholarship and placid devotion, on his mother's something more brilliant with a hint of the exotic, a whiff of the Bohemian. His mother herself made no pretence to be intellectual, but she had two accomplishments not uncommon in the Victorian gentlewoman; she spoke perfect French and she had an exquisite singing touch on the piano.

'Delight in learning came to me from her,' for she taught her children at home. Family life was all in all to her. 'The five things most precious in a woman – family love, faith in goodness, music and poetry, high courage in adversity were all hers.'

The Fishers moved, presently, to Blatchington near Seaford in Sussex, to enjoy 'the best kind of country life' on means not ample but adequate. The beneficent effects of low taxation upon domestic life has never been fully estimated. Blatchington was still in eighteenth-century England, with memories of the smugglers, even a hint that one local worthy *was* a smuggler. Whether or not he was, he was an expert bird-nester, climbing down the cliffs to take the eggs of a peregrine falcon for H. A. L.'s collection. The mummers came on Christmas Eve to play *St. George and the Dragon*.

There were visits to Cornwall, when Fisher senior was appointed to a Judgeship as Vice-Warden of the Stannaries; this meant, as a rule, four sessions of a fortnight each in Truro. They used to stay with the Leslie Stephens at St. Ives, the scene of Virginia Woolf's *To the Lighthouse*. Then came another move to a house in the New Forest inherited from an aunt; an unattractive house and the boys missed the sea, but the Forest itself made up for all other insufficiencies, and when the boys went to Winchester it was near enough for their coming home on leave-out days.

Tennyson was among the illustrious friends of this family, and H. A. L. went walking with him at Farringford, the poet sweeping along in his cloak, reciting his own poems with occasional comments: 'Isn't that grand?' Tennyson received much adoration from the soulful, but himself 'liked strong language and strong drink', and a weekly hot bath. The round, shallow tub was set out, cans of hot water fetched, and the coachman poured the stream over 'the stalward frame of the seated Laureate'.

A golden age it seemed, in retrospect from the grim first year of the Second World War; but in any retrospect it must have appeared mellow in happiness and security. War was remote; it might happen overseas, but it was unimaginable that this country should ever again be involved in close conflict. The world of politics was distant, social problems did not trouble the minds of this family, except for some disapproval of the wretched condition of the cottages on a neighbouring estate.

The boys' education in the classics was solid; they inherited a love of books and music, and these were found at home. The assumption of this lay beneath the exclusive classicism of Winchester. Science was almost untouched, history lightly touched. 'The vast field of modern knowledge was a closed book to us.' Whatever its limitations this education, and still more this way of family life produced men and women not only of intellect and talent but of strong personality. One sister was extremely musical and had a literary gift, too closely hidden but which expressed itself in a series of country plays, true to life and to the country. She was single-minded or eccentric to the point of genius. A passionate lover of birds and beasts, she once, according to family legend, chaperoned her daughter to a ball carrying a tray of newly hatched thrushes which she proposed to rear by hand and would not let out of her sight. After animals there came, in the scale of her affections, gypsies and other vagrants; then the villagers and country folk, and last of all townspeople.

One brother was Admiral Lord Fisher; another was Charles, a scholar and a ripe character who was killed in the Kaiser's war, and is commemorated in one of the great poems of that war by another great scholar, J. S. Phillimore.

Diversity of character, talent and achievement made this, and many another Victorian household a microcosm of humanity. The golden age of the aristocracy was in the eighteenth, continuing into the nineteenth century; the latter age saw the zenith of the minor gentry, of the upper-middle class, the scholars, clergy, and professional gentlemen, people of gentle blood if not of illustrious lineage, of moderate fortune, with leisure but with disciplined habits of mind, with tradition and an easy culture, an inherited love of letters and the arts, of nature and country life. Theirs was a goodly heritage.

7

Episcopal Journey: From Don to Priest

From Fellowship to priesthood, from married quarters in Oxford through vicarage to episcopal palace makes the pattern of life for one of the greatest of Victorian Bishops, Mandell Creighton. He was a Fellow of Merton, recently ordained, when, at one of Ruskin's lectures he met Louise von Glehn; she was wearing a yellow dress which to him indicated an original, even a daring taste, and he sought an introduction. This was in 1871 when Oxford Statutes made it possible – with the permission of their own colleges – for Fellows to marry. The Creighton–von Glehn engagement was one of many, and the don wrote to his Louise in some dismay:

'Merton has always been regarded as the most advanced and maddest College in Oxford; but the spectacle of all its Fellows rushing headlong into matrimony at once will make everyone in Oxford die with laughter.'

This did not deter them, and they were married in January 1872, taking a house in St. Giles' Road which they named Middlemarch, after George Eliot's new novel. The bridegroom's college servants supervised the removal and his 'white Persian cat was comfortably established on the hearthrug to welcome us'. Mrs. Creighton recalls in her *Life and Letters* of her husband that he 'always knew how to get himself well served'. He himself declared: 'Experience at Oxford has taught me how to treat male servants; it is by being fearfully strict with them, though never losing your temper or being put out.' To keep his temper was not easy for him; he was quick on the draw, but it was his family who knew that best: 'Those who were nearest and dearest to him alone seemed able to arouse his irritation' – from their very nearness, their being part of himself. With his servants he might threaten a most tremendous blowing up' but when the culprit appeared, he would 'speak in the kindest and gentlest way'. His college servants went on doing jobs for him: 'would come and help him to bottle a cask of claret' and bring him flowers from their gardens.

The young Creightons were very regular in their way of life. He

attended chapel every morning, breakfasted in college and lec-
tured all morning, lunched at home then went for a walk, or to a
public lecture with his wife; his pupils came to him in the late
afternoon, and in the evening, if they had no dinner engagement,
he worked, often dictating to his wife while he wandered about his
study from bookshelf to bookshelf. There were, however, many
dinner engagements, both in college – 'where I was sometimes the
only lady, for ladies were still rare in Oxford', and in the houses of
the married dons. College dinners might be luxurious, but the
domestic were simple:

'We were all comparatively poor, we were acquainted with one
another's pecuniary position and there was no desire for pretence.'
The hour was usually seven – 'only the great people dined at
seven-thirty' and the Creightons left at ten. Unless the weather
was very bad they walked to and from their dinners.

Among their hosts and guests were the T. H. Greens, the
Humphry Wards, Walter Pater and his sisters, and Jowett. They
were visited occasionally by J. R. Green the historian, by C. P.
Scott of the *Manchester Guardian*, by George Saintsbury and by
Robert Bridges. Marriage gave Creighton the best of both worlds:
he still belonged to Merton, dining in hall once a week; and at
home he found peace, a true companionship of heart and mind, an
easy and congenial social life.

'He was very particular about all the arrangements of his domestic life; his habits were simple, and he never expected personal
attendance, but he liked what was done in the house to be well
done, he accepted no excuses and overlooked no shortcomings' –
a fairly formidable husband. His wife proved adequate from the
first, for he wrote to her mother (whose comments we should
have liked to hear) that he was finding married life 'much better in
every way . . . in reality than in my anticipations I had ever hoped
for. I find everything much nicer than I expected; the troubles are
fewer, in fact, almost none. Louise is so admirable at managing
everything that I find I have less worry than I used to have among
my multitude of servants at College'. He realized that her solitary
breakfast might be dull, 'but she sees the usefulness of the arrangement and does not mind'. Altogether he found her 'a hundred
times better on closer acquaintance than ever I had though
beforehand. I keep on seeing new reasons for adding more and

more respect and moral and intellectual approbation to my feelings towards her'.

Of their children, the two eldest daughters were born in Oxford, and both named from Dante: Beatrice and Lucia. The latter was born in their second house, Beam Hall, which belonged to Corpus Christi, was close to Merton and altogether more convenient than Middlemarch. Creighton 'could be in and out of College constantly, and keep a watchful eye over the conduct of the undergraduates. Even in bed at night he would listen with anxious ears for possible fireworks or other unlawful noises'. Comment here could be ribald.

It was a hospitable house, the men coming in, very often, on Sunday evenings. This proved, however, a brief phase of academic domesticity. Creighton was offered the college living of Embleton in Northumberland; very near his own calf country for he had been born in Carlisle, of Scottish descent. His choice between Oxford and Embleton was not easily made. His wife's inclination lay towards Oxford, and while he was staying with his father he wrote to her:

'You give me reasons against Embleton which, you will permit me to say, are futile.' One was that he was irreplaceable at Oxford: 'But never was a place where men are so easily replaced and so soon forgotten.' There was the question of where he would be more useful: 'I answer, a man is equally useful everywhere if he is doing his best.' As for what that might be – 'Do you mean best for my fame or my happiness?' Fame, certainly, so far as that is concerned with being talked about by the set of people who do the most talking, would be best served at Oxford; as for abiding fame, if any, and for happiness he was unsure: 'If you helped me on these points with your views, you would be doing more that was definitely useful.'

His vocation was breaking out of its academic shell and the struggle in himself went deeper than he realized. This was more than a choice between two homes, academic or rural, or between two forms of a clerical don's career; it was between a mere continuance in scholarship and the complete fulfilment of his priesthood. Happily for the Church and for his soul's welfare the priestly vocation triumphed. There was still a strong pull towards academic life, and the essential matter of priestly duty was not clearly apparent. His private desire for change, for quietness and study was stressed:

'Your considerations omit the most essential point. By going to Embleton I get quietness and security.' At present there was little of either. The first was threatened by administrative duties, the second by the fact that 'I am, though nominally a Fellow, really a subordinate official in the employment of the unmarried Fellows' some of whom thought they had power to dismiss a tutor, as a governing body might a headmaster. A new Warden might make difficulties: 'If I were unmarried, I could hold my Fellowship and do work for other colleges' but not without the Fellowship, and in seven years more 'I shall have to sue for re-election'. There was little chance of a University post.

'Really, the state of things is this: I want to lead a literary not an active life. Which helps me most, Embleton or Oxford?'

It is a singularly unpriestlike question from one who was to become so great a priest and so great a Father-in-God. He summed up the relative advantages: in Oxford, the stimulus of intellectual society, the facilities of libraries; in Embleton, the quiet, the opportunity for concentrated work, the saving of energy. Louise, he knew, loved Oxford society:

'You are younger and have not had so much of it. I have long felt how trumpery it is . . . an interchange of things meant to be clever but not containing much that is real or true.' To discuss schemes of education in a drawing-room was easier than to work them out in a parish. Here was the first hint of pastoral vocation:

'Society gives you all the advantages of looking very wise and good, without much cost or actual effort.' His wife may not have relished the irony.

Merton and Oxford urged him to stay; it was hinted that he might become Warden. What finally tipped the scales towards Embleton was the desire for concentrated work, unbroken by lectures or tutoring. He was contemplating a *History of the Papacy*. 'A desire for less mental dissipation led me into the country.'

One friend told him: 'You will end by being Archbishop of Canterbury'; another – Mark Pattison – was gloomy: 'You can't study history without a library, and you can't get an adequate historical library unless you spend at least £1,000 a year on books.

Creighton went off to Embleton, to reconnoitre, in the Christmas vacation of 1874. After spending a night in the Bishop's Palace at Durham, he reached his future parish in a snowstorm, sooner than he expected, and so was not met. He started walking to the vicarage but was nearly lost in the snow. He found refuge with one of the churchwardens, and next day 'made a kind of Arctic expedition' to the vicarage where he camped alone for a week or two, making the acquaintance of several parishioners and correcting the proofs of an article. By this time he was established in the scholastic literary world, contributing to the more learned periodicals, editing a series of historical biographies for Rivington, his own being a *Life of Simon de Montfort*, and writing (in three weeks) his famous *Primer of Roman History*. This sold enormously, because, as he used to assert, it was of a size so convenient for schoolroom missiles that it had constantly to be replaced.

'Yesterday afternoon I staggered over to Falloden to see the Greys,' he wrote to his wife. 'Lady Grey is a brisk, talkative, active old lady, very Low Church, with a great interest in the souls of old women. . . . I find the villagers very kindly, with a general desire to be hospitable . . . but they will not accept one without fair criticism, and their approval will never be without reserve.'

He liked the country and the vicarage, although that would need a good deal of furnishing. The last incumbent had been there for forty years. It was a large house, of unusual type; a modern part of black basalt built on to an old red sandstone tower or peel.

'These towers were built as protection against the raids of the Scots' which may have amused one of Scottish name and ancestry. It was one of three such fortified vicarages in Northumberland. On the ground floor was a vaulted chamber for cattle, with two rooms above for the people taking refuge. The Creightons trained creepers over the grim black walls and made the house comfortable and comely.

And so began a new chapter, almost a rebirth, for the scholar began at once to fulfil his vocation as pastor and priest. Embleton was a country and seacoast parish, bleak, at first glance, with little beauty but the gleam of the sea: 'But it is a country which takes hold of the heart,' clear and spacious, a country to be discovered and loved through every change of season. The winter could be menacing, with icy winds from the Cheviots and frequent mists or 'sea-frets'; but the sea also could temper the cold and the vicarage was sheltered by a cliff and by trees.

The parish was made up of some five villages with a number of farms. Embleton itself was 'a forlorn-looking place', a scatter of cottages, a few shops and five pubs: 'a sort of metropolis for the district'. Most of the men worked in the basalt-quarries and this, and stone-breaking were well paid. There was easy work for boys, too, driving the carts of stone blocks to the station, and so, little ambition to learn any skilled trade. The morals of the place were low: 'terrible, almost animal.' There was no resident squire, and the employers in the quarries did little or nothing to raise the tone; often they paid wages in one of the pubs, where money was soon turned into drink. The new vicar began his warfare against evil by helping the young people in the school, the choir, the Girls' Friendly Society.

Three miles away lay the fishing village of Craster, a separate almost a peculiar community, much intermarried, little travelled. Some of the old women had never been in a train, never travelled more than a few miles from home. Then there was Newton-by-the-Sea made up of two hamlets, Upper Newton and Sea Houses, the latter a tiny place 'built round a square which was filled up with pig-styes and middens'. The people's livelihood was the herring fishery, and the women worked in the curing yards, dressed in oilskins, cleaning, salting and packing the fish to be sent to Spain and Italy as Lenten fare. There was work for everyone and a good harvest from the sea meant wages as high as ten shillings a day. To any suggestion that it was dirty work the reply was: 'Aye, but the money's clean.'

In winter came the haddock fishing and here too the women had their work, that of baiting the hooks, three to six hundred on long fishing lines; hours of patient work which would be lost if a three days' storm kept the men from putting to sea.

'A fisherman's wife had a hard life,' the vicar's wife discovered. 'It was seldom that love led a man so far to forget prudence as to choose a wife who had not been brought up to it.'

When the Creightons visited the women sitting at work on the baits, the man of the house would sometimes emerge from the box bed in the kitchen, having had his sleep after fishing all night

In spring came the crab and lobster fishing. It was dangerous work in winter; a father and son might be sharing a boat and a storm drown them both.

There were a few railwaymen in a village close to the North-Eastern Railway, and there were the employees and dependents of Sir George Grey of Falloden; the rest of the parishioners were farmers and farm-labourers, or hinds, to use the north-country word. These were hired by the year and were tenants of the farmer. Women workers were called bondagers. A group of them would share a cottage with an elderly woman as housekeeper. Married women were not expected to help but a man's family were, and this made a constant shift of population, as the family proved too large or too small for the particular work needed.

Wages were about twenty-five shillings a week, and were paid even if the worker were off ill. Children could earn from eight to ten shillings a week and more at the harvest. There was little distinction of sex, the girls sharing the roughest work. They wore short petticoats and large straw sun-bonnets with 'uglies' or shades over their faces and the back of their necks. These could prove becoming – by showing a pretty young face under the uncouth headgear. On Sunday they all dressed very fine.

The cottages were like those on the Scottish side of the Border, not like those in a south-country village. Some had only a kitchen, with box-beds shut off like tiny, separate rooms. Even when there were other rooms the family gathered in the kitchen. The good housewife had a back kitchen or 'back end' for rough work, and kept the main kitchen clean and comfortable, often well and solidly furnished. The Creightons thought the cottages ill-cared-for, perhaps because, being held rent free and only for a year or two, they stirred no pride in either landlord or tenant.

Morals varied from one village to another. The farming community indulged freely in fornication and adultery with neither shame nor apology, and with no great expense when the consequences arrived. On a farm there was always plenty of milk, plenty of food, plenty of work; a new member of the family, even if what is kindly called in Scotland 'a wee mistake', need not be a burden. Better housing made little difference; even when roomier cottages were built the sport continued. On the other hand, at Craster, in one-roomed cottages, illegitimacy was unknown. It

was the attitude which mattered, and that of the fisher-folk was
austere.

The women, as a rule, were good housewives, and, as in Scotland, good bakers, The smell of newly baked loaves was delicious;
baker's bread was at once an extravagance and a treat. But the old
ways were beginning to change as shops came near, and the
people gave up their old country diet of porridge, barley bread
and milk. White flour was replacing barley and oatmeal. Tea was
now the favourite drink, bacon and red herring made the staple
food. The Creightons let the vicarage pasture to a woman on
condition that she sold the milk of her cows in the villages; but
it was a difficult campaign in dietetics.

There were still distinct local dialects, one of the fisher-folk, one
of the farmers. The vicar liked the Northern speech with its
cadences, its softness, its caressing phrases: 'My comely jewel';
'My canny hinny.'

The two communities differed in character; the fisher-folk had
'the most heart and the most imagination', the farm-people were
reserved, almost unapproachable. The Creightons found that they
were expected to greet people on the road, and the response was
always friendly, but there was no touching of hats or pulling of
forelocks, no bob or curtsy. There was nothing of the feudal feeling of the south. They were a strong people, both fishers and
farmers, and they respected strength of mind and character in
others.

For the former Fellow of Merton there could hardly have been
a greater change of work or environment. He came utterly in-
experienced as a pastor, with little knowledge of working-folk,
but he came with good will, and in a way, his very inexperience
was a help. He had no set ways or prejudices. The little family
settled down in their peel-vicarage at Easter 1875. The vicar began
a weekly Celebration of the Eucharist instead of the mere monthly
one which had been the rule. He had a mixed choir and taught
them to chant the Psalms; held a service on Sunday afternoon in
the little church at Craster, and taught in the Sunday School – this
proving his hardest task. His curate shared these duties, and
lunched and had tea in the vicarage. After Evensong they separated; to meet again at supper would have meant too much shop-
talk, and Creighton declared that by this time he had 'an irresistible

temptation to talk nonsense and eat jam'. He not only did so, but played with his children afterwards, and read aloud to them, usually poetry, some of Browning, and some of Morris's early poems which he loved.

Louise, however much she may have pined for Oxford at first, became the perfect clergy-wife. She shared the visiting with her husband and his curate; they used to walk together to one point in the parish, separate each to visit different families and meet again at a fixed time. They were well, almost too well and hospitably received. It was difficult to refuse a glass of wine, but gradually the parish accepted the fact that they preferred tea. The former don adapted himself to homely talk, as that perfect parish priest George Herbert had advised.

'Mr. Creighton is a very good crack,' one woman pronounced. 'But Mr. Green (the curate) he's a fair old wife's crack.'

The vicar knew his people: 'Remember that in dealing with ordinary folk you do not gain their confidence at once,' he told a friend. 'You must begin anyhow, gradually you can advance to serious things. If so speak out naturally what is in you, you do a great deal of good by showing a higher standard of life and duty.' There may have been a faint, unconscious condescension, but he did let a body talk, and about bodily ailments as well as spiritual problems.

'Mr. Creighton he says it's my digester that's out of order, but I say it's my whole cistern.'

He used to prescribe and bring them simple medicines.

'A bottle mixed and brought by the vicar was thought of sovereign efficacy. The larger the bottle and the nastier the taste, the better.'

He acted lawyer as well as doctor, filling all the manifold parts of the parish priest.

He loved children, played with them in an exuberant manner which terrified timid parents, and told them long nonsense stories: a gift which, if not peculiar to the Victorians was at least highly developed in them. His characters were diverting creatures with such names as Timothy Toozelwits, Tuttery Buttery and Kezia Hubbock. 'No children ever had a more delightful playmate than we had,' his eldest daughter recalled. 'All our best games and romps are bound up in our minds with him. . . . We cast aside

toys and bricks when he was there – he himself was all we wanted.'
He used to play ball with them, the child being the ball. One can
understand the apprehension of some parents. He could become
a giant or a rocking-horse, with several exuberant riders.

'Sunday evenings in the drawing-room were always a great
time for romps, and the wildest and most furious took place there.
Perhaps he found them a rest and relaxation after his Sunday
duties.'

Like Sir Walter Scott he was patient of interruption in the
study, and would lay down his pen to answer questions or give a
lesson, then return, unflurried, to his writing. Certain faults did
bring down wrath upon the children: being noisy in the passages
and on the stairs, wandering in and out of the room in an aimless
manner, being 'disorderly and futile'. This daughter enjoyed her
Greek lessons, begun when she was six; she sat on a stool beside
him to read or recite verbs. But if she forgot too often, or made
excuses, the book would be flung across the room and she would
be told to go.

There were six children, by this time, and the vicarage was not
a place of subdued silence; but they 'were never allowed to behave
as if the house belonged to them'. They were never 'managed';
his respect for the individual was too strong; but they must
respect his commands. He ruled the house with laws which were
few but which must be obeyed.

Like many another scholarly cleric possessed of a large house
and a not over-large income Creighton began taking pupils. They
worked in the study where he sat writing his sermons, the various
brief histories and biographies of that period, the first volumes of
his great *History of the Papacy*. He would break off work to discuss
their reading, giving not so much formal tutoring as endless
stimulus. Among the daughters of the neighbouring country
houses he had other pupils; visiting them in their schoolrooms,
sometimes, no doubt, to the embarrassment of their governesses
whose slight learning quailed before his scholarship, setting them
a course of reading, making them write essays for him.

'Any reading worth mentioning must be hard work,' he told
one girl, prescribing for her Stubbs's *Constitutional History*. 'I
have chosen for you the hardest subject and the stiffest book that I
know of in connection with English History.' He deplored her

lack of interest in Church History – 'the most important part of all history.'

The discipline and the enlargement of the mind were both good things. Much of the trouble in village life came from narrowness of interest. The vicar gave lectures and Shakespeare readings and arranged concerts, and made over the gatehouse of the vicarage to the men for a reading-room. Teaching, except religious instruction, in the schools had to be given up, for the vicar, his wife and the curate all found that nothing they taught could satisfy the inspector. With whom lay the blame? Each side had its own point of view, but the vicarage thought it impractical and unnecessary to make these village children learn the capes of China.

On the lighter side, they gave a Christmas ball for the choir; the vicar led each of the twenty-five ladies in turn out into a country dance, then carved at supper, so that he found this 'the most severe physical exertion of the year'. The Creightons believed in parties, but they risked unpopularity by stopping some local customs. Certain parishioners were disappointed by being offered nothing to drink when they called at the vicarage: 'A dry visit this,' was one comment. A peculiar wedding rite was stopped: that of making the bridal pair jump over a form at the church door, as they came out. It was said to mean a leap over future troubles, and it was not always decorous. Even less seemly was the custom of making some vagrant into the mayor of the village on a local feast day. First made drunk, he was wheeled round in a barrow by men and boys who demanded drink-money at every house. The feast was reformed into something like a holy day as well as a holiday, for it fell at Trinity – which was also the feast of dedication of the parish church.

The girls wore fine, new frocks, there were rich cakes for tea in every house, and on Monday there were sports by the sea. Another treat occurred in Lent when the women gave the children 'carlins' – beans fried in sugar and brandy. The vicar had started a Temperance Society and it was feared he might put down this treat; but he knew when to relax a rule. 'As carlins were not drink they might be allowed.'

There were good friends in the neighbourhood: the Greys of Falloden and of Howick, the Crasters who gave their name to the fishing village, the Fosters of Newton – who had sheltered him that snowy night of his arrival. Lady Grey of Falloden was mildly shocked when he introduced French novels into her husband's library. The Creightons drove to dinner-parties in an open pony carriage. Guests came to stay, filling the large vicarage, drifting in and out of the study, which was also the smoking-room. In the afternoon they were taken on a round of parish visits. In the evening they played whist; when alone, Creighton worked until bedtime.

This chapter of his life ended in 1884 when he was appointed Professor of Ecclesiastical History at Cambridge. He returned to academic life, enriched by experience, prepared, though he did not know it, for his greater pastoral charge to come. Mrs. Humphry Ward wrote to him about 'the humanizing, educative life at Embleton' which had shown him 'the elemental human things nearer far than most men of letters have a chance of seeing them'.

The house in Cambridge was little and poky after the space of the vicarage with its garden, but it was made as pretty as possible. It was in these years that Mrs. Creighton was one of the Ladies' Dining Club; this was Cambridge of the new colleges for women. Creighton was sympathetic, and gave lectures, most of them at Newnham. 'We felt as if we had more of a share in him in any but his own College,' said one of the staff, Alice Gardner. His own college was Emmanuel to which he had been elected a Fellow. He used to dine in hall on Sunday, and in the Combination Room delighted some of the dons and shocked others by his talk. 'A perpetual fountain of light' was one description; but another was: 'Professor Creighton is so frivolous.' One remark is worth cherishing: 'The Tudors are awful! I really do not think anyone ought to read the history of the sixteenth century.' He, for his part, found that 'people in Cambridge are too serious for me; they don't often make jokes, they think it right to be very wise, and I never was wise. . . . I still feel fearfully on my good behaviour . . . I think people look on me as a sort of strange beast . . . I can see that any approach to humour is like a slight magnetic shock to the company'.

Cambridge was a dining society. The Professor grumbled, but accepted invitations, and nearly always enjoyed his evenings. He and Louise still walked to parties when the weather was not forbidding, and talked over them on the way home. Creighton was a stimulating guest, a drawer-out of others, sometimes in the Socratic manner.

'Cambridge was a little afraid of him,' one friend said; and another: 'If people knew they were to meet him they might rejoice or they might be alarmed, but they could not be indifferent.' If severe, however, he was 'beneficently severe'.

He was still the companion of his children. The boys were not sent to prep school, but to Marlborough when they were twelve; there were still six at home, and frequent guests. Their father took them for long walks. Expeditions somewhat beyond their powers – to country churches, to Audley End, to Ely – were shared with his pupils or with students from Newnham and Girton.

In 1885 he was made Canon of Worcester which meant a second home, for three months of the year, always in the vacation. The house in the Precincts or College of Worcester was Queen Anne, mellow and dignified, with a walled garden. He loved it, and loved every detail of the ritual of life in the Precincts. It was a friendly community with many children running in and out of each other's houses, so that their parents declared they had to count them at night 'to make sure that the right ones were in their own homes'. The difficulty here was to find time and quiet enough for work. Everyone knew he was at home after Matins, everyone could see him in his study from the College Green.

'I shall have to put up a notice that it is not fair to shoot a canon sitting'; but the shooters were so pleasantly welcomed that they felt no compunction.

The Creightons began to spend every vacation in Worcester which meant six moves in the year, back and forth.

'Organization and habit made the move rapid and simple, and by the evening of the day of transit, we were always completely settled down.' The contribution of the servants to this happy consummation is not given in detail, but may be imagined. In 1891 this godly way of double life ended, when Creighton was consecrated Bishop of Peterborough.

The Palace was huge and daunting, and although it had 'some interesting features, there was much about the house to grieve anyone with a feeling for architecture'. The new Bishop made improvements; he had the plaster stripped off the stonework of the front, discovering a lancet window; he furnished and adorned the bare chapel; and collected books and pictures of the diocese. In his view, he held the Palace in trust for the diocese and his successors, and he and his family lived as simply as possible. He kept no carriage – one of the first signs of austerity or retrenchment in a genteel Victorian household. The Palace was near the railway station and the Bishop travelled by train. He took no man servant with him, fearing to burden the smaller clerical houses he visited. In the Palace there were, necessarily, many servants, but the children were bidden remember that this stateliness belonged to his office and its smooth functioning and was not of the essence of their domestic life. He deprecated this official grandeur for his children. Before every ordination the family were sent away, and the Palace became a retreat house for the ordinands, as many as could be lodged there; others stayed with the Dean and the Canons and spent all day in the Palace.

The final change came in 1896 when he was made Bishop of London. The Palace at Fulham was so large and rambling that he never learned his way about it. He made London House, in St. James's Square the town house of the see where he could be accessible to his clergy and others. From there he used to take long walks about the city and in the parks. At Fulham, he walked on Wimbledon Common, and played hockey with his children and their friends. There were many parties, dinners and garden-parties (some of these for four thousand guests with hosts of children), week-end parties where London guests could easily fancy themselves in the country, among the trees of the great garden. The work on *The History of the Papacy* continued and was completed. The Bishop and the scholar were one. Above all he was Father-in-God to his people, and he took very much to his heart the apostolic injunction about hospitality.

8

Yorkshire Parsonages

The most famous vicarage in England is one of the poorest: the
oblong, stone house with stone roof, its small garden in front and
the surrounding graveyard, with the moors beyond, which Mrs.
Gaskell saw when she came to Haworth to stay with Charlotte
Brontë:

'Oh! those high, wild, desolate moors high up above the whole
world, and the very realm of silence.'

Within, there were four rooms on each floor. On one side of the
door was Mr. Brontë's study with the kitchen behind it, on the
other the parlour, and behind that a little 'sort of store room'
which, on her marriage, Charlotte made into a study for her
husband. Upstairs were four bedrooms and a tiny room over the
passage, which was known as 'the children's study' – never the
nursery, even when the eldest student was only seven. There,
and in the warm kitchen was woven 'The Brontës' Web of Childhood'; the foundations laid of the hidden countries of Gondal
and Angria. Toys were few; Branwell had his soldiers, the famous
Young Men, and sometimes shared them with his sisters; but
they were creatures, characters in a play, not toys.

'I suspect that they had no children's books,' wrote Mrs. Gaskell; but few children of that period had. The wealth of books
written for and about children belongs to later decades from the
1840's on to the end of the century. There were always a few,
but children in the early nineteenth century simply adopted certain
classics as their own; and this family liked to browse and feed in a
real library.

'The well-bound [volumes] were ranged in the sanctuary of
Mr. Brontë's study'; but even the best bound book may grow
shabby from frequent handling, and find a humbler home on
bedroom shelves. 'Up and down the house were to be found
many standard works of a solid kind.' Scott, Wordsworth and
Southey provided 'the lighter literature'. The children's aunt,
Miss Branwell, had her private store of evangelical books and

periodicals, transferred by Charlotte to the vicarage in *Shirley* where Caroline Helstone has access to 'some venerable Ladies' Magazines . . . some mad Methodist magazines full of miracles and apparitions and preternatural warnings, ominous dreams and frenzied fanaticism'. These had their influence on the poetry of the sisters. Margaret Lane has pointed out that many of Emily's poems are written in the metre and pattern of Methodist hymns.

These pious byways were, however, less followed than the great high roads, plains and mountains of literature. Charlotte's own taste, and that of her sisters is reflected in a letter written to Ellen Nussey:

'If you like poetry, let it be first-rate, Shakespeare, Thomson, Goldsmith, Pope (though I don't admire him), Scott, Byron, Campbell, Wordsworth and Southey. Now don't be startled by the names of Shakespeare and Byron. Both these were great and their works are like themselves. You will know how to choose the good and avoid the evil. . . . Omit the Comedies of Shakespeare and the "Don Juan", perhaps the "Cain" of Byron . . . and read the rest fearlessly.' One is more likely to be startled by the inclusion of Thomson, Southey and Campbell among the first-rate, and by the avoidance of Shakespeare's Comedies. For history, there were Hume and Rollin, 'and the *Universal History* if you can; I never did'. Only Scott was recommended in fiction. 'All novels after his are worthless'; and there is no mention of Jane Austen. For biography, there were Boswell's *Johnson*, Johnson's own *Lives of the Poets*, Southey's *Nelson*, Lockhart's *Burns*, Moore's *Sheridan*, and his *Byron*.

The young Brontës were not starved mentally, nor were they stunted. Maria, the eldest, used to read the newspapers and give a précis of their contents to the others. Her father told Mrs. Gaskell that he could talk to her as to an adult.

Their schoolroom was Aunt Branwell's bedroom where she spent most of her time; the kitchen was their nearest approach to cosiness, fun and childishness. A fragment of a diary, kept by Emily and Anne, gives a reassuring glimpse of lapses in self-discipline:

'It is past twelve o'clock. Anne and I have not tidied ourselves, done our bed work or done our lessons, and we want to go out to play. We are going to have for dinner boiled beef, turnips, potatoes and apple pudding. The kitchen is in a very untidy state' – and Tabitha expected them to peel the potatoes.

Tabitha or Tabby Aykroyd came to the parsonage when Charlotte was nine, and stayed for the rest of Charlotte's thirty-nine years of life, herself reaching ninety. 'She ruled the children pretty sharply, yet never grudged a little extra trouble to provide them with such small treats as came within her power.'

Poverty, with innate asceticism, ruled the household. Ellen Nussey, Charlotte's first and lifelong friend, described the almost conventual bareness and cleanliness. There were no curtains or other draperies for Mr. Brontë had a dread of fire, and 'not much carpet anywhere except in the sitting-room and on the study floor'. The house was solidly built, with thick walls and 'the pleasant old fashion of window-seats all through the house', massive frames and shutters, wainscoted walls. The stone stairs and hall floor were 'done with sandstone, always beautifully clean as was everything about the house; the walls were not papered but stained in a pretty dove-coloured tint'. The furniture, mostly of mahogany and horsehair, was austere: 'scant and bare indeed . . . yet it was not a scantness that made itself felt. Mind and thought, I had almost said elegance, but certainly refinement, diffused themselves over all.' The cleanness was more than the mere absence of dirt and dust, it was a positive quality, an essence, a sparkling grace. As Mrs. Gaskell saw it: 'Everything about the place tells of the most dainty order, the most exquisite cleanliness. The doorsteps are spotless, the small, old-fashioned windows glitter like looking-glass. Inside and outside of that house, cleanliness goes up into its essence purity.'

The Brontës might be doubly Celtic in blood through their Irish father and their Cornish mother, but Yorkshire made them as well; with their passion and imagination was mingled a strain of practical homeliness. They did not merely accept or endure housewifery, they performed it with zest.

'I have quite a talent for cleaning, sweeping up hearths, dusting rooms, making beds,' Charlotte once told Ellen. It seemed, at one time, as if they would have to send Tabby away; she had broken her leg, she was elderly, she ought, Mr. Brontë declared, to be sent home to her sister; but his daughters began a hunger strike (was this the first in feminist history?) and Tabby stayed.

They had, however, to agree to her going home until the leg was strong again and her health restored; but they would have no one else in the house.

'I manage the ironing and keep the rooms clean,' Charlotte reported to Ellen. 'Emily does the baking and attends to the kitchen.' Emily learned German while kneading the bread, and hers were the lightest loaves baked in the house.

'We are such odd animals that we prefer that mode of contrivance to having a new face encouraged amongst us. Besides, we do not despair of Tabitha's return.' It was not a harsh discipline for them: 'Human feelings are queer things; I am much happier blackleading the stove, making the beds, and sweeping the floors at home than I should be living like a fine lady anywhere else' – happier than she ever was or could be as a governess. Housework might take up time and energy but it left the mind free, and there was a pride in being a good housewife.

In later years when Charlotte was modestly enriched by royalties, a little comfort and colour stole into the house; the sadness was that Emily and Anne were no longer there to share it.

'I don't know that I ever saw a place more exquisitely clean; the most dainty place for that I ever saw,' wrote Mrs. Gaskell. How much this effect depended on austerity of furnishing, as well as on cleanliness, we may realize better than she did; even in the best-run Victorian house there must have been a certain stuffiness. Could those heavy curtains, those rails and pelmets be entirely free from dust, or those laden mantelshelves, that heavy, carved furniture, and many pictures?

'To be sure, the life is like clock-work,' continued Mrs. Gaskell. 'No one comes to the house; nothing disturbs the deep repose; hardly a voice is heard; you can catch the ticking of the clock in the kitchen and the buzzing of a fly in the parlour all over the house.'

Mr. Brontë lived a great deal apart, in his study, having his dinner sent in to him. Charlotte and her guest dined together in the parlour, where 'all the small table arrangements had the same dainty simplicity about them'. It was midday dinner, with tea at six o'clock After dinner, they sat talking by the fire. 'It is a cold country, and the fires give a pretty warm, dancing light all over the house. . . . Everything fits into and is in harmony with the idea of a country parsonage possessed by people of very moderate means. The prevailing colour of the room is crimson to make a warm setting for the cold, grey landscape without.' There were two pictures: the Richmond portrait of Charlotte, and an engraving of Lawrence's portrait of Thackeray. On either side of the hearth were shelves filled with books: 'books given to her, books she has bought and which all tell of her individual pursuit and tastes, not standard books'.

Quietness, purity, order made it almost conventual.

'Her habits of order were such that she could not go on with the conversation if a chair was out of its place; everything was arranged with a delicate regularity.'

The parlour was full of memories for Charlotte. The three sisters had sat here with their books, their sketch-blocks, Emily, perhaps, at the piano; here they had walked up and down together, after their father had gone early to bed, bidding them not be late; walked and talked of their plans for a school:

'They thought by a little contrivance and a very little additional building, a small number of pupils, four or six, might be accommodated in the parsonage.' Emily had recorded this very sober day-dream in a paper she wrote, as did Anne, every fourth birthday; the paper to be read four years later:

'I guess that at the time appointed for the opening of this paper ... we shall be merrily seated in our sitting-room in some pleasant and flourishing seminary, just gathered in for the midsummer holyday'.

From that parlour Charlotte and Emily set out on their first adventure to Brussels and the *Pensionnat Héger*, which was to be the first stage in their higher education as schoolmistresses. In that parlour Mr. Brontë had rejoined his daughters from the study, where Charlotte had brought him a copy of *Jane Eyre*.

'Girls,' he told them, 'do you know Charlotte has been writing a book, and it is much better than likely.'

This little grey, stone house with its austere beauty of purity, order and quietness lies behind all the rooms and houses Charlotte created in her novels: Mr. Helstone's vicarage and Shirley's elegant mansion; the crimson and white drawing-room 'all fire and snow' and the dining-room with its purple chairs and curtains at Thornfield; the sober comfort of the refurnished Moor House;

Lucy Snowe's sea-cave of a bedroom in Mrs. Bretton's house, and her own exquisite dream-home. No other houses in fiction or in biography hold the same poignancy.

Charlotte, when she married, was very housewifely:

'I have been very busy stitching; the new little room is got into order, and the green and white curtains are up; they exactly suit the papering, and look clean and neat enough.'

She was to become in her brief months of marriage a very dutiful and willing parson's wife to the husband who gave her devotion and tenderness, security and protection, though he could not give her the perfect sympathy of mind she needed. It is futile to try to imagine what further history – of happiness or frustration – that little parsonage would have held had she lived through child-bearing into her forties. One can only see her with Emily and Anne in their girlhood and young womanhood; or tranquilly with this new friend and fellow-novelist who gave and received such pleasant intimacy; or alone with dreams and hopes and memories.

It is impossible to see her in the draped and cluttered rooms of later Victorian domesticity. Even had she lived and flourished, in fortune as in health, her taste would not have changed. In her house there would always have been that delicate austerity, that exquisite frugality: clear, warm colours, the comfort of carpets, easy chairs, a sofa or two, fine linen, many books, a few prints and some porcelain, a piano, order and quietness everywhere.

In another Yorkshire parsonage lived a young clergy-wife endowed with a delightful talent and lively mind. She became the mother of a daughter in whom talent flowered into genius, of a delicate but undoubted kind. Ecclesfield Vicarage was the home of Mrs. Margaret Gatty and the birthplace of her second daughter Juliana Horatia, who became Mrs. Ewing and was the author of some of the best-loved books for children written in the golden age of such literature. She was usually called Julie, or, for special by-name, Aunt Judy, and when Mrs. Gatty became editor of one of the first magazines for children, she named it for this daughter *Aunt Judy's Magazine*.

Mrs. Gatty did not know Miss Brontë, and, it would appear did not greatly desire to know her, or warmly approve of what she heard. Ecclesfield Vicarage was a more lavish house than

Haworth, but was also more casual in its ways; never, one imagines, in that state of exquisite order. Mrs. Gatty came there as a bride in 1839, her husband newly ordained and presented to the living. Twenty-four years later she was writing ruefully:

'The dining-room has never had curtains yet, and those in the drawing-room are twenty-one years old.' But there was ease, even exuberance about the house. Among the most cherished pieces of furniture were two old black leather arm-chairs which had belonged to her father, Dr. Scott. He had been Nelson's chaplain on the *Victory*, and Nelson had died in his arms. From him came Juliana's second name, bestowed also, in its proper masculine form on one of her brothers. In those chairs the Admiral and his chaplain had sat together, in the cabin, working; and when Dr. Scott thought his Admiral over-tired he made him lie down on a sofa made from the two chairs with a stool between them.

Mrs. Gatty and her husband together wrote the Life of Dr. Scott, which gave them their first taste of publishers' blood. It appeared in 1842, and nine years later she published her book of tales *The Fairy Godmother*, which is by no means forgotten today and still holds its charm. Then came a series of *Parables From Nature* and other books for nursery and schoolroom. From the vicarage, too, was issued *Aunt Judy's Magazine* which, with Charlotte Yonge's *Monthly Packet* is one of the twin peaks of periodical literature for the young.

Dr. Gatty (he was, in due course, 'doctored' by Oxford) also continued to publish. At the request of his parishioners he brought out a volume of sermons which found its way round the world. One copy was presented to the actor Charles Keane; he took it with him on a world-voyage and used to read a sermon every Sunday to the ship's company: 'They came from the heart and they went to the heart' was his pronouncement. Another copy, sent to a doctor in Berwick, a friend and correspondent of Mrs. Gatty, was gratefully acknowledged by his wife as 'a resource for reading to the servants on Sunday evenings'; which floods with unearthly light the ways of a Victorian household. Clerical friends used to borrow one of those sermons when they came unprepared for the pulpit. A railway edition or shilling paperback was printed and dedicated to the Bishop of Ripon; but there is no record of any sales on station bookstalls, and one day in London,

the author knew 'the ludicrous humiliation' of seeing copies
hawked for a penny each.

Mrs. Gatty had a passion for both literature and natural science;
they are fused in her *Parables From Nature* – a truly original and
utterly delightful form of story. In 1863, after years of research,
she published a *History of British Seaweeds* which took her into the
professional ranks of naturalists, went into many editions, and
continued in use far into our own century. Her granddaughter and
biographer, Christabel Maxwell, found that it was being consulted
at a Marine Biological Station in 1945.

Her output was admirable, almost formidable: over twenty
books in thirty years, with the care of a large family on her
shoulders as well as that of a vicarage; and she was very much the
clergy-wife, with no idea of literary seclusion. Her granddaughter
thinks she was a scientist rather than a writer, for all the charm of
her tales, 'a frustrated Madame Curie, hampered by the times in
which she was living' and finding an outlet in literature. That,
certainly, was the one art and intellectual exercise which a gentlewoman could practise, and practise for money, without incurring
the faintest shadow of blame or hint of being unwomanly. Mrs.
Gatty might, in a later generation have been a doctor. She was
actively interested in medicine, was a pioneer in the use of chloro-
form for herself in childbirth, an advocate of its use by women in
the parish and of homeopathy. Her diary is full of such entries as
these:

'Went to see Mrs. Potter and gave her good advice. Went to
see Mrs. Fawley and dosed her with conversation and homeopathy. Saw Mrs. Potter and Mrs. Fawley. Homeopathy.'

She was, at the same time, no faddist or rebel but worked along
with the doctor who used to send her cases to treat. A boy, nearly
but not quite recovered from inflammation of the lungs, was sent
'for some of the medicine I had already given. Globules for ever!
(Especially when combined with mustard plaster and hot beer for
supper!'.)

Her children were encouraged to dose themselves, which
sounds a major risk. Juliana who was delicate, made such lavish
use of this encouragement that she was nicknamed The Countess
of Homeopathy.

Juliana has portrayed her mother and the vicarage in one of her most delightful tales: *Six to Sixteen*. Margery, the heroine-narrator is brought home from school by her friend, Eleanor Arkwright, to her Yorkshire vicarage. They travel by train through 'the black country' to 'the stone country' with its noble, austere scenery and pure air. There is a description which both Charlotte and Emily Brontë would have loved, and indeed they would have relished this book. The old church is like a miniature cathedral; the big, stone vicarage is set in a garden 'almost over-grown with vegetation like the palace of The Sleeping Beauty'. The girls are welcomed by Kezia who had been housemaid for five years, gone to seek a change, disliked it, and returned to settle down for life in the vicarage. Then comes the more tumultuous welcome of 'the dear boys' – not brothers but dogs, large and small, all of them exuberant. Eleanor's favourite retriever sleeps outside the girls' bedroom door.

'"Would you like a dog to sleep with you?" Eleanor politely inquired. "I shall have Growler inside and my big boy outside. Pincher is a nice little fellow, you'd better have Pincher . . . If Pincher snores, darling, hit him on the nose. . . . If Growler *should* get out of my bed and come on yours, mind you kick him off, or he and Pincher will fight through the bedclothes."'

Cook tells Eleanor 'the way them dogs behave is scandilus' but she feeds them well. The girls are feasted on 'strong tea and abundance of sugar and rich cream. We laid the delicious butter on our bread on such thick clumps that sallow-faced Madame [at school] would have thought us in peril of our lives. There was brown bread toast too; and fried ham and eggs, and moor honey and Yorkshire tea-cakes.' Eleanor's parents are from home, at the time, but the house is more than adequately run by Cook and Kezia.

Margery is charmed by Eleanor's bedroom: 'As is the case with the "bowers" of most English country girls of her class, it was rich in those treasures which, like the advertised contents of lost pocket-books, are 'of no value to anyone but the owner': prints of sacred subjects in home-made frames, knick-knacks of motley variety, daguerrotypes and second-rate photographs of "the boys" [brothers], i.e. Clement and Jack, at different ages, and of "the dear boys" [dogs] also.'

In the morning the girls' garden, in the afternoon go up to the moors 'to get some *Batrochosperma* and paddle a bit and give the dear boys a bathe'. Margery sheds her crinoline 'because Eleanor said we might have to climb some stone walls', and borrows a pair of Eleanor's country boots. They paddle in the river with little fishes swimming between their feet, collect the precious *Batrochosperma* or freshwater alga, and give the dear boys their head. Coming home, they go into the old church, large and noble, full of prayer and quietness.

Eleanor's parents return 'to a very confused and noisy greeting'. The vicar says affectionately 'God bless you' and almost in the same breath, 'Do call off the dogs, my dear, or else take your mother's beasts.' The beasts are 'crassys and Serpulae and two Chitons and several other things' in the way of marine zoology for Mrs. Arkwright's aquarium. They have been carried by the vicar in a tin can 'which had made him look like a particularly respectable milkman' and among the luggage is a large stone bottle full of sea-water.

As a picture of a Victorian vicarage this hardly fits into the conventional pattern of primness and piety. The arrival of 'the boys' – Clement and Jack is even more tumultuous. The girls drive in a donkey-carriage to meet them, wearing flower-wreathed hats, and there is a triumphal process through the village. Jack greets Kezia with a throttling hug which makes her declare that 'now the young gentlemen was home there was an end of peace for everybody, choose who they might be'. Madame from school is invited to stay, and is taken by the children to the Fair. She buys toys for all the village children – twenty-four halfpenny things, chosen by Jack, balls, whips, dolls, tiny churns, monkeys-on-sticks; Jack distributes them after making the children answer or part-answer a question from the catechism which is a sound vicar-age way of doing things.

This was the sort of life known to the young Gattys, though not the young Brontës; full of exuberance, indoors and out-of-doors, of active companionship with each other and with the village. It is decided that the girls will not return to school but have lessons at home. Mrs. Arkwright teaches them, and the read widely in the vicar's library, learn French and Italian, sketch collect plants and 'beasts'. Margery begins to write her account of it all, sitting in the great kitchen:

'There is no room so comfortable. . . . We first used it for paro-
chial purposes, small night-schools and so on' as did the real
Gatty girls at Ecclesfield. 'Then one evening cook said: "You
can sit here if you like, Miss Eleanor. We always sits in the
pantry on winter nights, so there'll be no one to disturb you."
And as we had some writing on hand which we did not wish to
have discussed or overlooked by other members of the family, we
settled down in great peace and comfort by the roaring fire which
the maids had heaped to keep the kitchen warm in their absence.'

Jack and Clement, like conventional schoolboys, disapprove:
'Who ever heard of ladies sitting in the kitchen?' In some
south-country kitchens, Margery agreed, perhaps not:

'But we have this large, airy, spotlessly clean room with its
stone floor, its yellow-washed walls, its tables scrubbed to snowy
whiteness, its quaint old dresser and clock and corner cupboards
of shiny black oak, and its huge fireplace and blazing fire all to
ourselves. . . . We cover the table and commonly part of the floor
with an amount of books, papers and belongings of various sorts,
such as we should scruple to deluge the drawing-room with.'

Cook 'stoned' the floor regularly and 'pot-moulded' the hearth
in fantastic patterns and polished the furniture to brilliance. The
vicarage dined early, and supper was cooked in 'the second
kitchen'. The vicarage had once been a farmhouse and this great
kitchen had been the living-room. It is ampler and comelier than
that at Haworth, but the Brontës would have been at home in
it, and at ease (after their first shyness) with Eleanor and Margery
in their bookish mood; walked happily on the moors with them,
and responded to 'the dear boys'. Brothers unlike Branwell, of
the mould of Clement and Jack, might have drawn them into full
vitality of body and of high spirits. But that is almost impossible
to imagine, as it is to wonder what a mother like Mrs. Arkwright –
or Mrs. Gatty – would have made of them. They would not, in
such a case, have been the Brontës.

The vicarage at Ecclesfield was so loved by its children that
they were homesick for it all their lives. There was an Ecclesfield
look. Christine Maxwell recognized it from time to time in her
mother, who was a sister of Juliana. They would not have chosen
any other home, although Mrs. Gatty herself pined for the sea
and for the warm south.

This biographer points out that their life was not one of 'Victorian ease and leisure . . . but a bustling, vigorous existence which influenced all those who came in contact with it', that it was a household where 'the women were more exciting than the men', and the animals as individual as the humans. There was never quite enough money or quite enough time for everything that was wanted or everything which should be done, but this lack was balanced by zest and vitality.

Mrs. Gatty's activity as a clergy-wife began at her first Christmas in the vicarage, when she and her husband gave a dinner to the Sunday School teachers 'to encourage them, and he [the vicar] will dine with them and give them a little good advice'. She herself took a class on Sunday and had her girls to the vicarage once a week. There was no national school in the parish – 'which I am sorry for; although it would not go on so well here, as the children are employed in the factories from five in the morning to half-past seven at night, which precludes the possibility of their learning much' – a notable meiosis. This was just before the passing of the first Factory Acts against the exploitation of children in mines and factories.

The house was run with the help of Bella, Mrs. Gatty's own maid since her childhood, and a housemaid. Accounts had to be kept, for parish affairs as well as the house. Juliana may have thought of her mother's methods when she described Miss Jenny, the parson's daughter, in *Daddy Darwin's Dovecot*; as she partly described herself or one of her sisters in the busy young heroine.

These children, like the small Brontës took to writing as well as reading very young. They produced a family magazine – of a lighter sort, infinitely less intense in imagination than the little books of Haworth Parsonage. A Court Journal recorded the doings of their royal selves: 'The Princess Margaret, in Her Majesty's absence, [took] it upon herself to perambulate the drawing-room, stuffing everything under the sofa-cushions or behind the books, as she thought it probable someone might call.'

In one issue was a notice of *Lost*: 'By the Reverend A. G everything he wants at the moment of his wanting it' with the addition: 'Nobody need look for anything as all the missing article are under his Rev. Nose.'

The four boys were sent to school, to Eton, Winchester, Charterhouse and Marlborough respectively; the girls were educated at home sometimes by a governess, more often by their mother. Like Eleanor and Margery they read widely and solidly:

'We are doing all we can over the boys' education, looking upon it as money laid out to interest,' their mother reported. 'The girls are pretty well; they teach, and visit the sick, and are as good as four curates' – aged from thirteen to twenty-one. Jenny in *Daddy Darwin's Dovecot* is motherless, and has no marked literary or artistic gifts; but in her occupations she is a mirror if not a portrait of any of the Misses Gatty.

On Saturday night Jenny sits 'balancing her bags. The bags were money bags' (was this Mrs. Gatty's way of keeping accounts?). 'The country parson . . . is responsible for a great deal of his work that is really done by this helpmate – woman.' Jenny ran the affairs and finances of The Savings Bank, the Clothing Club, the Library, the Magazines and Hymn-Books, and the Three-Halfpenny Club as well as the house itself. 'She could not bring her mind' to accountancy on paper; if each fund were kept in its own bag she knew exactly where it and she was, and could take the proper tenth from her personal funds to give to charity. Having duly balanced her bags she set about her other duties, which were to brush and comb the dog, wash her own hair, study her Sunday School lesson, and lay out her Sunday clothes, Bible, prayer-book and class-book on the oak chest at the foot of her bed; these done, she spread a coloured quilt over the white bed-cover for the dog – who resented the implied doubt of his cleanliness – and so to bed and to sleep 'as one ought to sleep on Saturday night who is bound to be at the Sunday School by nine-fifteen on the following morning, with a clear mind on the Rudiments of the Faith, the history of the prophet Elisha, and the destination of each of the parish magazines.'

This story, like all Juliana's tales is full of country scenes, almost of country scents of roses, clove pinks and sweet-smelling herbs. In this village the women carry posies to church: 'Country-women take mint and southernwood to a long, hot service as fine ladies take smelling-bottles.' The small girl, Phoebe, in the story copies her mother:

'My mother always says there's nothing like red bergamot to

take to church,' and she makes her posy of this mixed with red roses, pink hollyhocks and 'pheasants' eyes'.

The two eldest Gatty daughters drew two of the illustrations for their mother's new edition of *Parables From Nature*; the third, Dot, corrected proofs. Then Juliana burst into print in Miss Yonge's *Monthly Packet*. Mrs. Gatty was already a contributor though not a contented one, she wanted higher payment. She tried *Good Words*.

'Why does an orthodox parson's wife write for *Good Words*? When orthodox magazines value her services at £1 a page and copyright reserved – instead of 2s. 6d. (*Monthly Packet*) then you may wonder but not till then . . . Why does Miss Yonge's publisher pay authors so badly?' Perhaps because Miss Yonge herself had a mind above money, being a spinster of ample means who gave the greater part of her own earnings to the Church and her missions.

These two gifted women met in 1861 when Miss Yonge and her mother paid an over-night visit to Ecclesfield. They brought their maid, which complicated domestic arrangements, but offset this by their willingness to share a room. It was not an easy visit in any way for Charlotte was intensely shy and reserved: 'Her consent' to coming, Mrs. Gatty commented, 'is to be considered entirely due to Aunt Judy's fascination.' The acquaintance was courteous rather than cordial. Mrs. Gatty resented Miss Yonge's success as a best-seller, when she herself needed the money so much more, and was jealous of her position as 'the arbiter of juvenile literature'. However, the visit proved in the end a happy one and left a pleasant impression – due, perhaps to Aunt Judy. Charlotte, like her hostess, loved nature-study and collected shells; Mrs. Gatty presented her with two fine specimens. Looking at her guest with semi-medical eyes she found her excitable and over-strung:

'She writes more than she should and a year's holiday would do her good,' especially when she had no need to work. 'They are extremely well off, came here with a maid and keep a carriage. Indeed she must make six or eight hundred a year by her writings. So, so – that will do' – and better not show jealousy; but six or eight hundred a year would have been very welcome to this orthodox parson's wife. The parson, incidentally, used to annex her cheques for the general fund, and one of the first acts of rebellion in this household, a gentle but successful one, was when Juliana quietly held on to her own.

There was a defective sympathy between these two good churchwomen in church matters. Charlotte Yonge was a disciple of Keble, trained in the High Tractarian way; Mrs. Gatty was Low Church and disapproved of the new devotions which seemed to lead so near Rome:

'All England is crazy about the attempted innovations in the Church,' she had written in 1845. 'It has nearly come to a "No Popery" cry, and thankful indeed one feels English people of middle and lower orders are prejudiced on the right side. . . . A great many people, however, are getting frightened now that they see the results of Puseyism, and how nearly it borders on Popery.'

She and her husband had been reading, with marked disapproval, Ward's *Ideal of a Christian Church*; Ward himself – still, then, an Anglican – and many more moderate Tractarians than he, would have been shocked by the aspect of Ecclesfield Church: the chancel closed, the nave darkened by heavy galleries; and by the old font set up in the vicarage garden.

'You have no idea, no, not the faintest, what this place is like now,' its mistress had told her sister: 'the beautiful garden all lawn and flower beds' and 'the old stone font, handsomely carved, which we found thrown by and neglected in the old hearse house'.

In time came some outward reform: the font was restored to its proper place, the galleries were removed, the chancel was opened. Finally, in 1872, the vicar dared to preach in a surplice.

Catholic ritual and ceremonial might be ignored, but the homelier observances of the Christian year were cherished. One Shrove Tuesday which happened to fall before St. Valentine's Day, Juliana wrote in her diary:

'Did Valentines all day. Pancake bell. Sent a pancake to Inkey [the curate]. They were tossing pancakes from the church tower this morning.'

The church was always decorated for festivals and there was special music. The Gattys were all musical. The four boys, one of whom was Alfred Scott Gatty the composer, used to give concerts, and the whole family took part in theatricals.

Aunt Judy's Magazine published poems and songs, including a setting by Alfred for *The Walrus and the Carpenter*, as well as stories and articles, and it was illustrated. The bound volumes are a treasury of Victoriana. The entrancing *Lost Legends of Nursery Rhymes* by M. Clark appeared there, and there was a most hilarious serial about a family of bad-with-the-best-intentions children called *Scaramouches at School*, from whom E. Nesbit's *Treasure-Seekers* and *Would-Be-Goods* are in true descent. Best of all were the stories of Aunt Judy or Juliana herself, both short stories and novels for children: *Jackanapes; Jan of the Windmill; A Flat Iron For a Farthing; Six to Sixteen; We and the World; Mrs. Overtheway's Remembrances*, and the rest. Mrs. Gatty as editor was paid £10 a month, contributors were paid 10s. a page for original work, 5s. for translations and 'scissor-work': not quite such good terms as those of *Good Words* but better than those of *The Monthly Packet*. Lewis Carroll contributed a story *Bruno's Revenge* to one number, and in another appeared a glowing review of *Alice in Wonderland*. Some of Hans Andersen's tales were published in translation.

Aunt Judy's Magazine flourished for twenty years, a shorter life though a merrier than that of *The Monthly Packet* which lived from the early fifties to the nineties. Besides bringing joy to many nurseries and schoolrooms it endowed a cot in The Sick Children's Hospital, Great Ormond Street.

Mrs. Gatty enjoyed one exalted literary friendship besides the somewhat tepid one with Charlotte Yonge. A friend who knew Tennyson told her of his admiration for one of the *Parables From Nature* – 'The Unknown Land' – and she sent him a copy of the book. It was courteously acknowledged, and some time afterwards she happened to meet him on a journey, and introduced herself:

'I dare to do anything, after daring to introduce myself to the Laureate.'

This led to an invitation to stay with the Tennysons at Faringford:

'Walked three or four miles with Tennyson on the downs, and sat down. To the beacon and sat in the turf house. To the shore with Hallam and his nurse. *Maud! Locksley Hall! Vivien and Merlin!*' Bliss!

The friendship ripened to the warmth of 'a pleasant fight' about contemporary scientists, Tennyson attacking them as men 'of an eye well practised in nature, a spirit bounded and poor', Mrs

Gatty defending them as friends from whom she had received much kindness and encouragement. She came near converting Tennyson to her own interests:

'I found a few anemones in a stroll on the shore, and he was interested. I left them with him, an aquarium in a soap-dish, bringing away only one as a memorial.' According to Christine Maxwell they 'bickered' about some of the poet's descriptions: 'sea-blue bird of March', and 'daffodil skies'; but Mrs. Gatty's attitude on the whole was one of hero-worship:

'His home was her Mecca, he was named the Apostle, and her greatest happiness was listening to Mr. Tennyson.'

Dr. Gatty sometimes accompanied her, and he shared her admiration. He used to lecture on Tennyson's poems, and sent him a volume of his sermons. In return Tennyson sent an advance copy of the dedicatory poem in the *Idylls of the King*, and over this the vicarage ladies wept luxuriously. On a later visit, Mrs. Gatty permitted herself to be a little critical, even mocking, referring to the Apostle as 'The Great Panjam', making fun of his solemn reading or mouthing of a newspaper account of the wedding of the Prince of Wales. Perhaps, as her granddaughter suggests, she was now aware of herself as a lioness who might be permitted to roar a little. But when the poet presented her with a signed copy of his *Welcome to Alexandra* the astringency was mellowed by rapture. This visit was happy, even jolly, with the boys, one of the young Gattys among them, acting charades. Stephen Gatty played a doctor in Tennyson's own famous hat and cloak.

Other new friends were the Moberleys at Winchester, who were the inspiration if not the prototypes of the families in Charlotte Yonge's novels:

'They all chat just like the people in her books.'

Juliana knew and visited them too, going to Winchester from Charlotte Yonge's home, Eldersfield, at Otterbourne:

'Tea. Chat. High tea' is the record in Juliana's diary. One evening they read Dr. John Brown's *Marjorie Fleming* aloud to each other. Juliana was paid £16 for a story in *The Monthly Packet*; this was 'The Brownies' which has had a long life and influence. In our own century it gave Lord Baden-Powell the idea and the name for the juniors of The Girl Guides; the children in that story did all the things he wanted small girls to do, and performed a proper rite and ceremonial. So this daughter of a Victorian vicarage stands behind one of the liveliest Youth Movements of today.

Charlotte Yonge, though eighteen years older than Juliana outlived both her and Mrs. Gatty, and her admiration endured, though tempered by criticism. In her *catalogue raisonnée* of *What Books To Lend and What to Give* – years after the death of both mother and daughter, she mentioned their books: Mrs. Gatty's receive temperate praise, Juliana's much more cordial, though still with a slight sting:

'These exquisite pieces are too delicately worked for the ordinary style of children or the poor, though they may be appreciated by those who have time to dream over them, and, as it were, imbibe them.' But there must have been many 'ordinary', even some poor children in the multitude of Juliana's admirers through many generations.

The four daughters of this vicarage all married. Juliana's husband, Alexander Ewing was a soldier, a musician, cousin to a Bishop (of Argyll and the Isles) and composer of a hymn tune: *Jerusalem*; an impeccable list of qualities. It was a happy marriage, though childless. Juliana took happily to the wandering military life which gave her fresh material and varied backgrounds for some of her best stories. It was the soldier's wife who wrote *Jackanapes* and some of *Mrs. Overtheway's Remembrances*.

Mrs. Gatty died in 1873, a weary, somewhat battered old lady, afflicted by a muscular disease in her right arm, but valiant to the end. Juliana died in 1885, only in her forties; she had been delicate since her girlhood.

Ecclesfield Vicarage has neither the shadows nor the almost blinding light of Haworth, but it has the fullness of domestic life, with much happiness and a little sorrow, fun and work, great affection, bright talent, a gleam of genius. We see Haworth Parsonage, through Mrs. Gaskell's eyes, the more clearly for its austerity, its solitude, its silence. Ecclesfield vicarage itself can hardly be seen for the crowd of its inhabitants. It is full of cheerful talk and music, brimming with activity. Both houses are loved, both touched by enchantment.

9

Vicarage Variety

The vicarage could be anything from a small country mansion to a poor cottage. Mr. Crawley is not unique in his poverty. The average was a fair standard of comfort and dignity, partly because so many of the clergy were of the gentry, with private means; and with low wages it was easy to have servants. Mrs. Peel in her *Hundred Wonderful Years* describes, in a contemporary letter, a vicarage of the late 1840's which was neither grand nor bare, leaning towards wealth rather than poverty. The vicar had a stipend of £800, and could keep a one-horse carriage with a groom to look after it. The house had three family bedrooms, two dressing-rooms, a drawing-room, dining-room and study, with a parish room for meetings and other parish business. The nurseries were in a wing, and there were two servants' bedrooms, but there was no bathroom. Nurse, cook and house-parlourmaid received respectively £18, £16 and £6 a year; a gardener was employed, and a woman came in to help with the cleaning and baking. The drawing-room was elegant in its buff and gilt paper and red and buff carpet; the dining-room had buff paper and a Turkey carpet.

Social life was regulated by the moon, dinner-parties being arranged for nights of full moon – because of the risk of driving home in the dark on bad roads – and so were known as 'moons'. There were also grape dinners, given when the hothouse grapes were at their best. In summer, people gave archery and syllabub parties; afternoon tea was not yet in vogue, callers were regaled with cake and wine.

The vicar's wife and daughters did most of the parish work, teaching in the Sunday school and arranging the annual treat, training the choir, visiting the sick. Mamma held a Mothers' Meeting. The parish room was much used, for the villagers came to the vicarage for help and advice on many matters. There were, of course, family prayers, duly announced: 'Prayers are on the table, sir'; and the servants had their own pew in church.

Sometimes a son followed his father, making it, in a special way a family living. The father of Canon Anson succeeded *his* father as Rector of Sudbury near Derby, and held the charge for forty years. His was a true parish priesthood. He loved his people, knew them and all their problems intimately, loved the poor more than the rich, and this country parish more than the society of Windsor where, as Canon, he lived for three months in the year.

Social life in the parish was limited. The Ansons were related to many of the county families but the visiting radius could not easily exceed five miles; if they did not call their dinner-parties 'moons' they still regulated them by seasons of light. It was a new way of life for Mrs. Anson. The daughter of a rich and eccentric peer, Lord Vernon, she had been brought up in Italy: the Italy of Papal rule, unchanged since the eighteenth century, very grand and cultured and un-Victorian. She might have made a brilliant marriage and continued to live in the great world; but having experienced 'a puritan and evangelical conversion' she chose this unambitious though very happy marriage with a clergyman, and 'passed suddenly from a sort of Renaissance atmosphere in Rome . . . to a remote country village', where she became the mother of fourteen children, of whom eleven survived infancy. It is hardly surprising that much of her time was spent on a sofa; but after the birth of her last baby she renewed her activity, managed her large household, taught the girls French and German, wrote every week to the boys at school, looked after the women in the village. There were, her son admits, some gaps in her own education; but 'to be able to run a great household, to prescribe and weigh out medicines for a village, to talk fluently in two or three languages, to be all that men seek from a woman in the way of encouragement and sympathy and inspiration' while producing 'quite in the day's work, and almost as a *parergon*' those fourteen children, was a finer achievement than any academic honours.

Not many clergy-wives, perhaps, were of such exalted lineage or exotic background, but most of them were accomplished gentlewomen, full, too, of practical common sense, able advisers to their husbands' parishioners; true 'loaf-givers', dispensers of food, comfort and medicines, of garments, counsel and admonition. Teaching was a common employment; the village schoo was among Mrs. Anson's responsibilities, and in most parishes the parson's wife taught in Sunday school, had classes in the parsonage, found the village girls places as servants, generally looked after them.

The church at Sudbury was of pre-Tractarian simplicity: 'Ornaments were none, except a red velvet cover for the Holy Table, with a cushion for the pulpit and an hour-glass.' The village orchestra in the gallery had given place to a barrel organ which played twelve tunes, and this, in turn, to a real organ blown by a small boy who used, undetected, to suck sweets. There were few dissenters and nearly everyone attended Morning and Evening Prayer. The 'Early Celebration' of Holy Communion, was coming into use in some parishes, but not yet in Sudbury:

'It was taken for granted that only two hours in the day were acceptable to the Almighty' – 11 a.m. and 3 p.m. Morning Prayer consisted of matins, ante-Communion and sermon, this being preached in the black gown without surplice. There was a monthly Celebration of the Eucharist, after matins, known as 'The Second Service' and this 'Sacrament Sunday' was a solemn day, but on no Sunday might the young Ansons read novels or even secular biographies.

The annual move to Windsor was 'a colossal affair, almost like Noah's entering into the Ark, except that, as far as we were aware, it excluded the unclean beasts.' Children, about a dozen servants, cats and dogs, horses and carriages were all included in the expedition. Harold and his younger brother, the babes of the family, drove with their nurse to Burton-on-Trent where the carriage complete with occupants was put on a railway truck, and so by rail to Windsor via Birmingham, Oxford and Reading. 'It was like the migration of a tribe.'

Elizabeth Wordsworth, the first Principal of Lady Margaret Hall, grand-niece of the poet, recalled a parish of similar conservatism. Her father too held a double charge; he was Canon of Westminster and Vicar of Stanford-in-the-Vale, a Westminster living. The family had come to Westminster from Harrow where their father was Headmaster, but that phase was not clearly remembered or described. The house in the Little Cloister of Westminster 'was very picturesque, but even then hardly up-to-date' – or in plain words, had little or no sanitation, and an outbreak of fever was the result. At Stanford, the country air made up for most defects. It was pleasant country; the village was highly immoral, or perhaps merely natural in an uninhibited way:

'We learned a good deal, by visiting the poor, of the ordinary facts of practical life.' What with parish visiting and the reading of that unrefined repository the Old Testament, the Victorian girl can hardly have been as sheltered from the facts of life as tradition maintains. Both occupations make for realism.

In church they kept to the old ways, singing the Canticles and the Tate and Brady Psalms to a pitch-pipe, but no hymns ancient or modern. 'Altogether we were a very primitive people.' The mummers and carol-singers came round at Christmas, in summer there was Club-day: a procession with banners and a band of the local Benefit Club, to the church; after the service there was dinner, then dancing – by the men only – solemn, and heavy-footed, on the vicarage lawn. Many of them still wore the smock, the old women the scarlet cloak, the young women sun-bonnets.

'We saw a good deal of country life, and simple, primitive human nature at Stanford; and at Westminster we got most interesting glimpses of a bigger world . . . Few things are more educative than living near an old historical building.'

The girls, educated at home had been taught to read seriously and with purpose. As they grew up they acted secretary for their father, copying, for the printers, his Commentaries on the New and the Old Testaments. They were taught New Testament Greek.

The vicarage at Stanford was enlarged by Canon Wordsworth. It was adorned in most of the rooms with carved texts. Over the door lintel was carved: *Nisi Dominus Aedificaverit Domum Vanus Est Labor*; the dining-room had texts enjoining its guests to do all things, both eating and drinking, to the Glory of God, to speak evil of no man, to remember that those were blessed who should hunger and thirst after righteousness. In the store-room after the name of Martha in Greek letters was an injunction to the housewife not to be careful overmuch; in the study the vicar was bidden to 'buy back the opportunity' and reminded that 'If anyone be in Christ he is a new creature'. In his dressing-room he was told. *Nolumus exspoliari sed supervestiri* – 'Not for that we would be unclothed but clothed upon'. It was a somewhat austere house all its riches lying in books.

In 1869 Canon Wordsworth was made Bishop of Lincoln, and the family moved to the palace at Riseholme. One of their first visitors was Professor Conington, the great Virgilian, 'the most complete personification of a scholar as distinct from a man of the world', but able to talk on many subjects besides the classics. Elizabeth recalled Sunday evening walks in Buckland Woods lovely with rhododendrons, while the professor discussed the poetry of Cowper and some 'modern novels, Miss Austen's among them'. He was a faithful churchgoer and it was said that 'Conington attends to or remembers every sermon he goes to'.

There were quiet evenings at Riseholme, with the Bishop 'a very early riser and hard worker' dozing by the library fire, the others making 'as little noise as possible so as not to wake him'; so little that a mouse used to come out, and 'find its way to the tea-table in the corner, and enjoy the crumbs it was sure to find there'. But this church mouse went too far – 'so forward that he had to have a trap set for him – too much prosperity having had as bad an effect on his character as it seems to have had on the British public'.

The progress of a clerical family from schoolhouse to Close and thence to palace is repeated in the story of the Bensons. Edward White Benson was a junior master at Rugby, then Headmaster of Wellington before going to Lincoln, in 1872, during Bishop Wordsworth's episcopate, as Chancellor of the diocese. His son Arthur remembered the Chancery in the Close as one of the most beautiful houses he had known: a large house of Tudor red brick and much fine panelling, it ran far back from the street, set in a great garden, with stables and loft, coach-house and granary behind. On one garden wall grew peaches and apricots with wallflower on the top. Both houses and garden were cared for and improved by the Bensons, and in digging and clearing part of the ground a quantity of Roman coins and pottery was discovered. Within, the new Chancellor furnished a chapel which had not appeared necessary to his predecessor. Prayers were held morning and evening; E. F. Benson remembered their mother's proposing once in their father's absence: 'We won't have prayers tonight for a treat.'

Dr. Benson, like Bishop Creighton imposed the utmost possible simplicity on his family – 'no horse or carriage and only maid-servants', two clear indications of voluntary or necessary restraint. After five years in that lovely house there came a move to Cornwall when he was consecrated Bishop of the new see of Truro. There was no Bishop's Palace, but the large vicarage of Kenwyn was made the Bishop's House, enlarged by the addition of new wings, the turning of stables into kitchens, and the old kitchen into a chapel. It was renamed Lis Escop or Bishop's Court.

'No sweeter place could well be imagined.' In the soft Cornish air camellias and hydrangeas flourished out of doors, and 'no severity of winter ever emptied the beds of flowers'. The climate, however, did not suit the Bishop who disliked the moist warmth, and suffered from depression. He overworked, as always, and he was bewildered by the moral atmosphere: 'the people religious, but religion having no more *controlling* power than if they were studying theology'. Dissent was strong.

It was a brief episcopate though one of intense apostolic labour. After six years, in 1883, Benson was made Archbishop of Canterbury, and the family knew two homes more: Lambeth, and Addington near Croydon, the latter being the country seat of the Archbishops. It was a vast place, the house 'rather ugly in front, rather stately behind', surrounded by great gardens, a park of six hundred acres and a home farm. Inside, an ante-room full of books led to the Archbishop's study, also book-lined, with a Greek inscription over every section of shelves; full of tables, too, the Archbishop's facing the door. He was sensitive to draughts and had a sandbag placed to exclude them: a trap for the unwary who were prone to stumble and 'fall into the presence of the Primate'. The mantelshelf was crowded with little things, family gifts and mementoes, and 'a marble clock and a bronze statuette of a sitting nymph which my father loved because of its exceeding ugliness'.

Addington, with its country peace and the greenness of the quiet hills, was more loved than Lambeth; but that was beautiful too, and comfortable, cool in summer, warm in winter, with a garden of unexpected space and quietness, there in the midst of London. The new Primate was a born improver; in every clergy house he took action. At Lambeth he ransacked the attics, bringing to light hidden treasures of furniture and he rehung pictures. There was a great library, but he made his dressing-room into

ily prayers by Samuel Butler

ounty Cricket Match, Sussex by J. R. Reid

A Victorian interior as displayed in the Geffrye Museum

his study, an austere one with only a writing-table and chair, a sofa, a prie-dieu and some devotional books. The chapel was 'a very exquisite building, full of colour, with painted walls and stained glass windows'.

E. F. Benson recalls the archepiscopal dinners, very stately yet with a touch of austerity. The gentlemen sat for only one round of port after the ladies had withdrawn, and there was no smoking; in the drawing-room the company sat only until ten o'clock when a bell summoned them to the chapel for Evensong, after which they departed. Only once was a cigarette conceded and that was to Royalty in the person of the Duke of York, afterwards George V. There *was* a smoking-room but its existence was ignored by the Primate. E. F. recalls also their first Easter at Addington when the drawing-room was not yet in order, 'but we managed with the ante-room, the Chinese room, the school-room, my father's study and her own room by way of sitting-rooms' – which seems adequate to us, but to Mrs. Benson, accustomed to high, wide and handsome household ways, it was informal, almost a picnic.

Archbishop Benson's love of Addington was not shared by his successor Frederick Temple who found it 'an expensive luxury' and thought, besides, that the Primate should live in Canterbury when not at Lambeth. He sold Addington and had the old Palace at Canterbury rebuilt. Lambeth, incidentally, became a family house only in Victorian times; the first Primate to bring his wife to live there, instead of relegating her to a private domicile else-where was Archbishop Howley who crowned the young Queen.

Temple's successor, Randall Davidson, knew only the statelier homes of the Church of England. He was chaplain to Archbishop Tait (Benson's predecessor) and married his daughter Edith, bringing her as bride to the Deanery at Windsor. From a deanery they moved to a bishop's house. Davidson was appointed Bishop of Rochester, and decided that the proper place to live was the centre of South London. Two large houses in Kennington Park were made into one, not altogether conveniently; before his departure to the ancient see of Winchester, the Bishop planned and saw the building of a new Bishop's House.

At Winchester that was much state. Farnham Castle, the residence of the Bishops, was (in the words of Davidson's biographer,

Canon G. K. A. Bell): 'one of the most lovely of all episcopal houses . . . a beautiful building of fair, red brick with a Norman keep, most romantic of castles', and set in a deer park. Auckland Castle, in the see of Durham, was even grander and had a river in the park: 'But I wouldn't change Farnham for this house, grand as it is', the Bishop once wrote to his wife from Durham; he was contented with his comparatively modest state. In Durham the Castle was the centre of hospitality and life for the diocese, and the Davidsons began to make a like use of Farnham. Church and social workers, clergy and their wives, missionaries home on furlough, all needing rest, comfort and counsel found it there in a generous hospitality, and 'the Castle also came to be a centre of friendship for the town as well as for the diocese'. The palatial life of the episcopate endured through Victorian into Edwardian times, but the splendid isolation of the eighteenth century was giving way to a pastoral hospitality, a stately homeliness.

The pattern of late-Victorian clerical life was clear in the holiday rectories where Winifred Peck and her sister and brothers spent most of their holidays; a clergy-family themselves, the children of Bishop Knox (as he became) they delighted in the rural change from their home in Birmingham. In retrospect those country rectories were much alike, with two particular features: 'a college oar hanging in the hall, to tell of the rector's prowess at Oxford or Cambridge, some thirty or forty years ago,' and 'a drawing-room scented with that peculiar camphor in which sequin hangings, tiger-skin rugs, Benares screens and brass ornaments and buddhas arrive in packing-cases from the distant corners of the Empire'; gifts from the sons of the rectory serving the Empire overseas.

Holidays meant 'detective work about the family of our hosts'. It was forbidden to ask direct questions of any servants left in the house, but family portraits and photographs could be used in evidence and these were numerous. The children always hoped to discover a skeleton in the cupboard: 'any grim, unidentified building in a picture was held to be the gaol or penitentiary in which the rector or his son had served their time.' The discovery of a French novel tucked behind 'Milman's interminable volumes was perhaps startling, but much more frequent and edifying wa the finding of Charlotte Yonge's novels in the schoolroom. These visiting children diagnosed the nature of the absent owners: 'Benevolence was shown by flowers and writing-paper left to welcome us, parsimony by an empty biscuit-tin on the sideboard, frivolity by a hidden hoard of old snob magazines.'

Writing in our own day the author recalls, wistfully, the end of many of those rectories, their transformation into lay country houses, or their continuance, shabby and burdensome to unaided mistresses.

'It is not so much the shy shades of rural deans which haunt these houses, it is the still more intangible shades of maids, gardeners, nurse-maids and large families of happy children.' A clerical-domestic pageant included:

'A whitewashed, straggling house in Devon, bordered by scented tobacco plants; the old peel tower, flanked by a small modern wing in the thin and shining air of the Northumbrian coast; a compact Cotswold mansion of silver-gilt stone; a low little Cornish home, half-hidden in white jasmine; and a dignified Georgian residence near the Welsh border. . . . Does the church clock, we wonder with Rupert Brooke, still stand at ten to three, and can the present rector possibly afford honey for tea today?'

We come far from stateliness and from country sweetness and quiet in the vicarage in the slums where Samuel Barnett and his wife fought so valiantly against poverty and evil. This warfare of the Church of England in the second half of the century was steadfast, and was at once a source and renewal of her spiritual life. She became a missionary Church at home as well as overseas.

An Oxford man and a scholar, Barnett was tempted by the offer of a living near Oxford. Country life within reach of the academic was the desire of many good men. But both he and his wife had a vocation to this special and urgent work of mission to the poor and neglected slum-dwellers. When the Bishop of London offered him the parish of St. Jude's, Whitechapel, he accepted with a whole heart, though well warned by the Bishop:

'It is the worst parish in my diocese, inhabited mainly by a criminal population, and one which has, I fear, been much corrupted by doles.' This was in 1872. The Barnetts were married in 1873 and after a honeymoon tour of the English cathedrals, settled down in their parish, though not at first in their vicarage, as the previous vicar had not yet moved out. They took lodgings in Finsbury, temperately described by Mrs. Barnett as 'small and frugal'. The condition of the kitchen may be guessed from one incident:

'I'm sorry, sir,' said the landlady, 'but a mouse has drowned itself in your rice pudding. We have such a lot of them.'

To this the vicar's Franciscan reply was: 'Poor little mouse!' Mrs. Barnett who had been a social worker under Octavia Hill, was prepared for most of what she had to face. Every day, she and her husband 'traversed the terrible courts between the parish and our rooms', exhausted, when night came, less by work than by their discovery of the degradation of the people.

The parish was a microcosm of slumdom. There were a few narrow streets of 'fairly decent cottages occupied entirely by Jews'. Otherwise it was 'a network of courts and alleys'. In some, the houses were three stories high, barely six feet apart, and had, for sole sanitation, a cess-pit in the cellar. Others were of wood, and a pipe in the court provided all their water. Windows were repaired with paper or rags, banisters were chopped up for firewood, the walls were tenanted by vermin. Each room held a family; some were let, for eightpence a night, to anyone for any purpose.

'In these homes people lived in whom it was hard to see the likeness of the Divine.'

Some of the men worked casually as dock labourers, more often they lived by stealing or by receiving stolen goods; they hawked, begged and gambled, drank and fought, were moved on or moved themselves when police attention came too close. An agent of Octavia Hill reported on those 'wrecks of houses' in what was pleasantly called Angel Alley, as being 'once a den of wild Irish', partly stables and partly rented rooms. In another alley, no rents had been collected for years, the landlord being afraid to enter. 'His wife was suffering from an Irish attack of poker and broomstick.' The agent added that 'a more hideous collection of heads and more horrible-looking rooms it would be impossible to conceive'.

In the midst of this desolation and abomination stood St. Jude's Church and schools. The former was opened with a congretation of six or seven old women who expected to be paid for attending. A year later this had increased to thirty in the morning

and from fifty to a hundred in the evening, with a choir in training.
The schools were opened with a hundred and forty-two children.
Adult classes, girls' night school and mothers' meetings were
begun; a nurse and a mission-woman were engaged, a maternity
society organized, a library opened. Concerts and oratorios were
performed; there was a group of lady visitors with a plan of relief
for the poor. And the driving force of all this activity was love.

'The end we have in view is that everyone may know God as
Father.' People were not 'cases', they were fellow-members of the
family of Christ.

Disappointments were inevitable, with many failures, heartbreaking discouragements, but the warfare was valiantly waged.
The vicarage, which was the focus and centre of all the activity,
was a small, dark house, with a basement kitchen, no bathroom, no
pantry. The Barnetts had no children, but they had the care of a
sister of Mrs. Barnett's; childish in mind, with her nurse. The little
house was always full of people coming and going: poor parishioners, distinguished and helpful friends. The concerts and
oratorios were not given by amateurs alone, but by such celebrities
as Fanny Davies and Clara Butt, and by famous choirs who, having
made music in the church came to the vicarage for hospitality and
friendship.

'We spent a great deal of time, thought and money on creating
pleasures,' which was a new way of evangelizing, and one not
always or by everyone approved. Feed and clothe the poor by all
means, instruct them and put them to honest work; but to amuse
them to delight them with music and beauty was, in some eyes, a
vanity.

'As yet the rich don't recognize that the poor are their equals in
human powers of enjoyment,' the vicar declared, and himself
encouraged these powers. The vicarage could not be made other
than small and dark but it was filled with bright and lovely things:
inherited furniture, the new Morris papers, Liberty silks and
cotton. One working girl remembered the flowers and sprays of
leaves which filled the rooms 'with the story of fields and gardens'; the drawing-room with opal-coloured walls and primrose
silk curtains; and the generosity with which the beauty was
shared. Not the least heroic part of Mrs. Barnett's charity was her
resolute blindness to the greasy head-marks on her Morris papers,

and the dirty garments sprawled on fresh upholstery. She did not even take such measures as moving chairs away from the walls and covering them with washable cotton. The Barnetts gave parties, bringing East End and West End together. Informal suppers were served, and there was no over-entertaining.

'Too often are the poor invited for an evening's pleasure and then set down in rows to be entertained by songs or parlour tricks which chiefly entertain those who perform. People must talk together if they are to break down the class barriers built by mutual ignorance. . . . There is nothing which people find so interesting as their fellow-creatures.'

The vicarage was a place of fun and refreshment as well as of prayers and spiritual counsel. There were larger parties besides, held once a month in the school for the whole parish. To these all the helpers came, some of them gaily, others jesting with difficulty.

'I think you make a mistake,' the vicar wrote to one of the latter. 'The conversation with another guest may seem to be dull work by the side of what can be done for vice and misery, but it is nevertheless the kind of work which prevents evil. The sense of fellowship, the power of quiet enjoyment, the realization of higher modes of life depend on simple intercourse.'

The Barnetts spent many holidays abroad, bringing back portfolios of prints to be shown, with travel-talk, to their guests. Distinguished folk came and were friendly – Lord Ripon, Walter Crane, Herbert Spencer, the Holman Hunts. Sometimes the visiting entertainers were stupidly unkind; it was not courteous or amusing to mimic the accents of the people, to sing comic songs about them, 'to pretend to be vulgar in the belief that it was sympathetic'. On parish outings, too, there were varying standards of courtesy and hospitality on the part of the hosts. At one great house the guests were given tea in the stable-yard, the tea, already milked and sugared, poured from watering cans; at another the hostess herself received the guests, and took the women to a bedroom to leave their outdoor things.

'Look, mother, here's a bed with a room to itself,' exclaimed one child. A third hostess had the table set as if for a ball supper with what Mrs. Barnett feared was a dangerous amount of 'portable plate'. Nearly always, the guests repaid courtesy with courtesy. 'The old people behaved like true gentle-people.'

The Barnetts used to send out formal At Home cards with R.S.V.P.: 'Reserved seats, very pleased' was one translation. Their 'wooden wedding' or twentieth anniversary in 1893 was celebrated by a party where wooden gifts were bestowed on the guests: paper-knives, napkin-rings, picture frames all put into a lucky dip from which everyone somehow managed to extract exactly what he or she had wanted. There was no 'pi-jaw'.

Toynbee Hall, which was largely the creation of the Barnetts, may fitly be mentioned in a study of Victorian households, for it was in origin and atmosphere domestic. It was, in effect, a product of that small, dark vicarage which was so full of the light of kindness and gaiety.

'We shall live in space, comfort and quiet,' Canon Barnett wrote to his brother, 'and we shall have about us the salt of the earth in the shape of Oxford men.' There were thirteen residents, all working in the parish, and they and the Warden (Canon Barnett) formed the Grand Committee which made rules. One of these was that no one coming late to dinner might have soup; the Warden had a way of ladling out the soup very slowly, as the laggards slipped into their places. Breakfast was taken at small separate tables: 'No one was good enough to breakfast together'; lunch and dinner at the long common table. Mrs. Barnett was housekeeper.

There were parties here too, all masculine, for the Warden thought that women would be 'too distracting for each other as well as for the men'. Each resident invited four guests, and once a year there was an enormous party for all the students at Toynbee Hall and all its filial clubs. There were exhibitions of pictures and all the handiwork of the clubs, music in the great drawing-room, and outside, 'the quadrangle hung with fairy-lights and coloured lanterns which glowed softly among the Virginia creepers along the old brick walls; the lights gleamed out from the latticed windows over which the gables rose against the stars; round the quaint dovecot opposite the clock the pigeons sleepily clustered; while above all, with the tower of St. Jude standing out darkly, the moon rose through a ripple of white clouds. . . . The roar of London was all unheard; and the crowded streets hard by, with their long lines of costers' barrows and their flaring lamps, seemed far away indeed.'

It might almost pass for a description of a college at Commemoration or in May Week, or of a party at some country house or vicarage – which is only to point the family resemblance, for Toynbee Hall was the offspring of college and vicarage united.

'St. Jude's and Toynbee Hall and the Exhibition were all built on my wife's tea-table,' Canon Barnett declared.

There were other foundations: The Children's Holiday Fund, established to send poor children to cottages in the country or by the sea, for a fortnight in summer – a homely hospitality, the cottage hostesses kind, the children happy; St. Jude's Cottage Hampstead, opened in 1889, at first to train girls in housework, then growing into a rest house for workers and tired people in general. Mrs. Barnett's tea-table continued to be surrounded by guests. 'The garden was small, but the drawing-room was large in this house, and so was its hospitality.'

No work of beneficence, no action against misery taken by good Victorians, and they were many, is more deeply rooted in domesticity and pleasant culture than that of the Barnetts. Country house and vicarage, century old college are in the background. It is a unique and invaluable quality in English and Victorian social work.

10

Houses of the Poor

'Our streets are infested with miserable creatures from whose faces almost everything human has been erased, whose very presence would fill us with shame, but for familiarity with the sight.' So Cardinal Manning wrote of the London poor whose numbers and miseries alike increased during the century of the Industrial Revolution. London was not unique; in every great town and city, old and new, the people swarmed in warrens which could hardly be called houses. They came from the country to the mills and factories, came over from Ireland, piled and huddled together in sub-human conditions which would not have been tolerated in any stables or cowsheds; for in these every horse or cow had its own stall, the place was from time to time cleaned out, the creatures were fed and cared for.

In Glasgow, at the beginning of the Queen's reign, the slums were, according to the Superintendent of Police, 'unfit even for sties'. In those 'fetid wynds' – to use Thomas Johnston's phrase, some fifteen to twenty people were herded together in one room. They slept on straw. Edinburgh was scarcely more refined. In some lodging houses in the Tron parish in High Street, the stench was so powerful that a policeman fainted. Sanitation barely existed; the old cry of 'Gardyloo' was a euphemism, for it was by no means mere water or *l'eau* which descended from the windows. Within, the walls were thick with filth, glistening with damp, and vermin flourished. This was breeding-ground for germs, with resulting cholera and typhus. Disease and starvation between them achieved – again to quote Thomas Johnston – 'a massacre which might have appalled even King Herod' who, after all, limited his victims to the age of two. In Glasgow half the poor children died under five, and among the survivors many were dwarfish and deformed. They were starved of food, they were starved of clean air and light; some of those miserable rooms were windowless or had a window about as large 'as the crown of a man's hat', open drains and cesspools were common. With no damp course, the houses, even by the hearth, were continually sodden.

The horror spread to the Black Country in both England and Scotland, to the mining villages, to the towns growing up around the new steel works, factories and mills. Miners' 'rows' were no better than huts, some below street level, stone floored, with damp-mouldered walls. Rents in some places were 6s. or 7s. a month for one room. Wages were about 4s. a day; a man might earn 24s. a week, if working full time, but this was rare; his wage might fall to 2s. 6d. a week and a shipbuilding strike meant a lock-out with no work for anyone.

In this miners' world, for it was a separate community like that of fisherfolk, the first Labour leader, Keir Hardy, grew to young manhood, on his way 'From Pit to Parliament'. He was born in 1856 near Holytown in the black centre of Lanarkshire, of very poor folk. His father was a ship's carpenter with only intermittent employment, his mother worked on a farm, and went on working after the birth of this, her first baby; she left him in the care of his grandmother, and ran home at intervals to feed him. At the age of six, after a few months at school, he began to earn money as an errand boy. His mother taught him to read and he continued to learn, by reading the newspaper placards and the pages of books open in booksellers' windows.

The family moved to Glasgow, and Keir found a job as messenger with the Anchor Line Steamship Company; then with a baker, delivering the early morning rolls to customers. He worked from seven in the morning till seven or half-past seven in the evening for a weekly wage of 3s. 6d. much needed at home. One morning the exhausted child over-slept; he was warned that a second offence might mean dismissal. Again it happened, and he arrived late at the shop, was sent upstairs, to his employer's warm dining-room above the shop, where prayers had just been said and the baker and his family were sitting at a well-spread breakfast-table. The boy was dismissed – 'and to make you more careful in future, I have decided to fine you a week's wages'; and so home to a house without food or fire, on a wet, bitterly cold December day.

He remembered that home: his mother in bed with a new-born baby, both stricken with fever, himself doing the family washing.

He remembered another home, an attic in the village of Quarter where his father found work as a joiner, and young Keir went down the pit – from six in the morning till half-past five in the evening, so that in winter he never saw daylight. He could see his mother, in these early mornings making breakfast for his father and himself at a fire of cannel-coal, his father saying with irony: 'You hae this consolation at least, that sailors and colliers are the twa classes that ministers pray maist for – if that's ony guid.'

His recollection was of an average wage of 15s. a week, of families of five or six children, of brick houses with brick floors, straw beds, and the coal kept under the bed.

Conditions were not much better a generation later, in the English Black Country where D. H. Lawrence was born. His wife Frieda wrote in her reminiscences of him: 'Vividly he would present to me all the people he had known in his youth . . . his mother, such a queen in her little house, and his father down at the pit, sharing his lunch with the pit pony. It all seemed romantic to me. And the colliers being drunk on Friday nights, and battles going on inevitably it seemed, every Friday night in nearly all the houses like a weekly hysteria.' There are many concepts of the romantic. Lawrence's high-born German wife may have listened to his recollections as to tales of some strange underground dwarfish people. She did, however, realize the harshness of his poverty and its results: 'Lawrence would never have been so desperately ill if his mother could have given him all the care he needed, and the food she could not afford to buy for him.'

He was born in 1885 at Eastwood, near Nottingham; his grandfather a tailor to the Coal Company, making the heavy clothes worn by the miners, his father a miner, not precisely a ne'er-do-well but incapable of advancing far, with a tendency to drink, to grumbling and self-pity; he was not ungifted, he was musical and sang well. Lawrence's mother was distinctly superior; she had married beneath her which did not cause harmony in the home. She had been a teacher, her father an engineer of a social grade above that of his son-in-law; clever but intolerant and some-times harsh she could not forgive the conditions to which her marriage had reduced her.

The spiritual background of Lawrence's childhood was the

local Congregational chapel. He used to tell his wife about the evangelical missions or 'revivals':

'A collier's wife in a little sailor hat, in a frenzy of repentance would clatter down the aisle, throw herself on her knees in front of the altar, and pray:

'"O Lord, our Henry he would 'ave come too but he dursn't. O Lord, I come as well for him, O Lord!"'

At one time Keir Hardy's mother kept a little shop in her house and Lawrence's mother did the same; she sold caps and aprons in her front room. She was the dominating influence in her son's boyhood; a 'Victorian *bourgeois*' as he described her, opposed to the 'industrial proletarian' in her husband and his family. They quarrelled a good deal.

> 'My father was a working man
>   and a collier was he,
> At six in the morning they turned him down
>   and they turned him up for tea.
>
> My mother was a superior soul, a
>   superior soul was she
> Cut out to play a superior role
>   in the God-damned *bourgeoisie*.
>
> We children were the in-betweens,
>   little nondescripts we,
> Indoors we called each other you,
>   outside it was *tha* and *thee*.
>
> But time has fled, and our parents are dead,
>   We are risen in the world all three,
> But still we're in-betweens, we tread
>   between the devil and the deep cold sea'.

A famous Scots minister coming from a long line of Highland clergy, Dr. Norman Macleod, had his first parish in another special community, that of the Ayrshire weavers (or websters in the Scots tongue). He was appointed to the parish of Loudoun: covenanting country, and the weavers were most of them 'thrawn commentators sweir to 'gree', ready to argue at all times and on all points of politics and theology. They were well read, for the village or parish library was well furnished and they had no notion of escape-literature. Their intelligence, the minister noted, was 'strongly coloured with self-conceit which was characteristic of the old race of Scotch websters'. Those who were not of the Strait covenanting tradition were agnostic, following the teaching of Tom Paine. Moral standards were low; 'vital godliness was a rarity'.

The young minister began Sunday school and other classes and kept a strict church discipline, which meant that the erring and the lapsed were brought before the Kirk Session to be admonished; and not only for gross carnal sin and open scandal, for living together in sin, dispensing with the rite of marriage, but for forestalling that rite – as proved by the too early arrival of a baby. The minister faithfully visited his parishioners, was some-times welcomed, sometimes snubbed, and often put through his theological paces; as when he called on a contemporary Mause Headrigg, a deaf old woman who put her trumpet to her ear and bade him 'gang ower the fundamentals'.

The cottages were mostly two-roomed, with a but and a ben – 'the loom in the but (or room) the wife in the ben (or kitchen)'. One man in such a house made the minister go over not the fundamentals of theology but the seven points of Chartism. These, Norman Macleod declared, would 'drive the country into revolution and create, in the end, national bankruptcy'. 'Nay-tion-al bankruptcy! Div ye think sae?' replied the weaver. 'Dod! I'd risk it.'

After five years, in 1843, the minister moved to the parish of Dalkeith. The immediate background was respectable, with streets full of good shops and the houses of prosperous tradesmen, but the hinterland of wynds and closes held 'dens of as miserable a class as can be found in the purlieus of Edinburgh or Glasgow'. The working-men here were inferior in character and intelligence to the weavers; the lowest strata 'appalling' in their 'poverty, ignorance and squalor, easy to reach so long as the question was one of almsgiving, but which it appeared almost impossible to reform'.

Drunkenness was the root of the evil, and springing closely

from that root were bad housing, poor clothing, lack of food. Macleod urged the prosperous to help the poor; he started a loan fund to help them; he preached, not only in the church but outside 'to fifty outcasts in the wynds' who would not enter God's house in their rags. One poor boy he rescued, handing him over to his housemaid Jessie, in the manse; Jessie promptly stood the boy in a tub of hot water, where he appeared 'like a ghost among mist', scrubbed him clean, borrowed a shirt for him gave him a meal and a shake-down.

The problem of poverty, ignorance and misery became larger in this minister's last parish, the large one of The Barony in Glasgow. His own house or manse was in the pleasant West End of the city, in Woodlands Terrace, high above the streets, looking to the hills. Below, on the Clyde, were the great shipyards, where every morning could be heard the thud of the steam-hammers and all the stir of labour; heartening, this, for it was the lifeblood of Glasgow and a fine and honourable craft. But there was the grim area of little work, little money, little hope. Again he urged or compelled his wealthier parishioners, some of them merchant princes, to give the money he needed for his poor; he started schools (this was in mid-century before the coming of free and compulsory education), he opened a penny bank, established a club with a refreshment room which served men with good, cheap meals, and a reading-room to keep them out of the pubs. Education, for girls as well as for boys, would cure many ills:

'We want a higher class of industrial schools, in our large towns especially, for our females, where, in addition to the ordinary branches of learning they must also received instruction in shaping and making clothes, in washing and dressing them, and in cooking too, so as to fit them to become cleanly, thoroughly intelligent wives, and in every respect helps meet for an artisan, who could make his home more attractive to him than the whisky shop. . . . We require a wider education for our artisans themselves, so as to train them up to such fixed ideas as may fit them to meet the actual temptations to which they are exposed, to perform their duties as workmen, parents, citizens; and so as to enlarge, too, the field of their enjoyment as human beings.' The dignity of human nature, of personality must be guarded; there must be for everyone an individual world of private and domestic interests.

The best of wives could do little in some houses, and to reproach them with failing to make an attractive home would have been a stupid impertinence.

J. L. and Barbara Hammond quote a Report, of 1845, of the Health of Towns Commission on the poorer kind of house in Manchester, built 'with a rapidity that astonishes persons who are unacquainted with their flimsy structure'. These were not 'underground dwellings' like some of the miners' dwellings, but went to the opposite extreme of 'having neither cellar nor foundation'. The walls were only half-brick in thickness, they were built back to back, without drainage or ventilation. 'Like a honeycomb, every particle of space is occupied. Double rows of these houses form courts with, perhaps, a privy at one end and a dump at the other, common to the occupants of about twenty houses.'

The window tax, which was not repealed until 1851 meant the minimum of light and ventilation through few and tiny windows, and none at all in privies, passages and cellars.

There were some good landlords; as the Ashworths, quoted by the Hammonds who found that 'habits and conditions were closely connected', decent houses producing decent behaviour. A house with living-room, kitchen and three bedrooms was the best type.

But where there were no building restrictions houses could be packed together, open spaces built up. Within there was squalor, without not a sign of greenness, not a whiff of fresh air. With no space for recreation there was only one refuge, the public-house or the gin-shop. They were warm, brightly lit, and sociable – until the fighting began, and even that might be considered a form of sociability. The vicious circle whirled round and round in a terrible vortex.

The miseries of the poor recur vividly in fiction, especially those of the drunkard's home. Mrs. Henry Wood's *Danesbury House* is a tract rather than a novel and starkly black and white in its attitude to any form of alcohol, however mild; but its description of the gin palaces with their flaring lights, of ruined homes, and of a roaring case of *delirium tremens* has a lurid reality. George MacDonald's Scots novels give clear pictures of domestic life in town and country. In the opening chapter of *Sir Gibbie* we see the depth of poverty and degradation reached through drink. The dumb waif who is the hero, heir, though he does not know it, to an ancient estate and baronetcy, brings his father, Sir George, home from the pub on Saturday night, pushing, pulling and guiding him, back to their wretched attic; there he contrives somehow to heave him on to their bed, covers him with an old plaid, and curls up to sleep beside him in perfect contentment, his filial duty done. He awakes, to find his father dead; and in dread of what may be done to him through misguided philanthropy, for he has a horror of losing his freedom, runs away, holding north towards his lost ancestral home in the hills of Aberdeenshire. In his wanderings he plays the Brownie, doing tasks at night on a farm; is caught and cruelly thrashed by the gamekeeper; finds refuge in a shepherd's cottage.

There, MacDonald gives an idyllic picture of the Scottish country poor: a prose version of 'The Cottar's Saturday Night'. It is a tiny cottage, only Robert the shepherd and his wife, Janet, living there, now that their family are up and out in the world, working on neighbouring farms; they are all well-doing, devoted to their parents, coming home on Saturday night for supper and family worship. Gibbie has been put to bed in Janet's and Robert's own bed, but the sons go out and cut heather to bind thickly together in a box and make a small bed for him, covered with coarse, clean linen. He is given food, oatcakes and milk, he helps the youngest son Donal at the herding and is blissfully happy until he is found and taken into ward by a guardian, to be educated for his true station in life; but that is another and sometimes dull story.

Had he not so often strayed off into exhortations and musings – excellent in themselves and in their place – MacDonald would have made a fine domestic novelist, a *genre* painter in fiction, and filled a sad lack in Victorian Scots literature. In his *Alec Forbes* he describes more than one interior: the comfortable, kind and genteel house of the hero's mother, the grimness of that to which the child-heroine, Annie, is brought by her uncle. The grimness does not come from poverty or drunkenness; the uncle and aunt are the limit of respectability, they are well-to-do enough on the proceeds of their shop, but they are mean to the core, and the bleak discomfort in which the child lives is colder than any poverty. Annie is stowed away in an attic with the barest furnish-

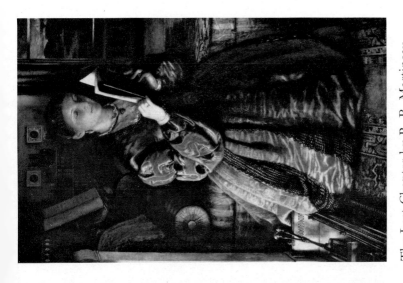

The Last Chapter by R. B. Martineau

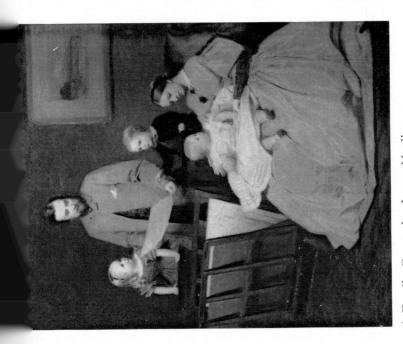

A Family Group by James Hayllar

Victoria & Albert Museum, Crown Copyright

An easy chair, carved walnut and marquetry with a porcelain panel inset with a portrait of Prince

ing, lit only by the moon and stars at night, seen through the skylight, and shared with rats. Everything else she could bear but that is unendurable horror. Mercifully there is a cat, and puss becomes one of her most cherished companions. This particular interior might well claim to be the meanest in fiction.

Country poverty was less grim than in town, because there was fresh air around if not within the house. Here too the cottages were cramped, insanitary and damp; wages were low and food frugal. But here, more often than in the towns, conditions could and often were improved by a good squire. His tenants were kept at least tolerably housed, the roof repaired, the walls sound. Workers on a farm had milk enough, and with a patch of garden to grow vegetables a family might have wholesome if meagre fare.

George Bourne in *The Bettesworth Book* records the memories of a Surrey countryman who, as a boy in mid-century, lived and worked on a farm: it was hard work but good living: 'any amount of bread and bacon, and plenty of home-brewed beer, and in the winter a sure, drowsy place by the kitchen fire . . . the open hearth with its chimney corner, the fire-shine glowing out dim and ruddy upon flitches of bacon hung around the room, and reddening upon the faces of sleepy boys. It is likely that never again was Bettesworth in such good quarters'. Bettesworth had never been more than a labourer or an odd-job man, and when he talked to George Bourne he was old and living in 'distressful poverty, that cynically grinning life-companion of the labouring people'; the degree of poverty revealed by his pathetic delight and gratitude over a strip of worn carpet, given him to cover his potatoes from frost, but accepted as a luxury his home had never known.

Conditions did not change rapidly. A recent book of memoirs, or fiction or of both skilfully interwoven, *Miss Clare* (by 'Miss Read'), describes a childhood of the nineties in a poor but extremely well-doing family. Miss Clare remembers the tiny cottage where she and her sister grew from babyhood into first childhood. It had no water, no sanitation, and was far from weather-proof:

'The autumn gales had lifted several slates from the roof and had driven rain into the bedroom through the gaps. The window frames had shrunk with age and fitted poorly, and many a keen draught whirled through the rooms. There was no damp course and the walls of the scullery glistened with moisture. The strip of matting which Mary had spread on the flag-stone floor there was dank and musty.'

The landlord's reply to any complaint or request was:

'What d'you expect for two shilluns a week? . . . And how far d'you reckon two shilluns is going to go when it comes to putting a new set of slats on the roof? . . . If that ain't grand enough for you, you know the answer.'

The rent was high enough for a labourer, a thatcher as the children's father, Francis, was at the time. There was a black winter when he was out of work, laid up with a broken leg; he had fallen from a ladder while thatching. His father did as many of his jobs as he could, giving Francis the wages, and the kind farmer's wife for whom Mary his wife had worked before her marriage, sent piles of mending, with generous pay, and gifts of vegetables, eggs and butter; but still it was a hard winter.

Things improved in time and the family moved to another house in a healthier village: a solid and comfortable cottage with kitchen and parlour downstairs, two bedrooms above; a bathroom was not even dreamed of, and in many a larger and better house of the period would still be absent, or if it existed be of a primitive sort.

"'Tisn't a palace. . . . Two up and two down, but a pump inside and good cupboards,' and the rent still two shillings a week. In the same cottage Miss Clare, grown old, lived and remembered her youth.

Her mother, Mary, had been a servant in a farmhouse where she was kindly treated and well trained in housewifery by her mistress. There was plenty of wholesome food, the great kitchen was always warm, for coal was cheap, and logs were sawn and stacked.

'At Michaelmas the pigs were killed, salted and jointed, and hung in clean muslin from the beams in the kitchen. Strong beer was brewed in an enormous copper from home-grown barley and provided a nourishing drink for the men. There was milk in abundance and butter was made once a week. . . . All the bread, the massive pies and puddings were made from home-grown wheaten flour. Vegetables and fruit were picked each day from the garden, and the farmhouse kitchen seemed always to be filled with the fragrance and the clatter of cooking.'

In the evening, with the lamp lit, they all sat round its light; Mary and her mistress had their mending, there was talk, perhaps some reading until drowsiness sent everyone to bed, and by ten o'clock the house was dark and still. Morning came too quickly, with many jobs for Mary, the kindling of the fire, cooking and cleaning. She was happy and would have stayed there contentedly for years, had she not met young Francis. Their marriage was approved, and Mary was given many things by her motherly mistress: 'There, my dear, put that aside with your things. 'Tis a bit shabby, maybe, but it'll prove useful, I don't doubt' – which it did, and was treasured, whether it was linen or crockery. When they married Francis had saved ten pounds, and Mary had a wedding-gift from the farmer and his wife of five golden sovereigns.

In the Highlands and western islands of Scotland life went on very much as it had done for two or three centuries. In some parts, notably in Skye and Lewis, the black house was common: a round house divided inside by a partition, the hearth set by the wall. In other houses the hearth was in the centre of the floor and the peat smoke went up through a primitive chimney hole in the roof. The peat stack by the door was the only fuel. The cow lived next door, beyond a partition.

Angus McLellan writes of his childhood, in the 1870's on South Uist: 'My father had neither croft nor land, he was only a squatter on the land of John Ferguson the farmer. He had to pay rent for every cow he kept' – £2 a year, and was not allowed to keep a horse at all. 'He was allowed to cultivate all he could dig with a spade, and that was not much.'

Potatoes made the staple fare, and the misery of the people during the potato famine is beyond telling. At the time of Angus's recollection they were plentiful, more so than oats, for to grow oats the earth had to be broken in and made soft with potato crops. For manure the people used kelp or burned seaweed. The other staple was fish. Most families had bread and tea for breakfast, fish and potatoes for dinner, porridge and milk for supper, but oatmeal was not plentiful. The sea, indeed, gave more than the land in both work and food. The lamps, small iron cruisies or cruisgeins burned fish liver oil, for paraffin was hardly known.

'It's surprising how happy the people were' – poor in material things but rich in traditions, in their great inheritance of Gaelic poetry and legends, tales almost as old as the hills, beliefs in another world – neither earth, heaven, nor hell – that were frowned on by the Kirk but still persisted. There was a wealth of music, of songs of labour: for milking and churning, for laying and for smooring the hearth, for spinning and weaving and fulling the cloth; cradle-songs, too, more tender and lovely than any others. Even when Calvinism officially banished Our Lady and the saints, she and they were invoked in songs and blessings: St. Bride, St. Columba, St. Patrick, St. Michael and all the angels.

There was the ceilidh, the gathering of neighbours round one hearth to tell stories and sing or hear songs. Sometimes the young folk gathered in a barn for a dance – Alexander Carmichael in his *Carmina Gadelica* tells how they used to hang a blanket before the window lest the minister come along and see, and denounce them. But in some places the minister was sympathetic and encouraged the old traditions and diversions. Anyhow, the ceilidh went on.

Angus McLellan recalls poaching adventures. He shot a rabbit, was reported by an unfriendly shepherd to the gamekeeper and the factor, was had up and fined £2 or fourteen days in gaol. He chose to pay the fine. His brother lent him a gun, and he went out in the boat to shoot shags (cormorants). 'I took in what would pay it within the year.'

The island pattern of life was twofold, on the croft and on the sea. There was lobster and herring fishing; once there was so great a herring harvest in Loch Eynort 'that the loch was dry; they were so plentiful that when the tide ebbed, the shore looked white with them' and this continued all one winter and spring. For such abundance there could be no market. 'It was food enough, better than nothing, that's all', fresh and salted, until, in the end, 'we were dumping it in the sea.'

Sometimes they caught flounders and cod was plentiful. Fishing was hard, cold work and often dangerous, and it brought in little money. Even lobsters were sold at 7s. a dozen. Once a whale surfaced near the boat: 'She was as long as the net, and her two eyes were nearly as big as that chair.'

Angus and his mates had a great love of stories and used to go to hear a noted seannachaidh or story-teller, Alasdair Mor. One night they were so enthralled that they forgot time and tide and a rising storm; when they came out they found that the sea had swept up on the shore, and filled and sunk their boat, while the nets were dragged into the deep water. They managed to recover the nets, which were anchored, and, with great effort, to refloat the boat; but 'we were fed up with the stories of Alasdair Mor' for a time.

11

London Families

I

The London poor make frequent appearances in Victorian fiction, especially, we have seen, in Dickens. A Dickensian novelist of our own century, himself Victorian by birth, set some of his tales in a Victorian background. William De Morgan in his *Alice For Short* and *Joseph Vance* created in each case a poor child, one with a wretched home, the other with delightful parents, and brought them into comfort and dignity: a variant of one of the enduring themes of fairy tale.

Alice is a late Victorian child. We meet her carrying home a jug of beer from a pub in Soho: 'She did not like bringing it; and though her eyes were blue and she was a nice little girl, she could almost have found it in her heart to stop and drink some by the way. But she was afraid of her mother.' When some boys on a slide knock her down and break the jug she is almost too terrified to go home. Charles, the hero of the book, and his friend Jeff who have their studio lodgings in the house, come to her rescue. Her mother 'old Mother Gingham, looks blotchy, smells of threepennyworth of rum shrub' as Charles describes her, is a drunken drab. 'She suggested but came short of the Seven Dials, old St. Giles' type – the sort that used to wear a red handkerchief round its neck and no head-covering.' Charles's defence of Alice is backed by money, and vengeance is stayed; but he is troubled about the child.

Jeff and he are enjoying their holiday in Bohemia with a little work thrown in. Charles's own home is wealthy, his father a silk merchant, and he can afford to rent 'the old state drawing-room of this old Soho house'. Alice's parents occupy the basement, as caretakers. Her father had been a journeyman tailor in a very good business, until dragged down by his wife's drinking habits; now he works at home on odd jobs. His wife had been the daughter of a prosperous publican. The basement smells of 'varieties of decay' and here Alice, who hardly remembers the good days, 'has passed her small new life, mostly weeping in the darkness'. Her father is not unkind. He insist on Alice's being given supper – kippered haddock and bread scraped with butter; 'if her father hadn't given her some off his own slice, it wouldn't have been no butter at all in a manner of speaking'. Her mother drinks and drinks, until a quarrel flares up. That night Alice is wakened by the 'airey-bell' and the voice of a policeman.

'Alice jumped out of bed – it was so nice and warm and such a pity to – and pulled a rag stopper out of a pane of glass to answer through.' Charles comes down, and they find her mother unconscious, with a bad wound in her head, her father dead of cyanide poisoning. The mother is taken to hospital, and Charles takes Alice to his parents' house in Hyde Park Gardens, to be welcomed and cosseted by his sister Peggy. Alice, undoubtedly a poppet, so captivates the family that without any definite plan she becomes one of them, and when Peggy marries a young doctor, who proceeds to Harley Street, goes to live with her and become 'Aunt Alice' to her children.

But in those first weeks of her new life of semi-adoption she is taken by Peggy to visit her mother in hospital. It is almost certain that the woman will die of her injury, but there has been a flicker of recovery – and recovery of mind and soul. The true woman in her is full of gratitude and contrition, and she tells Peggy her story: 'It was drink . . . I had been a total abstainer, Miss, and Samuel I made of him a total too, or near it' – because her own mother had died of drink. They had been happy and comfortable at first, but with too frequent childbearing she grew weak:

'What can a woman do, Miss, when her strength is not enough? And when the doctor comes and says: "You must drink stout." "You must take port"? And what could you hope for from a man but follow on?' So the degradation began; the older children had escaped but Alice had paid for all.

Alice herself is completely detached, in an unchildlike way which startles Peggy. She makes no complaint against her mother, but simply assumes that 'justice or vengeance was her mother's function, and love was her father's' because he had never illtreated her, and had given her some protection and kindness. She is too young to understand or feel compassion. Peggy is deeply moved:

'The creature that Charles had seen . . . was much more Alcohol than a woman. When Peggy spoke with her at the hospital, on her death-bed, the obsession had been removed, and the woman had come back again, as truly as the demoniac's sane soul returned to him when the Gadarene swine rushed to the lake and bore his curse away for ever.'

The small Joseph Vance knows nothing of such misery. He would have been surprised at being called poor for he is rich in parental love, has enough to eat, lives in cleanliness. His mother is not only good to the core but one of the most endearing comic characters in fiction, his father, Christopher, wayward but irresistible. They are of the respectable poor who can and do emerge from poverty when Christopher takes himself in hand.

The story begins with a fight in a pub between Christopher and a sweep. It is all told by Joseph himself, in age, recollecting his youth. Christopher is laid out flat, by a foul, and taken to hospital; Mrs. Vance manages somehow, thanks to the Workman's Benefit, Club. Christopher has lost his job, which troubles him very little for he comes home to an agreeable convalescence, 'ate more than his share of breakfast and dinner, as an invalid who required feeding up' and 'seemed to take kindly to doing nothing at other people's expense' until the doctor suggested 'that he wouldn't recover the use of his legs until his allowance was stopped'.

Mr. Vance is resourceful and a profound psychologist, who knows that most people will believe what they are told they believe and accept as fact what is convincingly presented to them. From a 'Licensed 'Awker, but some they do prefer to call me an Itinerant Marine Store Dealer, some a General 'Ardware,' he buys for one and three-pence an old signboard: 'C. Dance, Builder. Repairs, Drains promptly attended to', has the Dance altered to Vance and the board 'done all over' by a friendly sign-painter for a shilling, and sets it up outside his house. People are convinced that it has always been there; among them Dr. Thorpe who looks after the local Savings Bank, and who tells Mrs. Vance – as she reports it: 'They was inquirin' up at the 'ouse for someone to see to the nursery chimney, likewise the drains in the basement' – and employs Christopher. Somehow or other, helped by a capacity for bluff which comes near genius, Christopher does that job and others, and so begins the new life of prosperity. Joe is taken by his father to Dr. Thorpe's house, Poplar Villa.

'What's a Willer? It's a 'ouse with a stables for a one-'orse shay, and a green'us and a gardener and some scarlet geeraniums', Christopher informs Joe. 'And what's geeraniums? Well, geeraniums is what they sells on the barrers. And what's a green'us? Well, it's glass, and there's a grapewine in it, and it's where they shoves the garden-pump away when not in use.'

Joe is taken up by Dr. Thorpe – a Doctor of Science not of Medicine – who discovers in him a born mathematician, sends him to school and, in time, to college. His younger daughter, the adorable Lossie, adopts Joe as her younger brother. Meanwhile Christopher continues to ascend. His bluff succeeds, his building and repairing business flourishes. The family move to a villa themselves, with 'the little orfice round the corner' for business, and indoors 'ackchly a back and front drawing-room, breakfast-room level with the kitchen, three large and two small bedrooms, commodious kitchen and scullery, at the moderate rental of forty-five pounds per annum' as the somewhat dazed Mrs. Vance describes it. An excellent housewife, entirely without ambition or snobbery, she wonders what she will do with a servant: 'Your father says I must learn to be waited on like my betters, but it's hard to reconcile myself to it at my time of life, after all these years of cooking and cleaning up.' With wifely submission she accepts the change: 'As your father says, it's only habit, and we must all get accustomed. But it don't seem natural to leave off cleaning, and very likely a girl with followers and a cook the worse.' When her husband insists that he wants 'a 'ansum girl to open the front door', Mrs. Vance, a realist, makes the immortal statement: 'Then Followers. So sure as the sort you describe, Followers. And if Followers, then Consequences.' She would prefer a servant like one she had known 'whose appearance was security itself, and avoided strickly by gentlemen and young men alike, but twelve pounds a year and not a penny less, being indeed honest and sober'. Apparently when a girl was 'such that followers are out of the question' then higher wages were expected on that account alone: a new theory of domestic economy.

A little maid is found, Seraphina by name, to be known as

Feener, who pleases everyone, but poor Mrs. Vance does not long enjoy her change of fortune. The years of work and poverty have been too hard, and she dies of tuberculosis, to the intense grief of her husband and son, and to the bewilderment of the former.

'I really believe', Joe reflects, 'he thought that settees covered with Utrecht velvet, walnut chiffoniers with curvilinear marble tops, buhl, marqueterie, ormolu and so forth, had in them the antidotes to pulmonary disease.'

II

For real London families we may begin with the delightful recollections of M. Vivian Hughes. On her mother's side she was Cornish, and holidays in her childhood were spent in Cornwall at the family house which was more than an ordinary farm; a homestead, a community, self-supporting with its poultry and pigs, cows and dairy, and vegetable garden. The house itself had grown with the generations, and was a mixture of old and new, rambling and homely. Housekeeping was lavish. Fish was rare, sometimes a local catch of pilchards, sometimes a gift of trout; 'the staple food was pig-meat in its endless variety, and poultry'. An old family cookery book advised: 'If you have nothing in the house and company should come, take a cold turkey.'

Bread was baked every day in batches of manchets or loaves moulded by hand, not baked in a tin. One of these once cut was never served again at table, but always a fresh loaf, the broken bread being made into mash for the turkeys. The narrator, Molly remembered the great stone dairy with its slate shelves, set with vessels of milk at every stage, from the newly drawn, in pails, to the dishes of cream and the butter made, not by churning but by turning the cream in a big bowl. Skim milk was sold for a halfpenny a quart or given away. One must not speak while turning the cream, or the butter would not come.

Sanitation was primitive, baths were taken in bedrooms, the water fetched from a rain barrel. Windows were kept closed; fresh air was for out of doors. The germs would appear to have disliked this, for there was no illness. But then life was lived largely out of doors, in play as well as in work. Picnics were frequent and opulent, with Cornish pasties 'that perfectly complete portable meal' as provender. Housekeeping in London was, necessarily, less opulent but no less skilled. Molly's mother cooked by instinct and found it difficult to tell an inquirer just how she made her delicious rice pudding. She put a piece of butter in. How much? 'Oh, a good bit' – and so on.

It was a family of four brothers and one sister. When their father died Molly was offered by her mother a choice between staying at home with her – the boys would see that they had adequate means – and doing lessons there, or going to school to prepare herself for wage-earning. Molly chose the latter, with her mother's warm approval, attended Miss Buss's famous London school, went to Training College at Cambridge, and so to various teaching and lecturing jobs. In 1897 she married Arthur Hughes, a barrister, clever and hard-working but not yet well-off. They chose to have 'a wedding without tears' or fuss or frayed nerves. Molly was lecturing in Bedford College and went on with her work until the end of term. Her trousseau was simple: a wedding dress of cream silk worn with a picture hat, a going-away coat and skirt in grey, with a little shoulder cape, designed by a French dressmaker: "E clothe the shoulder and 'e not make warm'; sufficient underwear, including an exquisite nightdress, hand-embroidered by her mother for her own trousseau. They were married in St. Alban's, Holborn:

'On the arm of an ideal brother I was walking to an ideal husband, and as I went, I was vaguely aware of quite a little congregation of old pupils and students and friends.'

The honeymoon was spent in Salisbury. Arthur, an absent-minded packer, had forgotten to bring a nightshirt and they had to rush out and buy one. The only shop open so late was a universal provider's who provided a garment in pink flanellette at 2s. 11d. reduced to 1s. 11d.

They took a flat in Ladbroke Grove; by no means modern in fittings. There was no gas, all the cooking and water-heating depended on the huge, old-fashioned range.

'Disraeli said that there were three things a man should never grumble at, because they were unalterable: the weather, his wife, and the kitchen range.' Arthur dealt efficiently with theirs.

He went off to the Temple, in the morning, leaving Molly to unpack their possessions, trying to tidy away the wrappings of paper and straw before being submerged. 'I thought of the story of the old woman whose square house became round; the explanation being that she thrust everything into the corners.' This danger averted she began to prepare the servant's bedroom about which she had 'a rooted idea' that it 'must have pink chintz covered with muslin round her table'. This was done, the bed made up, a supply of caps and aprons laid out when the maid, Emma, arrived from Norfolk; a fresh-faced country girl who had never left her native Dereham and who used Norfolk dialect: 'do' for 'if it should', and 'deen' for a scrap or small quantity: 'Not a deen of sugar left.'

Emma proved a treasure, not only knowing how to work but teaching her mistress the method. She worked steadily and without haste, with special days for special jobs, and she liked her mistress to go out and leave her in active possession.

Molly became a prudent shopper. She discovered the little shops in the neighbourhood where everything was cheaper than further west, where the customers were critical, refusing stale vegetables. Household bills were modest; Arthur paid the coal, and Emma's wages, Molly everything else, and out of an allowance of 30s. a week could save five or six shillings. She learned to cook and appreciated Emma's rhyme:

> 'She could make, she could bake,
> She could brew, she could sew,
> And found time to teach her three sons to say "No".'

The sons came in due time.

Remembering those Cornish manchets she made bread, so much to her husband's taste that she continued to bake it and to make her own yeast. Friends and relations were surprised that she, the former school-mistress and lecturer, could run a house so well; but her mother was in her, and so was the beloved aunt who had managed the Cornish house so superbly well.

London in the eighties and nineties was the world of Ernest Shepard's childhood and youth. He was born in St. John's Wood, the youngest of three children, their father an architect. His first childhood was spent in a house in Kent Terrace, which had a front door with two stained-glass panels, designed by his father

One, with an owl, represented Night, the other, Morning. The aesthetic note was continued in the drawing-room which had mantel-shelves filled with blue and white china. This London was still part-rural. The milkwoman went her rounds carrying two pails of milk on a wooden yore across her shoulders; the little shops round about Park Road were like a village. The barrel-organ man played his tunes, the muffin man came round in winter, the crossing-sweeper did his work, much needed in those days of horse-traffic. Open dust-carts were drawn by horses 'which seemed permanently to wear a nose-bag' driven by men with leather flaps at the back of their hats. When the rubbish bins were emptied clouds of dust arose, enriched by coal-dust when coal was shot through the hole into the cellar. An odd-job man sat in a chair in the Terrace, ready to fetch a cab, carry luggage in or out of the house, run errands. The children went to a school in Baker Street. Sometimes, for a treat, they went shopping with their mother in Oxford Street and Regent Street and had tea and cream cakes in a teashop.

The basement kitchen was large, warm and friendly. Through the window could be seen the feet of passers-by on the pavement above the area steps. Tea in the kitchen was a genial meal, with Cook and Lizzie the housemaid, and sometimes Lizzie's sisters dropping in. In front of the fire stood the large tin roaster on legs which raised it to the right height; it was open in front, with a little door in its back for inspecting and basting the joint.

People went to town by bus when they did not take a cab. There were two buses, the *Atlas*, running between the West End and The Eyre Arms, the *City Atlas* going to the city. It was fun to sit beside the driver. There were no fixed stops, people hailed the bus from the pavement, told the conductor where they wanted to get off, and no doubt conductor and driver both knew the regulars. The inside was stuffy, with velveteen seats and straw on the floor; stairs led to the knife-board top, but ladies did not make the ascent. The most delightful form of transport was the hansom, the open-fronted cab with the driver perched up behind.

The children paid frequent visits to their aunts in a big house in Gordon Square; a solemn house with a stone urn on a sideboard in the hall, to hold visiting-cards; a dismal ornament of a moth-eaten albatross's head, a cheerful picture of a little girl and a dog, from a Christmas Annual; and, on the hat-stand, two men's hats to scare off intruders and intending burglars. The dining-room was dark green, with several large prints and engravings on the walls, some of Biblical subjects, one by Landseer, one of the Duke of Wellington: all proper for a dining-room where everything ought to be dark and large. Light colours and gay little pictures and ornaments were suitable only for the drawing-room.

'All the furniture was of solid mahogany and not very comfortable, and there was always a slight smell of dinner.' The aunts dined at six, and the visiting children had high tea; then played card games in the drawing-room until a quarter to nine, when tea was brought in, and they went to bed. At ten there were prayers. The maids filed in, cook first, then the parlourmaid, followed by 'Alice and Mary and the little one at the tail' the little one being the tweeny shared between cook and housemaid. The house had a bathroom but it was considered more refined to have one's bath in one's own room.

The aunts did not care for travel. Their holidays were usually spent within driving distance of home; but that could be rural enough. One year they took the Vicarage at Highgate and drove out in a private bus: two of the aunts, four maids with their luggage which included boxes of linen and of provisions, two cages of canaries, a knitting machine and an invalid chair. The other two aunts followed in a fly with the fifth maid and a nurse. One of the aunts was something of an invalid. They might not enjoy travelling but they must be out of town in the holiday season. This convention was so strong that a stock subject of comedy was the family who could not afford a holiday, and who stayed in town, living in the basement, back parlour and bedrooms with the blinds pulled down in front.

These ladies, however, were in no need of retrenchment. Their summer quarters were not cramped. One vicarage – they tended to choose clerical houses – had ten bedrooms, and there was always a garden.

The children were taken farther afield by their parents. One delectable holiday was spent in a farmhouse in Kent, the two boys sharing a feather bed in a big bedroom; one wall was adorned with a text: 'The Lord shall preserve thee and keep thee.' Downstairs was the parlour where the boarders ate an enormous tea beginning with home-cured bacon and eggs, and continuing with bread and butter, home-baked buns, cheese, pickles, jam and plum cake. But the boys preferred the large kitchen, its great fireplace and a gun hanging above the mantelshelf, a clock on the wall painted with a picture of a volcano, hooks in the rafters for hams, geraniums on the window-sill and a cat curled up on the window-seat. Waking early, on their first morning they came down and out, to explore the farmyard, and were given an extra first breakfast of bread and milk.

There was endless fun here; and for variety there was the village, with a shop that sold everything from sweets to bootlaces, bonnets to fireworks; but the best sweets were made by an old man in his own kitchen, and they went to see him make toffee, pulling it from a hook and flavouring it with herbs.

A cosy, secure and contented childhood, it was shadowed by the illness and death of the children's mother. For a year they lived with the aunts, then their father took a house on the riverside in Hammersmith: three stories, a basement, a stone-flagged hall, a balcony over the portico and a studio in the garden. This was to be a very modern house; a bathroom was added. The drawing-room was elegant with its fine marble chimney-piece and tall bookcases in recesses. And there was a garden, neglected, almost wild, but with a cherry tree and a grape vine. Two faithful maids came with them, their mother's old nurse, Lizzie the cook, and a small girl called Virtuella.

There was a holiday with the aunts in a vicarage near Guildford – a far cry from Gordon Square – another in Hampshire in a big, old house with a garden to match; and most excitingly, the first holiday abroad, in Germany, with their father. Happiness returned. This artist narrator is singularly devoid of frustrations and complaints, his father was kind, his brother and sister were good companions. They were neither poor nor rich, they knew that solid comfort which was the heritage of a wide and varied middle class in the last decade of the old century, the first decade of the new.

Richard Church lived in a somewhat lower stratum; one removed from poverty, and further removed from squalor, and very conscious of that removal, acutely anxious in self-preservation.

'Social critics tend to overlook the result of the close, huggermugger home atmosphere in the child-life of the great masses,'

he says, in the first part of his autobiography *Over the Bridge.*
'It is that which makes them over-emotional, unadventurous,
matriarch-ridden. It makes them gullible too, thin-skinned and
hostile, yet at the same time almost embarrassingly kind.'

There could indeed be few greater contrasts than between this
lower-middle class he describes and the upper-middle to upper-
and-aristocratic world which is a very masculine one, ruled by
men, for the shaping of men and men's careers; an adventurous
world, the adventure beginning when the boy is sent to his first
school, an unemotional, or at least a laconic society. The home life
of Richard Church's background was simple, a unity of parents
and children, with grandparents, aunts and uncles very near. The
upper-class household was threefold: the realm of the parents,
that of the servants, that of the children with nurse or governess.
They touched each other at points, were ruled by a common law,
but with many minor or local rules in each realm. Children of the
poorer parents were rarely apart; no one in any way took the
parental place.

This house 'over the bridge' was in Battersea; it had been
bought with a loan from the Temperance Permanent Building
Society. The mother of the two boys, Jack and Richard, was a
serious, gentle woman, superior in background and education to
her husband. He was cheerful and casual and she loved him with
an almost maternal tenderness. He was illegitimate, probably of
gentle blood on his father's side; he remembered kind ladies visiting him in childhood taking a dutiful family interest in him, and
when he grew up they used their influence to have him employed
in the lower Civil Service, as a postman. His childhood had been
unhappy; his mother 'a person of humble mien and few words'
had married, giving him a harsh step-father. From the age of nine
he had knocked about the streets, gone to work and learned some
of the harder lessons of life. He could read and write and he had a
good singing voice, and sang in the choir of St. Luke's, Chelsea.
It was at a Christmas party for the church, given by those kind
ladies, that he met his future wife, Lavinia Orton.

His background was 'three squalid rooms near the Heath', hers
a genteel home, ruled by a tyrannical father, 'a holy terror, a
perfect example of the Victorian domestic tyrant'. He was Goods
Manager at St. Pancras, thought well of himself and poorly of his

daughter's choice of husband. In fact he forbade the marriage. This quiet girl, however, was fully as resolute as her father. She had already left home, trained as a teacher and was independent; she kept in touch with home only for the sake of her mother. This mother, Richard Church's grandmother, could claim kinship with George Eliot but did not care to do so; literary genius was all very well in its place but it did not condone living in sin. 'It seems to be a rule that whenever a middle-class *bourgeois* family throws off a sport . . . there is disapproval.' Lavinia continued to meet her young man in what must have been the gravest of wooings; she coached him in grammar and arithmetic, and thanks to her loving tuition he passed the examination for the Post Office. He was given a job, they married and set up house. . . . The stern parent relented.

Mrs. Church played the piano, 'pieces' of the key-rattling sort, on her 'Broadwood-White' which must have been first cousin to the Pooters' Collard & Collard – Bilkson, and sang drawing-room songs. It was all very cosy, very genteel, protected by anxious care, but it was still close to poverty and violence, and to a robust vulgarity almost equally to be deprecated.

The Churches had a maid, a 'daily', Harriet, 'a dry, sardonic Cockney', quick of tongue, kind and loyal, who diverted herself and the boys by playing the mandolin. Sometimes she took them to her home which gave them their first impression of class consciousness. Here was something very different from their own, here was a 'teeming mass of live creatures' with all its 'noise, restlessness, inconsequent good humour and occasional outbreaks of storm', with finances depending on casual employment. At home there was the security of regular work; his mother was still teaching, and that profession had dignity, not quite so high as that of a doctor or a clergyman, but with 'a magic, nevertheless', and authority.

In retrospect Church could see in Harriet's home 'the pedal articulation of the machine of snobbery which maintains the shape and movement of human society . . . These folks in the slums of Battersea had little to look down upon and everything to look up to.'

There was a lower stratum – that of violence. Coming home one Christmas with the unexpected, almost startling gift of an aquarium, Jack and Richard were followed by a gang, and saved, unintentionally, by another. The second gang was following a man, 'a navvy a hatless figure with features flaming and eyes distorted by drink and fear'. Pursuing him came 'the real cause of his flight . . . a woman, ragged and shameful, her hair torn down, her blouse gaping, and one eye laid open and bleeding on her cheek. She was mad with fury and screaming with pain; plunging wildly to right and left, but striving by sheer power of rage to follow her man who had thus ill-treated her. The mob was at her skirts, urging her on, making an Elizabethan sport of this horror.'

The hideous drama deflected the attack on the two boys who came safely home; but Richard was sick and hysterical with fright and horror, until healed by 'the closed world of home' where 'no horrors were entertained for long'. How sheltered that world was only the mature man could recognize. Looking back he could see 'how miraculous was the achievement of my parents', with what effort, out of what sparse material they had made this security. They were not unique in this; it was an achievement heroically common in their class, especially among the women.

'The most static institution human society has ever known must surely be the lower-middle-class household, consisting of a small family, at the end of the Victorian era in England.' Below that level was a too dire poverty, often crime; above it there was the separation of children from parents by nursery and schoolroom or school life, and by 'some degree of intellectual and cultural pre-occupation' in the parents. Life in the small house was communal. This class was 'a purgation group between the vast and still increasing masses and the true middle class of professional, administrative, employing folk'.

Their delicately balanced posture produced caution, reserve, even timidity and primness, for one false step might take them over the border into the undesirable land. It was better to look away from that border altogether.

'We overlooked the existence of the policeman, police stations, prisons and crime.' In Church himself this memory left a distaste for detective novels which have become almost the favourite upper-middle-class and upper-brow form of fiction.

'I think grimly of the small margin of safety which my parent struggled to maintain between their respectable little home and the hungry ocean of violence whose thunder never left our ears; the violence of the street, the crass mob', divided by so narrow a frontier from the Battersea they knew: 'a slumbrous suburb of clerks, minor civil servants and artisans'.

It is the world of the Pooters, though with more intellectual effort and no absurdity; and still the world of the Kenwigses and Cratchits whom Dickens knew – again without the exaggeration he added of comedy or sentimentality. It did not change for at least a decade of the new century.

12

Artists at Home

The friendship begun between two young men at Oxford in the
fifties, was not only to endure till their lives' end, but to become
the nucleus of a small artistic community which had immense
vitality, and a warmth and colour so radiant that it still holds and
enfolds us, making a magic world to which we continue to be
spellbound, even while our taste and judgement resist. Rossetti
may have been the dominating figure in the Pre-Raphaelite
Brotherhood, but it is Morris and Burne-Jones who hold us in an
affection and intimacy which no rejection of their work can spoil.
They were so alive, so ardent in their ideals, so creative – of things
and of poems, of pictures, furniture, books and tapestries, and of
a particular type of beauty that they truly seem to have made this
world of their own. The Burne-Jones girl and woman did appear
in the flesh. 'The curious thing,' his grand-daughter, Angela
Thirkell, has written,' is that the type my grandfather evolved for
himself was transmitted to his descendants,' most clearly to his
daughter Margaret, mother of Angela Thirkell. 'As my mother
grew up, she was the offspring of her father's vision and the
imprint of this vision has lasted to a later generation.' The women
in the early paintings reflect his wife, Georgy; but the hair is that
of Mrs. Morris, and how far the type was created by the artist or
by that strange and lovely woman can hardly be decided.

Before either of these real women came into the picture, the
two young men, down from Oxford, were living in three rooms
at 17 Red Lion Square, with a bedroom each, and a studio in
common:

'The rooms are so comfortable, not very furnished at present,
but they will be soon,' according to Edward Burne-Jones. The
furniture was being made. The fifties saw the nadir of taste:
'Ugliness and vulgarity reigned unchecked,' J. W. Mackail has
written in his *Life of William Morris*. 'Nothing could be had that
was beautiful, or indeed that was not actively hideous'. Unless one
had inherited furniture from an earlier and comelier period or

could acquire such treasures, the only way was to have things made.

'Topsy [Morris] has had some furniture (tables and chairs) made after his own design,' Burne-Jones continued. 'They are as beautiful as medieval work, and when we have painted designs of knights and ladies upon them, they will be perfect marvels.' They were – in their way. Morris's drawings were carried out by a local carpenter. Rossetti came, saw and laughed.

'Intensely medieval furniture' he called it – 'such as Barbarossa might have sat in,' with a round, rock-like table and the famous settle, a colossal piece, with a long seat and three cupboards above, the doors of which were to be painted. It reduced the size of the studio by a third. Rossetti 'laughed but approved' and made designs for the doors, of the meeting of Dante with Beatrice in Florence, and their meeting in Paradise. Some of the chair-backs were painted by him with scenes from Morris's poems, and a large wardrobe was painted by Burne-Jones with scenes from Chaucer's 'Prioress's Tale'. 'The theory that furniture should mainly exist to provide space for pictorial decoration was carried, in these chairs, to an extreme limit,' is Mackail's dry comment.

Comfort was stuffy, *bourgeois* and contemptible, the well-padded plush arm-chair of so many parlours being the lowest of created objects. This period was the beginning of the partnership between Morris and Philip Webb, the architect who was presently to build a house for him, and make some of its furniture; proceeding to design and make this new kind of furniture for others.

Meanwhile the two friends, Morris square, bluff, naval-type, bursting with energy, prone to tempers, Burne-Jones gentle and dreamy, prone to glooms, lived contentedly together. They had the luck to find a sympathetic housekeeper, soon to be known as Red Lion Mary, a personality as vivid as their own. She was benevolent, cheerful, imperturbable:

'Their rough and ready hospitality was seconded by her with unfailing good temper; she cheerfully spread mattresses on the floor for friends who stayed there, and when the mattresses came to an end, it was said that she built up beds with boots and portmanteaux' – so Lady Burne-Jones recalled in her *Memorials* of her husband. Cleanliness was limited to the tub – 'hers was not a nature to dash itself against impossibilities, so the subject was pretty much ignored'; but in the matter of food and fires, comforts and commissions she was entirely dependable and adaptable.

'Let's have quarts of hot coffee, pyramids of toast, multitudinous quantities of milk,' Burne-Jones suggested for breakfast, when Rossetti was staying with them, and the order was, within measure, fulfilled. Mary made dresses for the models, carried out Morris's designs for embroidery, and dealt with his tempers:

'Though he was so short-tempered, I seemed so necessary to him at all times, and I felt myself his Man Friday.'

Marriage created a quartet of friends. Georgina Burne-Jones, as generous as she was gentle, was captivated by the beauty of Jane Morris, and her own crystal clear personality must have been irresistible. Both young wives fell in with their husbands' way of life; both were sufficiently artistic to help them. They both did embroidery and other needlework.

The rooms in Red Lion Square were given up. Morris had a house built for him, in 1860, at Upton, in Kent, near Plumstead and Bexley Heath, and a group of cottages known, to Morris's delight, as Hog's Hole. The Red House, he called it, for it was built of red bricks, a departure from the Victorian stucco, a return to an older medium. Webb planned it L-shaped, high-roofed, with rooms facing on the garden, the house forming two sides of a square inner court with a covered well in the centre, and a rose trellis on the other two sides.

Indoors was a fine staircase leading to a large drawing-room which Morris proposed to make 'the most beautiful room in England'. But except for Persian carpets and some blue china, nothing beautiful could be found in shop or warehouse: 'Not a curtain or a candlestick; not a jug to hold wine or a glass to drink it out of, but had to be re-invented, one might almost say, to escape the flat ugliness of the current article.' Webb made a dining-table, some glasses, and some copper candlesticks; and the firm of Morris and Company was formed and registered, consisting of Morris, Burne-Jones, Webb, Faulkner Ford Maddox Brown. One of their aims was to make furniture 'either depending for its beauty on its own design, on the application of materials hitherto overlooked, or on its conjunction with figure and pattern painting. Under this head is encluded embroidery of all kinds stamped leather and ornamental work in other such materials, besides every article necessary for domestic use.'

Mrs. Morris, her sister, and Mrs. Burne-Jones worked the embroideries; so, for a time, did Morris.

'Top has taken to worsted work,' proclaimed Rossetti.

They used coarse, dark blue Yorkshire serge as background for their brilliant colours. Their friend William De Morgan made gay, fantastic pots and tiles, with birds and beasts and fish in vivid colours, sea-greens and purples, rose and blue. Later came the famous Morris carpets and wall-papers: the daisy and the pomegranate patterns, the rose-trellis with birds.

Wall-paper was to become the most popular and practicable hanging, but Morris had none of it in his new house; only embroidered cloths or painted walls were contemplated. The drawing-room was to be 'a continuous belt of pictures' from an old romance, painted as a frieze above a set of embroidered hangings. The bedrooms were to be hung with serge. The staircase was to be painted, by Burne-Jones, with scenes, in medieval style, from The War of Troy.

This was an open guest-house for friends, especially at weekends.

'It was the most beautiful sight in the world to see Morris coming up from the cellar before dinner, beaming with joy with his hands full of bottles of wine and others tucked under his arms.' Georgie Burne-Jones was to recall the almost idyllic happiness of those years. They were not many, for the Red House was found to be inconveniently far from London – ten miles was a long journey in the sixties. Morris must live near his business which was developing rapidly. A house was taken in Queen's Square, Bloomsbury, to be both home and place of business, the Red House with its wall paintings and the great painted wardrobe was sold. Morris never went back.

Meanwhile the Burne-Joneses had taken up house in rooms in Russell Place, with thirty pounds and no debts. The studio was in working order, the rooms were almost bare: no chairs in the dining-room, only a table 'sitting on which the bride received her first visitors'. Furniture was made at The Boys' Home, Euston Road, from designs by Webb: high-backed, black chairs with rush seats, a sofa of black, panelled wood, a deal sideboard on which Edward painted pictures of 'ladies and animals': kind ladies feeding them, cruel ladies torturing them. He painted, also, a small piano in unpolished walnut. Inside the lid was a design for the *Chant d'Amour*, and on the panel under the keyboard a painting of girls playing in a garden, with the veiled figure of Death knocking at the gate.

Georgie Burne-Jones remembered herself as a very casual young housewife, with a 'light-hearted indifference to many things generally regarded as essential' which 'lent boldness to domestic arrangements'. She drew and painted, as well as doing embroideries, and found it natural to ask 'our only maid – a pretty one' to pose for her in the middle of the morning.

In 1867 they took a house which was to be their home till the end, The Grange, in North End Lane, in what is now West Kensington. It had belonged to Samuel Richardson, long ago, and here he had read *Sir Charles Grandison* to his guests. North End Lane was a real lane or little street with little shops at one end and some pleasant Queen Anne Houses. There was something of a country air about it and the large garden behind The Grange. To the third generation, Angela Mackail (later Thirkell), and her brother, Sunday with the grandparents was like a day in the country. We see it clearly through her eyes; this was one of the *Three Houses* of which she has written.

The Burne-Jones's only daughter Margaret had married the classical scholar, J. W. Mackail, and they and their children lived in another of these three houses: 27 Young Street, Kensington Square, next to The Greyhound – 'It is not every one who has the luck to be brought up next door to a public house' – which was like a country inn. The house belonged to Thackeray's daughter, Anne Thackeray Ritchie. The Old Kensington of which she wrote was still, even in the nineties, half rural and romantic with red-brick houses, flowering gardens and little lanes.

On Sunday – 'a pale golden Sunday when the sun shone on an endless, leisured day' – the small Angela's pleasure began with a visit to her mother in the four-poster bed, with curtains patterned with birds; there she had 'conversations till the dressing-bell rang and the smell of sausages began to rise from the kitchen'. Sausages were essential to Sunday breakfast: 'sacred Sunday sausages I had almost said'.

Then came the formal, uncomfortable toilet-starched crackly petticoats with starched tapes, a white piqué frock, white frilly pinafore, black shoes and stockings, a straw hat with tight elastic and wreath of flowers; thus dressed, the journey by horse-bus, six a side, fourteen upstairs, to North End Lane.

The Grange had a square hall with a green earthenware stove. Grandmother – Lady Burne-Jones as she had become by that time – had a sitting-room with Morris wall paper, the pomegranate design on a dark blue ground. There was a Morris carpet on the stairs, covered, in the careful Victorian way with drugget. In the dining-room three extra places were always laid for any friends who might come. The Mackails were regular Sunday guests, Angela's place always by her grandfather. She had the privilege of blowing the froth off his beer, and of having the delectable crisp, brown top of the mashed potatoes browned in the oven.

The Grange had seen all but the first few years of the Burne-Jones's married life. Their children had grown up here; and here Edward had come to fame and a pleasant degree of fortune. The little painted piano was in the drawing-room, and he had painted his wife and daughter and son grouped round it: Margaret and her mother the incarnation of the feminine type he had portrayed – or created.

The Morris's had, during these years, moved again into the country. They were tired of London and wanted 'some little country place . . . which would release them from that incubus of middle-class London family life, the recurring choice of a place for summer quarters, and the discomforts of a holiday in lodgings'. There were two daughters, Jenny and May. Morris, following an advertisement, found his house of dreams, Kelmscott Manor, on the Thames near Lechlade, about thirty miles from Oxford.

'A heaven on earth', he told Burne-Jones: 'an old stone Elizabethan house . . . a mass of grey walls and pearly grey roof.' The garden went down to the river, and there was a boat-house and 'everything handy'. It was a three-storied house with mullioned windows, built of the local rubble, 'buttered over, so to speak, with this plaster which has now weathered to the same colour', with stone slates, 'the most lovely covering a roof can have', all sized down in perfect proportion like a fish's scales or a bird's feathers'. There was a dove-cot, there was a barn and the garden was divided by clipped yew hedges, looking 'as if it were, if not a part of the house, yet at least the clothes of it'.

Inside, Morris found a white-panelled parlour, and above it a room hung with tapestries of about 1600, not particularly fine, pleasantly faded: 'at any rate they make the walls a very pleasant background for the living people who haunt the room', besides giving it 'an air of romance . . . which nothing else would quite do'. Altogether it was 'a house which I love, with a reasonable love, I think'. He was to be homesick for it, even in Italy. 'Even in these magnificent and wonderful towns, I long rather for the heap of grey stones with a grey roof that we call a house north-away.'

He gave its name to the last house he acquired – Kelmscott House, Hammersmith – 'a large, Georgian house of a type ugly enough without being mean, familiar in the older London suburbs' – so Mackail describes it. The drawing-room upstairs had five windows over the river, which was so near that on sunny days reflections of the water played over the ceiling. The room was hung with Morris's own tapestries, and here came the great painted settle with its cupboards. The rest of the furniture was designed in harmony, making the room 'a mass of subdued yet glowing colour'. In contrast, Morris's study was austere, with neither carpet nor curtains, and little furniture beyond a square table of unpolished oak, scrubbed white. He had a tapestry loom set up in his bedroom. The coachouse and stables were made into weaving sheds to produce the now famous Morris carpets.

The Burne-Jonese's also felt the need of a holiday house. They had visited and fallen in love with the fishing village of Rotting-dean, near Brighton; still unspoilt, full of character and reality, not a sub-suburban art-and-craftery. Here they bought two cottages, to be made into one and called North End House: 'a most ingenious and rather confusing dwelling', Angela Thirkell calls it – the third of her Three Houses. The two cottages were linked by a little covered court; one could pass from one to the other through a room, or by going up the blue stair in one, through the nursery and down the brown stair in the other. They were called the blue stair house and the brown stair house. 'It all made a kind of rabbit warren, most enchanting to a child.'

Burne-Jones wrote of it to a friend:

'The magician's hand [that of the architect, W. A. S. Benson] has been laid upon it, and another house has been added, and new rooms built and windows turned south that were east, and there is a garden now and ilexes, and bay-trees, and fig-trees, and a man's garth where coarse friends may smoke. Also a bower for Margaret with a bow-window, and a study for Jack [Mackail], and a haunted room and a wide hall and a new dining-room with hangings round it, and a still-room for Georgie to make scents and jam, and a studio for me, and a sublime bedroom for Phil [their son] . . . Altogether it is very pretty and tiny.'

There was a study for Jack because Margaret had married from this house and it was still holiday home for her and her husband, and their children when they came. Her father wrote of the wedding day, in September 1888:

'We hung up curtains of needlework on the walls of the room and covered the wall above them with branches – all the room was myrtle and roses – and her big bouquet was white roses and jasmine. She looked so bonny. I behaved pretty well – and Margaret herself was quietest of all. I was up betimes, but she was alseep till her accustomed hour, and went about her wonted ways quietly, and dressed herself when the hour came . . . The hills were full of harvest, a broad, yellow land, the church looked a thousand times older than the hills. Oh, there is nothing but gratitude in my heart, my dear – her life has been so happy till now, and surely it will be happier than ever' – but 'as for us who are left, we are without doubt many years older.'

Elsewhere he wrote about the 'man's garth' – a glorified smoking-room 'that I call The Merry Mermaid, like a pot-house parlour where men can drink and smoke and be vulgar': a better idea than Mr. Boffins's amalgamation of tap-room and genteel parlour.

'Oh, you can't imagine what a room is that blessed pot-house room. . . . Such white walls, such red curtains, such wood fires of logs resting on the handsomest dogs – and the settle is there and the arm-chair and the long table and the new birthday cupboard, and the big dresser full of the madcappest pottery; there I sit grinning because the floor is brick and the walls whitewashed and the oak black and the fire crackling. . . . The long black table is such a model of proportion that I have had a big dining-table made just like it, only ten times as big.' The room had a half glazed door with red curtains. Above the hearth was a painted bas-relief of a mermaid.

'It is all so peaceful and pretty and tiny, but do you know that it is very trying to have two houses, and the blessing of heaven does certainly hesitate over such covetousness. I always want things that are in London: books, pictures, even sorry clothes; and if I replenish this place, then when I go back to London, I suddenly want everything I have brought here.'

He found The Grange lonely without Margaret: 'The house is silent, or full of echoes. . . . That seems such a heavenly way the French have of living all together in a big house, within reach and within call, and I want it.'

There was, however, a comforting amount of coming and going between the young and the parental household. To the Mackail children, North End House was even more part of their life than The Grange; for there were spent not merely 'pale golden Sundays' – long as these might seem, but weeks of holiday, both winter and summer.

From a child's point of view the Victorian house wins over the modern by its space, its rambling corridors, many and varied rooms, its steps and stairs. It was about a house with attic stairs that George MacDonald wrote his *Princess and the Goblin* story; and this Rottingdean house would have made a perfect setting for a domestic fairy tale: up the blue stair and down the brown one into – not the other part of the house but some realm of magic; perhaps into the house as it was a hundred or two or three hundred years ago. In the first decade of the twentieth century E. Nesbit was to use this way of enchantment. In her *House of Arden*, two children, Edred and Elfrida return to their ancestral castle; in an attic they find a chest full of old costumes, are compelled, by magic, to choose those of one particular period. Running downstairs they come into the parlour as it was a hundred, two hundred, three hundred years ago, and so go back, further and further into their family history.

But to return to North End House – there was magic enough in its form and contents to satisfy any child. Angela Thirkell recalls The Merry Mermaid room – the brick floor, the white walls, the hearth ruddled, in the local fashion 'with red whitewash if one may so describe it'. The 'madcappest pottery' was German: jugs and mugs of gay colouring, brought home by friends. There was very little of that sort in England then. In summer the door stood open on the garden, in winter the room was bright with firelight and candles.

The nursery had white walls, painted at the foot of the little girl's bed with an angel. In the morning, as light returned, the angel appeared to be pulling away the curtain of darkness. In the day-nursery was a painting of a water-mill and on the opposite wall a peacock in a tree. In a recess where a naughty child was stood, to face the wall, an indulgent grandfather had painted a cat and kitten, and a flight of birds. This was a snug room in winter with its sloping attic ceiling, its little, blue-curtained bow-window; the nursery bath before the fire, at bedtime.

Downstairs, her parents' bedroom was small, with room only for the beds, chairs and washstand. 'The bower' had Morris chintzes with yellow birds and red roses, and a casement window on the garden. The dining-room had an archway to the hall, hung with blue velvet curtains, and its walls were hung with dark blue cloth embroidered with flowers. Grandmamma presided at the oak table, in a high-backed Morris chair with blue cushions. Delectable meals were served – lobsters, prawns and shrimps. Georgie might be the incarnation of her husband's etherial vision, but she liked her victuals. One of her favourite dishes was a marrow bone, served on toast, the marrow picked out with a special, long-handled spoon. She liked also a sandwich of plum cake between thin slices of bread and butter.

Her grand-daughter remembered her in her widowhood, wearing a long, black grown trimmed with lace, and with lace swathed on her head and pinned with old paste brooches. She was utterly unself-conscious in her friendliness – 'could talk to working people in their cottages with as much ease as she received a royal princess who came to look at pictures' – the comment betrays a certain class if not self-consciousness – and she used to quote and preach Ruskin and Morris to them.

In the hall were a glass barrel of rosewater, a clock painted with the sun and moon, telling the days of the month as well as the hours of the day, some della Robbia casts, and the Watts portrait of Burne-Jones.

The drawing-room was a concentration of pre-Raphaelite art. The little painted piano had been brought there, and there was a clavichord made by Dolmetsch to a design by Burne-Jones, painted deep red, with a Latin poem inscribed on it in white letters: the poem by Mackail; and a laurel wreath encircling the pun *Clavis Cordium*. The paintings for Morris's Sangraal tapestries hung here; and best of all, in a child's eyes was the large toy cupboard – 'an enchanting sight . . . like a page from Nutcracker and Mouse King or a story from Ole Luk Oie.' It was filled with grandmamma's collection of toys and tiny things: Russian families of dolls in painted wood, the smallest going into the next in size, from tiny baby up to large grandfather; miniature Sicilian oxen and carts, Chinese mother-of-pearl fish, jugs, pans and coffee-pots: a true Land of Treasured, not Lost Toys, demanding a story by Mrs. Ewing.

The window-seat could become a fort, or an omnibus, or remain a seat and observation post looking right down the village street. But the furniture was not made for comfort. That, it would seem, meant little to the pre-Raphaelites. The wooden sofa by the fire was painted with pictures of the archangels in heaven, with a black hole to indicate where Lucifer fell, fascinating to the eye, but not reposeful to the body. The only comfortable piece of furniture in the house was a large, ordinary, stuffed sofa, otherwise the sofas were simply long, low tables with a little balustrade round two or sometimes three sides, made of plain oak. A few hard squabs or cushions were the sole concession to the body's needs.

'As for pre-Raphaelite beds it can only have been the physical vigour and perfect health of their original designers that made them believe their work was fit to sleep in' – the foundation being of wooden slats.

In the garden was a summer-house, the lower part used as tool shed, the upper a room which was 'a triumph of pre-Raphaelite discomfort', cold in winter, hot in summer, with windows that stuck in their grooves; furnished with wooden chairs designed by Burne-Jones for the cartoon for Morris's tapestry of the Knights of the Round Table, and made by a local carpenter High and narrow, they were 'suited to no known human body' The conclusion was that 'if that is how Arthur's court was fur nished, it is quite enough to explain the eagerness of the Knights to leave their seats and follow the Quest of the Holy Grail'.

The spell lingers. Our bodies might shrink from these austerities, our eye, taste and judgement reject some – though not all – of the work of the Brotherhood, no longer delighting, as once in our youth, in the melancholy sweetness of the Burne-Jones' paintings, reading Morris's poems selectively and sparingly, choosing, certainly, some of his designs and colours. Yet to re-read the *Life of Morris* and the *Memorials* of Edward Burne-Jones is to be captivated again by their charm. Theirs was so true a brotherhood; they so truly created a world of their own in forms and colours long neglected or overlooked: so startlingly in contrast with contemporary crudities that they appeared new, fresh, as bright as the colours of dawn and of spring, with all the richness of a garden or an orchard in their patterns. They lived with zest, these men, even Edward in his dreaming, sometimes melancholy moods, knowing the ardour of creation, the shaping of dreams. There was much humour in them and they lived in the light.

13

Authors at Home

I

'We see great numbers of people here, but are always most content alone. My husband reads then, and I read or work, or just sit and look at him which I really find as profitable an employment as any other.'

This first letter from a happy bride was written by Jane Welsh Carlyle, in December 1828, to her mother-in-law from the house in Comely Bank, Edinburgh, where Thomas had brought her after their wedding in October. Two months later, the same bliss was there: 'We lead a most quiet and even happy life here; within doors, all is swept and garnished; and without, the country is no longer winter-like but beginning to be gay and green. Many pleasant people come to see us, and such of our visitors as are not pleasant people have at least the good effect of enhancing to us the pleasure of being alone. Alone we never weary; if I have not Jean's enviable gift of *talking*, I am at least among the best listeners in the kingdom, and my husband has always something interesting to say. Then we have books to read. . . . There is a piano too, for "soothing the savage breast!"' – Jean was her sister-in-law from whom a visit was happily expected.

It was an idyllic beginning to one of the most debated marriages in literature. Carlyle's only reproach to his wife was that she could not or would not talk: a disability from which he did not himself suffer.

'Often when he has talked for an hour without answer, he will beg for some sign of life on my part, and the only sign I can give is a little kiss.'

Whether or not silent with her tongue, she could talk entrancingly on paper and her letters make a domestic chronicle for nearly forty years, from this honeymoon period in Edinburgh to the last days in Chelsea. Most of it is of a Victorian household, most of it in London. In 1828 the Carlyles left Edinburgh for Jane's own house and farm of Craigenputtock, Dumfriesshire, which Froude declared 'the dreariest spot in all the British dominions' but its owner found 'no such frightful place as the people call it. . . . The solitude is not so irksome as one might think. If we are cut off from good society we are also delivered from bad. . . . I read and work and talk with my husband and never weary'. Emerson visited them there, and wrote of 'the wild and desolate heathery hills' and the solitude; but also of Carlyle's fortune in his wife: 'a most accomplished and agreeable woman', and that 'truth and peace and faith dwell with them and beautify them'.

He was one of the first of Carlyle's friends to be captivated by his wife; very far from being the last.

Carlyle's brother Alick lived in a cottage near them and looked after the actual farm. Jane had a good servant; she kept house, baked bread and looked after her poultry very contentedly and capably; she shared the Brontës' pride and pleasure in good house-wifery. There were plenty of books to read, and if visitors were few, letters were many, from all parts of the earth, including Germany: 'It is so strange to see "Craigenputtoch" written in Goethe's hand.' And here Carlyle wrote *Sartor Resartus*.

He needed, however, the scope and stimulus of London, and after an exploratory visit in 1831, they decided to move there for good. In 1834 they arrived at 5 Great Cheyne Row, Chelsea, which became as much background and part of their lives as Abbotsford was of Scott's. Carlyle wrote of it thirty-two years later, when Jane was dead, recalling her genius for home-making, her 'beautiful thrift' (a very Scottish union!), her talent for keeping 'the minimum of money reconciled to human comfort and human dignity'.

He said that and more, in sorrowful remembrance; he did not say it to her at the time. The peasant in him who had seen his mother working long and hard in their cottage in Ecclefechan, took it for granted that his wife should do the same. It was a woman's job. Looking back, he realized something of her effort and achievement. It was and is a pleasant house: 'a most massy, roomy, sufficient old house' as he described it, and for all the pain and sorrow it held in those two lives, it has today a lovely peace, as if their suffering had been purgation.

Jane cheerfully tackled the business of packing and clearing up at Craigenputtock, and the settling in at 5 Cheyne Row. After three or four days of 'quasi-camp life, of gypsy life' Carlyle found that 'all was swept and garnished, fairly habitable; and continued incessantly to get itself polished, civilized and beautified'. Some of Jane's creative energy went into housewifery; the greater part of it into her letters. Had there been a little more – the subtle, extra touch of genius – she would have written entrancing, witty novels; she might have approached an earlier and greater Jane, and she might through such self-expression have attained peace.

Her letters are inimitable; they create the world of people and things in which she and Carlyle lived. They were written to her family and friends; many to her cousins, Helen and Jeannie Welsh in Liverpool; many to her husband when he or she was from home; some of the earliest and most delightful to her mother-in-law for whom she had a deep affection. To her she wrote proudly:

'Our little household has been set up again at a quite moderate expense of money and trouble; wherein I cannot help thinking with a *chastened* vanity that the superior shiftiness and thriftiness of the Scotch character has strikingly manifested itself. . . . To see how they live and waste here, it is a wonder that the whole city does not "bankrape and go out o' sicht" – flinging platefuls of what they are pleased to denominate "crusts" (that is, what I consider all the best of the bread) into the ashpits. I often say, with honest self-congratulation, "In Scotland we have no such thing as 'crusts'." On the whole, though the English ladies seem to have their wits more at their finger-ends . . . I never cease to be glad that I was born on the other side of the Tweed.'

London extravagance shocked her. 'From birth upward she had lived in opulence,' her husband was to write of her, 'and now, for my sake, had become poor.' The opulence had been no more than the solid and elegant comfort of her father the doctor's house in Haddington; the poverty was cheerfully accepted; and no degree of wealth would have made her extravagant except in an occasional, diverting burst. She was horrified by the shiftlessness of her new friend and neighbour, Mrs. Leigh Hunt; hers was a Bohemian way of life which did not commend itself to the Scotswoman, who foresaw the end of the friendship:

'She torments my life out with borrowings' – anything from tea and teacups, spoons and glasses, to a brass fender – and nothing was returned in full (except, perhaps, the fender). 'Is it no a shame to manage so, with eight guineas a week to keep house on?' It annoyed her, too, when dining out 'to see as much money expended on a dessert fruit (for no use but to give people a colic) as would keep us in necessaries for two or three weeks'.

There was a danger, indeed, of her being over careful, ungracious about a generous extravagance in others. Once when her mother was staying with her, she (Mrs. Welsh) brought in cakes and confections and wax candles to adorn the table for a dinner-party. Jane scolded her for thriftlessness, removed half the dainties and two of the candles, and her mother wept. It was one of those small unkindnesses that leave a lasting remorse; and the candles were to be used much later.

She was, however, well contented with her lot in London.

'Is it not strange that I am here,' she wrote to her cousin, Miss Stodart, in Edinburgh, 'sitting in my own hired house by the side of the Thames, as if nothing had happened; with the fragments of Haddington, of Comely Bank, of Craigenputtock interweaved with cockneyalities into a very habitable whole?' There was 'an everlasting sound' in her ears, of people and of traffic, of doorbells and raps – 'gentlemen-raps, twopenny post-raps, footman-showers-of-raps, of the whole devil to pay, as if plague, pestilence, famine, sudden death and wee Eppie Daidle were broken loose to make me diversion. And where is the stillness, the eternal sameness of the last six years? Echo answers, at Craigenputtock' – and there they could stay for all she wanted of them. 'This stirring life is more to my mind, and has, besides, a beneficial effect on my bowels. . . . I am more and more persuaded that there is no complete misery in the world that does not emanate from the bowels.'

This was a pre-Victorian house and it kept its pre-Victorian simplicity through changing fashions and rising prosperity. It is larger than Haworth Parsonage and it was more comfortable, though always with a certain austerity, but it has the same atmosphere, and under Jane's care it had that essential and shining cleanliness and order which are an essential part of beauty; quietness too, though not so absolute as that of Haworth, which Carlyle would assuredly have enjoyed and broken.

Her own description of the house was of 'an excellent lodgment of most antique physiognomy . . . all wainscoted, carved and queer looking, roomy, substantial, commodious, with closets to satisfy any Bluebeard, a china closet in particular that would hold our whole worldly substance converted into china'. In the panelled drawing-room stood her little, square piano, with green silk behind its fretted panel, on which she used to play the Scottish airs her husband loved. 'This large and comfortable tenement we have, without bugs, for some two or three pounds more rent than we paid for the pepper-box at Comely Bank,' the reason for this cheapness being that Chelsea was unfashionable; and the only inconvenience of that lay in being so far from most of their friends – who for all that contrived to find their way to Cheyne Row often enough. Some were within easy reach: the Leigh Hunts (perhaps too easy) Mrs. Somerville, a fellow-Scot, most distinguished and most delightful of women scholars, mathe-matician and astronomer; and 'one who lives in prodigious *shine* with wife and family . . . a grave, handsome man', a sculptor and architect, George Rennie, a sweetheart of hers fifteen years ago. They had met with some embarrassment: 'I was within an ace of fainting, and he looked like one of his own marbles. But neither of us, I believe, entertained a particle of tenderness for the other.' This 'faithless lover' now lived 'in the wretchedest atmosphere of "gigmanity"', and his wife was a fool.

Behind the house was a garden, long neglected, but possessed of two vines said to have produced two bunches of grapes which might be eaten, and a walnut tree bearing about sixpence worth of nuts. Here Carlyle liked to sit and smoke.

It was never a luxurious house, never over-furnished. The Carlyles, like many a couple of our own day, acquired things gradually. Jane wrote to her husband, on one of his absences, reporting the purchase of a sofa. 'You shall share the possession. Indeed, so soon as you . . . behold its vastness, its simple great-ness, you will perceive that the thought of you was actively at work in my choice. It was neither dear nor cheap, but a bargain nevertheless, being second-hand . . . Oh! it is so soft, so easy! and one of us, or both may sleep in it. With my velvet gown I shall require no great outlay for *Putz* this winter, so I thought I might fairly indulge *ourselves* in a sofa at last.'

There was another sofa, some years later, in 1843:

'I have realized an ideal, have actually acquired a small sofa!!' and lest Thomas think that 'this little woman is falling away from her hitherto thrifty character and become downright extravagant', reassured him that the seller had asked £4 10s. for it but would let it go for £2 10s. without mattress or cushions; she had a spare mattress and cushions, even so thought the price more than enough, then thought of offering, in part exchange, some old green curtains which were 'filthy, and what was better, super-fluous', and he took them for 30s. 'I do honestly think more than their value, but I higgled a full hour with him, and the sofa had lain on his hands'. The remaining pound was paid with 'Kitty Kirk-patrick's sovereign, which I had laid aside, not to be appropriated to my own absolute, individual use. So there is a sofa created, in a manner, by the mere wish to have it'.

It was from the first a most hospitable house, a magnet to draw people within its shelter: from the most eminent men of letters and science to shy schoolroom girls, from fellow-authors like Mrs. Oliphant to brides from America like Ellen Twisleton. Dinners were rarely given; people came informally for tea, those long evening parties of tea and tobacco and talk. It was an easy house to visit. Among the most intimate were the Sterlings, Carlyle's friend John, and his parents, his father at one time leader-writer for *The Times*; there were the Darwins, Charles and Erasmus; the Italian exiles: Mazzini who diverted his hostess with his highly idiosyncratic English – 'the cares of bread', 'there came to pass a sweep' and other pleasing phrases; and a beautiful Countess Clementina degli Antoni 'the woman to make my husband faith-less, if such a one exist – so beautiful, so graceful so melodious, so witty, so everything that is fascinating to the heart of man'.

Evening parties meant no elaborate preparation. '"The victual-ling" of so many people is here a trifle, or rather a mere affair of the imagination' – a matter of tea and biscuits. 'The expenditure is not of one's money but of one's wits and spirits.'

There began the procession of servants unmatched in literary or domestic annals. To Jane, her maids, good bad or middling were persons to be watched over, reproved, cherished, commended. First came Sareetha, or, more fully, Sarah Heather, 'that poor little Chelsea specimen' as Carlyle called her, nicknamed The Peesweep, who one evening brought up two extra teacups and when asked why, replied in surprise: 'Are there to be no gentle-men?' This was when Carlyle was away, in Scotland, and Jane, with her mother who was staying with her, was conducting a grand house-cleaning. Sareetha rose at half-past six and lit the parlour fire; her mistress at half-past seven, made the breakfast which gave her an appetite to eat it, and after breakfast 'mother descends to the inferno where she jingles and scours, and from time to time scolds Sareetha, till all is right and tight there. I, above stairs, sweep the parlour, blacken the grate, make her bed, and then could clean myself, as the servants say', and sit down to her Italian lesson. The beautiful Countess was teaching her. Mother and daughter lived very simply, a roast continued for two days cold, they had porridge for supper, made on the parlour fire, the kitchen one being let out when Sareetha went to bed at eight.

These early letters to her husband are full of her heart; their peculiar fascination indeed is in the occurrence of a note of passion in the midst of a domestic tale. How much strain and frustration lay behind them we can only guess. But of the mutual passion of this husband and wife there is no doubt:

'Try all that you ever can to be patient and good-natured with your *povera piccola Gooda* [she used to call herself his Goody] and then she loves you and is ready to do anything on earth that you wish; to fly over the moon if you bade her,' writing or un-writing (for Carlyle's periods of dryness have almost the force of his creative) he was difficult. Jane wrote once, just before her own return from a much-needed holiday:

'Oh, my darling, we will surely be better, both of us, *there* [at home] again'.

Sareetha was followed by Helen Mitchell from Kirkcaldy, one of the major characters in this domestic drama forthright and faithful, pungent in comment, given, alas, to tippling. Jane once reported herself as being so surprisingly well that Helen asked every morning if she had no headache yet. Helen was dismayed when Mrs. Welsh missed a call from the gorgeous Count d'Orsay, a 'most beautiful man, and most beautiful carriage! The Queen's was no show i' the world compared wi' that. Everything was so grand and so preceese.' She commented freely and favourably on Cousin Jeannie Welsh until her mistress could have wished her struck dumb for twenty-four hours:

'She spent a whole hour in removing the breakfast things, that she might have repeated *flys at me* with her Job's comfort: "Isn't it a pity now, but Miss Welsh were nearer – for it's quite surprising how fond she is about you!"' It was Helen who when discussing second marriages, gave it as her opinion that 'Mr. Carlyle will be a very desultory widow. He is so easily put about, and seems to take no pleasure in any females'. She was something of a Mrs. Malaprop:

'How expensive,' she exclaimed, before a painting of the Virgin and Child in the National Gallery.

She coped well and vigorously with the house-cleaning, the master of the house well out of it and the mistress persuaded by Mr. Sterling to leave it all for a few days, and go with him to the Isle of Wight; on her return – 'Helen screamed with joy, then seized me round the neck and kissed me from ear to ear'. Helen was, in Jane's phrase, 'the strangest mixture of philosopher and perfect idiot'. During another upheaval she remarked: 'When one's doing this, one's doing nothing else anyhow.' *This* was a major domestic operation. Carlyle driven almost mad by the piano rattling of the young lady next door, 'could neither think nor live', and a joiner was summoned to make a more or less sound proof study at the top of the house. Then after 'it was got through in the end', as Jane told Mrs. Sterling, Thomas found that 'devil a bit he could write in it any more than beside the piano; it was all so strange to him'.

Jane herself could hardly bear that piano: 'That horrible, squalling girl she rattles me up with her scales, vocal and instrumental,' she told her cousin. 'The idea of any creature out of Bedlam falling to work to practise at eight o'clock in the month of November!' But it was part of the common discipline of Victorian young ladyhood to practise for an hour before breakfast, whether the month were November or May. Carlyle one day banged on the wall with a poker. Then he wrote a 'seductive letter' – a most diplomatic one, begging the pianist as a fellow-artist to have pity on him and his writing, and to refrain from practising in the morning. The girl's father called, not, as Jane feared, in wrath but in contrition. 'He almost knelt to Carlyle to implore his forgiveness for having daughters who played on the piano,' and promised that his would not do so before two o'clock in the afternoon, when the worst of Carlyle's work was over.

To return to Helen – she left, after a time to go and housekeep for a widowed brother whom Mrs. Carlyle disliked and found 'a flustering, incredible sort of man', mean and undependable, wanting his sister only as a cheap housekeepr. Her forebodings were realized, and Helen left him, to return to Cheyne Row: but not for long. She was a perfect and pitiful idiot in her weakness for drink. The Carlyles came back from the country, one day, to disaster, no reply to their knocking until, at the twentieth knock, the door was opened and 'there stood Helen – her mouth all over blood, her brow and cheeks white with chalk from the kitchen floor . . . her hair hanging in two wild streams down her neck . . . and on her face a hideous smile of self-complacency' – dead drunk on gin. 'The whole house was beastly . . . she had been drunk every day in our absence, and having drinking-parties in the house.' On partly recovering, she rushed 'out into space for more drink' and came back, at ten o'clock, to fall insensible on the kitchen floor, having drunk half a pint of rum and a quart of ale.

It was the end, final and complete. Helen was given a choice between being boarded with a friend in Camden Town, and being sent back by steamer to Kirkcaldy. She chose the former, and her mistress took her to the house.

'I spoke hardly ten words to her all the way . . . and came away desiring never to see her again in this world. She may go to the Devil her own way – I have bothered my self enough in trying to hold her back.'

A new servant had already been found, Elizabeth Sprage, who proved satisfactory. It was she who picked up Nero, the beloved little Maltese terrier, when he chose to 'fly' out of the library window, and landed on the pavement, miraculously unbroken, though very sorry for himself. After an hour in bed with his mistress he recovered: 'But I don't think either my own or my maid's nerves can stand it' – if Nero chose to fly again.

Then there was Fanny, who, in 1852, dealt not only with painting and alterations in the house, but with burglars. Carlyle had taken refuge in Scotland, Jane was sleeping out for a night or two, coming home in the morning; and one morning found the police in the house, taking down Fanny's deposition. The burglars had taken a silver spoon, a fine table-cloth, and some of Fanny's own best clothes, but no more. They had broken in by the larder window, unheard by her, but 'something woke her', she reached out for a handkerchief on her bedside table, knocked over a brass candlestick, and the noise frightened the burglars away. Jane returned to sleep there, had the window barred, and let it be known that she had a pair of loaded pistols by her bed. The thieves paid another visit, gaining no entrance; as well for them, because Jane would have fired on them.

Later in the procession of maids came Charlotte; two Charlottes, the first of whom had to be dismissed, though reluctantly: 'She was needing to be put under some *stricter* supervision than mine, still she was and is warmly attached to us.' Drink again seems to have been the trouble. Gin was cheap and was the ruin of many a servant lass.

In her place Jane engaged a Treasure, so-called, who proved to be seventy-one, and 'an arrant old humbug! Couldn't speak a word of truth; couldn't even cook, and finished off by stealing eight bottles of ale! A great comfort for poor Charlotte who came and nursed me, and cooked all my food when I was too ill to take care of myself.' She nearly took Charlotte back, but reason prevailed over sentiment; instead came 'the new, tall Charlotte' and with her another maid:

'Now I am mistress of two servants – and ready to hang myself! . . . Both these women are good servants, *as servants go*. But the *twoness* I hate . . . with *one* servant, especially with one *Charlotte*, we were *one* family in the house. . . . Now, it is as if I had taken in lodgers for downstairs; and had a flight of crows above me upstairs! I ring my bell, this one answers, but it is the other's business to do what I want. Then the solemn consultations about "Your dinner" and "our dinner", the everlasting smell of fresh turpentine without anything looking cleaner than it used to be; the ever-recurring "we" which in little Charlotte's mouth meant Master and Mistress and self; but in the mouth of the new tall Charlotte means, most decidedly, "I and Sarah". Although you [her friend Mrs. Russell] had *two women* yourself, you can't understand the abstract disagreeableness of two London servants in one's kitchen. A maid-of-all-work, even in London, will tolerate your looking after her and directing her; but a "cook" and a "housemaid" will stand no interference.'

It was worse, as she discovered, in a great house with a hierarchy of servants. Staying, on one occasion with Lady Ashburton, for whom in any case she had little love, Jane fell ill, and lay miserably unattended, because none of the maids thought it her duty to wait on an invalid. On another visit, at Christmas, she helped her hostess to dress dolls for a Christmas-tree for children on the estate. The dolls had been bought cheap and unclothed – a meanness Jane could not understand in a woman of such wealth. None of the maids would help in the miniature dressmaking; it was not their place to do so, and their mistress, high-handed though she could be, would not risk their giving notice. The only concession was made by her lady's maid who supplied a bundle of scraps and remnants.

Jane, no doubt, scolded her maids when she thought they deserved it, and could be ruthless, as with Helen, when they were hopeless; but the relationship was always warm, personal, sympathetic on both sides. The house in Cheyne Row remained singularly un-Victorian in its simplicity of furniture; un-Victorian too in its smallness of staff. There is a modern ring about these chronicles. This housewife is closer to our generation than to her own in this matter. Today she would have managed very capably with a 'daily'.

She was Everywoman in her domestic cares and her domestic delight:

'I feel like a little Queen,' she wrote to Carlyle, sitting in her pretty, newly cleaned drawing-room, 'so far as what Mazzini called "the material" is concerned, indeed, I suppose, no queen ever got half the comfort out of a nice room; queens being born to them as the sparks fly upwards', and when all the bustle was over and he came back, 'it will be such a pleasure to receive you and give you tea in your new library.'

After the major operation of repairs, painting and alterations she wrote:

'You can't imagine how utterly strange and unhomelike all these improvements have made the poor house'; but she could see how well it would look in time: the pleasant, square, panelled drawing-room given a new window and chimney, her own room painted and papered pink, docked of some three feet of space, and further crowded by a large bookcase; but she was to move up to the former spare bedroom when it, in turn, was ready. Carlyle's room was painted a faint pink, 'and there are wainscot closets for his clothes running all along the room at the fireplace, and he has got my pretty green carpet, and Mrs. Carlyle's picture over the mantelpiece, and is very smart indeed'. The kitchen and back kitchen were flagged and painted. It was a workable house.

And the grace which Emerson had found in the farmhouse at Craigenputtock was apparent here. The Peesweep's surprise on finding that no gentlemen were expected was justified. Gentlemen – and ladies, and children – came and came again. This homely and brilliant Scotswoman skimmed, without effort, the cream of intellectual society. One evening, when Carlyle was dining out and she had stayed at home, not feeling over well, preferring 'a nice, long, quiet evening of looking into the fire', Tennyson and his friend Moxon arrived. Jane was overwhelmed with pity for her husband's having 'missed the man he liked best', and for the poet's probable embarrassment, for Tennyson was ill at ease with women, having 'at one and the same moment a feeling of almost adoration for them, and an ineffable contempt'. She decided that 'the only chance of my getting any right good out of him, was to make him forget my womanness'. So she 'got out pipes and tobacco – and a brandy and water – with a deluge of tea over and above', and Tennyson, with an apology for polluting her room, sat smoking 'for three mortal hours, talking like an angel, only exactly as if he were talking with a very clever man, which – being a thing I am not used to – strained me to a terrible pitch of intellectuality'.

But was it not her own magnetism which drew the angelic discourse? Her husband, when he came home to find her in 'an atmosphere of tobacco so thick that you might cut it with a knife', was considerably astonished.

Then there were the Darwins; Charles was not captivated, for some reason, but his brother Erasmus was devoted to her, and showed it charmingly. He could offer unwanted criticism, as when he called one evening and found her alone, he found fault with the brilliance of the lamp: 'It was surely far too much light for a *single* woman.' But 'light is one of the things I do not like to economize in when I am alone, just the more alone I am the more light I need'. But he could make a sound diagnosis; finding her jaded and weary, one day, he said she looked as if she needed 'to go to Gunter's and have an ice' – and the prescription worked.

Hearing Mazzini tell her, one day in January, that she ought t
wear a shawl in the house, he forthwith brought her one of gauz
white lambswool.

She flirted, adroitly and agreeably with him and others; inspir
ing a minor but agreeable poet to a minor but agreeable poem:

> 'Jenny kissed me when we met,
> Jumping from the chair she sat in'

was Leigh Hunt's way of celebrating her affectionate greeting.

She even kissed a Bishop, or future Bishop of Edinburgh
Charles Terrot when he called, during her first days in Cheyn
Row, to take letters back to Edinburgh for her:

'I sprang into his arms, and I believe almost stifled him with th
ardour of my embrace' – which the good man not only accepte
but returned 'with more sympathy than was to have been antici
pated.' Some years later she contemplated having recourse to hir
in a more spiritual way. Writing to her husband in one of he
devil-facing moods, she told him:

'Here, on the table before me . . . lay means enough to keep hir
at bay for a while: first,
Two series of discourses on
1st 'Christian Humiliation'
2nd. 'The City of God'
By C. H. Terrot, D.D., Bishop of Edinburgh!!!
and secondly, a pair of pistols with a percussion lock.

'Are not the Fates kind in sending me two such windfalls in
one evening? When I have made myself sufficiently desperate b
study of the one, I can blow my brains out with the other. Com
what may, one has always one's "City of God" left, and – one'
pistols'.

To one unbidden guest, or intruder, her manner was less thar
cordial. This was an American of the crudest sort. He arrived ir
her and Carlyle's absence, announcing to Helen that he woul
wait. Jane found him calmly seated at Carlyle's writing table, 'a
tall, lean, red-herring-looking man'. He rose to inspect her. 'Oh
you are Mrs. Carlyle, are you?' and, 'Do you keep your healt
pretty well, Mrs. Carlyle?' Undaunted by her chilly manner he
informed her that he had come a 'great way out of my road to

congratulate Mr. Carlyle on his increasing reputation' – hoping he
would soon come in, but in case not, he was writing a letter to
him, 'here, at his own table'. Presently Darwin and Mr. Wedg-
wood arrived, and were hospitably received by the intruder, to
their intense amusement. They and their hostess ignored him, but
he was impervious to snubs, broke in upon their talk, 'poured in
upon me a broadside of positive questions' – about Carlyle's
health: 'what does he complain of, Mrs. Carlyle? – Of everything',
uncrushed by 'the most churlish answers . . . which seemed to
patter off the rhinoceros hide of him as though they had been
sugar plums'.

Jane liked men, enjoyed – whatever her self-depreciation – the
most brilliant talk, flirted, was complimented; but she was by no
means only a man's woman, She liked her fellow-women, loved
some of them, had friends of the deepest affection and loyalty:
Mrs. Russell in Scotland, and Mrs. Aitken, formerly Miss Stodart;
her cousins Jeannie and Helen, younger than she, for whom she
had an almost maternal tenderness; and Ellen Twisleton, who
wrote with delight of her visits to Cheyne Row. She and her
husband called one Sunday evening about eight, and stayed until
eleven 'after a very agreeable evening' of very good talk, Carlyle
discoursing on Cromwell and Frederick the Great.

'I really think it the highest possible enjoyment to see these
people intimately and familiarly as I do. Mrs. Carlyle gave me an
old stone casket which was Dean Swift's cash-box.'

Her first impression had been of Mrs. Carlyle as 'a very ugly
woman with a broad Scotch accent' and Carlyle no better; but
that they were 'both overflowing with a store of agreeable conversation'. Carlyle had 'a face of sad sincerity'. She found their
background surprisingly poor: 'They live in Chelsea in the most
ordinary house and style imaginable – real poverty it is – the most
wretched neighbourhood' – but the intellectual wealth was there.
And the standards of this affluent young bride as regards prosperity and comfort, were considerably higher than Mrs. Carlyle's.

'Dear little diamond-eyed Mrs. Twisleton' Mrs. Carlyle called
her. Towards the end of her life she made a most congenial friend
in another Scotswoman and author, Mrs. Oliphant, who came to
live in Ealing, in the 1860's, with an introduction to the Carlyles.
There was an immediate and mutual affection. Even Carlyle liked

this valiant woman who, widowed, with three small children to bring up, was setting forth on her long career as novelist and woman of letters. He approved her work – she had written a *Life of Edward Irving*, to which Jane contributed memories – and her sense and general character. She, for her part, felt utterly at home with both husband and wife; and when Jane came to visit her and found her nursing three children sick with the measles, she took one in her arms with a poignant maternal tenderness. They spoke the same language, these two women.

Then there were the children: the little Leigh Hunts, the Macreadies – one of them her goddaughter who found it a high treat to come and spend two days with her – and Thackeray's daughters, Anne and Minnie. The former recalled, in her own delicious way, long afterwards, the journey taken by her small sister and herself through the lanes of what was to become West Kensington, on a snowy winter's day, to Chelsea, to 'the old house' with its 'stillness, its dimness, its panelled walls, its carved banisters, and the quiet garden beyond'. Their hostess had hot chocolate waiting for them: 'I thought ye would be frozen.' They sat in the panelled drawing-room where a portrait of Cromwell hung; but she herself was the best picture, sitting there 'in her corner of the sofa, by one of the little tables covered with nick-nacks of silver and mother-of-pearl', looking like a Gainsborough in her dark velvet and point lace. She could afford rich clothes then, and she loved them. 'She was not familiar, but cordial, digni-fied, and interested in everything' – a perfect hostess for girls as well as for great men and women. These girls loved her and they found her house entrancing; in the dining-room was 'that enchant-ing screen covered with pictures, drawings, prints, fashions, por-traits without end'.

Ugly – no; it was a singular lapse in Ellen Twisleton, who per-ceived her charm, brilliance and kindness, to find her so; not pretty, certainly, least of all by suave Victorian standards, but with an animation, a spirit that lit her like a flame. Mrs. Oliphant saw her more truly: 'her clear and expressive face, the ivory paleness the hair still dark, untouched by age, upon her capacious forehead the eloquent mouth scarce owning the least curve of a smile at the bright wit and humorous brilliant touches which left all he hearers amused and delighted.'

It could never have been a plain face with so much wit, so much ardour of mind and heart, so much tenderness behind it. So much tenderness – her husband knew it and her dearest friends, and the children who came about her; her dogs knew it. First came Nero who captivated Carlyle himself by dancing round him:

'A most lively, affectionate little dog, otherwise of small merit, and little or no training,' was his master's verdict. 'We had many walks together, he and I, poor little animal, so loyal, so loving, so naïve and true, with whatever of dim intellect he had.' Tough on a small dog to have his intellect assessed by Carlyle! Nero took part in a pretty domestic drama; his mistress, left a legacy of £100 wrote a cheque to her husband for £50 and sent Nero trotting up to his study to deliver it.

Like Elizabeth Barrett's Flush, Nero was stolen:

'I wish I had not set up a dog, I did not think there was so much superfluous sensibility left in me that I should lose my night's sleep for a dog's absence out of my bed.' Nero was found, and all was well, until, after eleven years of joyous and loving life he was run over. He seemed to be recovering, but was found to be in too great pain to live; and so was put to sleep and laid in the garden. It was no small grief to his master; to his mistress, heartbreaking. Another dog came into her life, hardly less beloved; and it was after rescuing him from threatened death under carriage wheels that her heart gave way, on that last drive in her own carriage.

Was her childlessness the root of her misery, deeper than that of bodily ill health, the misery of headaches and sleeplessness, the fret of nerves, the transient but bitter jealousy of the first Lady Ashburton? There remained, after all her kindness, her devotion to her husband, an unexpended fund of tenderness which a child, especially a daughter would have drawn forth.

These domestic letters tell of splendours and miseries; the splendours being of the mind, the miseries of body and mind inextricably mixed. Modern diagnosis would no doubt find the physical cause and cure of much of her illness; her nervous tension might have been relaxed, but it is a condition only too common today. Like many sufferers today she took drugs for sleeplessness and these brought on depression; her husband took the same medicines for the same trouble with like results, and added to that was his natural melancholy. Carlyle in his black moods was enough to drive anyone to dementia.

He should, his wife once told her cousin, have married a woman with 'a perfectly sound liver, plenty of solid fat, and mirth and good humour without end – men do better with their opposites. I am too like himself in some things – especially as to the state of our livers, and so we aggravate one another's tendencies to despair.'

But they were made for each other, Carlyle with a plump and placid wife is unimaginable, Jane with any other of her wooers would have been unsatisfied, even with Edward Irving. They needed each other, these two. But singly and together they went through many a dark wood.

'If one cannot make head against the Devil in a world where one meets him at every turn, one may as well take a little arsenic at once and spare oneself the sin and sorrow of being nothing but a Spooney in God's universe. For ten days I was nearly out of my wits with want of sleep – and I say this not *figuratively*, not even *exaggeratively* but in simple truth. For four nights in one week I never *once* closed my eyes, and *henbane* even in large quantities of no more use to me than cold water. The consequence was such a state of nervous exhaustion as nobody ever saw in me before – Carlyle declares me to have been "quite mad" for half an hour – and I can well believe him. I have for a long while back been dreadfully haunted with the apprehension of going mad some day.'

That was written to Jeannie Welsh in the spring of 1846; later that year, while staying with the Welshes in Liverpool she wrote to her husband:

'What a mighty problem we make about our bits of lives; and death is surely on the way to cut us out of *all that* at last, whatever may come after all. Yes, nobody out of Bedlam, even educated in Edinburgh, can contrive to doubt of *Death*. One may go a far way in scepticism; may get to disbelieve in God and the devil, in virtue and in vice, in love, in one's own soul . . . only not in death. The most outrageous sceptic – even I, after two nights without sleep – cannot go ahead against that fact – a rather cheering one on the whole – that, let one's earthly difficulties be what they may, death will make them all smooth, sooner or later.' The thought that beyond death might lie eternal sleep no longer dismayed her

'I am weary, weary, to such a point of moral exhaustion, that any anchorage were welcome, even the stillest, coldest.'

She had, no doubt, a tongue that could cut mercilessly, and she could take her husband's moods and glooms with a caustic and wholesome cynicism.

'If you wish for a quiet life, never you marry a dyspeptic man,' she told Anne Thackeray; and told her that when Carlyle grew a beard, he spent the time hitherto given to shaving, in 'wandering about the house, and bemoaning that which was amiss with the universe'.

But the depths of fear and despair were shown again and again: 'Oh my own darling! God have pity on us! Ever since the day you left, I have been wretched day and night, with that horrible malady. God help me, for on earth there is no help.'

And about the same time she wrote to her dear and good friend Mrs. Russell 'My darling, God for ever bless you and dear Dr. Russell for your goodness to me, your patience with me, and all the good you have done me. Often when I have felt unusually free from my misery of late, it has seemed to me I could not be grateful enough to God for the mercy, unless He inspired me with a spiritual gratitude far above the mere tepid gratitude I offered Him. And just so with you; I feel as if I needed God's help to make me humanly capable of the sort of sacred thankfulness I ought to feel for such a friend as yourself.'

Friendship and love were given her abundantly; and always there was her passionate pride in her husband.

'Oh, my dear, what a magnificent book this is going to be,' she wrote to him about *Frederick the Great*. 'Sparkling as *The French Revolution*, with the geniality and composure of *Cromwell*.' It took, surely, a very proud and loving wife to find geniality and composure in *Cromwell*!

Her faith gave her fortitude, her love and loyalty were deep and strong; together these virtues kept her natural tenderness and generosity from dryness and bitterness. She trusted in God; she lacked only the peace that passes understanding. And that came to her at the last.

Carlyle was in Edinburgh, after his triumph as Rector of his old University, and she was happy and triumphant in his fame, when she drove out that day in April 1866, her little dog on her

o   *199*

lap; and when she had picked him up, hurt but not grievously, sat so still and silent that at last her coachman asked a lady to look into the carriage and see if all were well with his mistress, who sat so quiet. All was indeed well, and they brought her home in that last stillness. When she had been laid out, her housekeeper remembered a bidding given her once, when Mrs. Carlyle was very ill. When the end came, she was to find in a closet in the spare bedroom the two wax candles that, long ago, had been put away from the table her poor mother had decorated. They were lit now, as she had desired, and gleamed by her bed as at last she slept profoundly.

II

For Mrs. Carlyle, whatever her unfulfilment of heart and mind and body, her house was her kingdom. She managed her domestic affairs not only with 'beautiful thrift' but with zest, and no access of wealth or resultant increase of staff would have kept her out of her own kitchen or away from the problems and affairs of her maids. Her comments on the housekeeping of a delicately distinguished poet and woman of letters, a generation later, would have been pungent. A holy Bohemia might perhaps describe the home life and background of Alice Meynell in the nineties. 'The pencilling mamma' as George Meredith called her was, more than any woman of genius before her, truly a woman of letters. She might be said to have literature in the blood, to breathe books. Like her husband she wrote for their joint living, but even in affluence she must have continued to write, she could not have lived without some form of the written word. Her culture was innate and instinctive, part of her body, her mind, her soul.

Her daughter Viola has written affectionately of the home she remembers, in London, shared with three sisters and three brothers.

'Journalism was the pleasant and constant companion of both my parents. At the time of their marriage it committed its act of confiscation for ever of leisure from my mother's life.' It was highbrow and Catholic journalism. Wilfred Meynell edited *The Weekly Register* and Alice wrote for it: leaders, essays, reviews; corrected proofs, translated Papal encyclicals, and contributed, besides, to other periodicals her fastidious, unique essays, her devout and lovely poems.

'We [the children] fitted into the literary life and business of the household.'

The house, in Palace Court, Kensington, had been built for the Meynells, a tall house of red brick, gabled, with small-paned windows. The seven children who grew up there might, by some standards, appear neglected. Their mother was more deft with a pen than with a needle, and the trimming she sewed on her daughters' hats more often than not came off.

There were of course maids: cook, housemaids, nurse. As a housekeeper she was vague, and her interviews with the cook were inconclusive. Meals, even dinner-parties occurred, but sometimes the food was just enough 'to serve to put away from you the desire of eating and drinking'. The Meynells were the most welcoming of hosts, but their hospitality was of the mind rather than of the table. One guest, promised a treat in the library, looked hopefully for a drink, but had read to him some of the poems of Francis Thompson. This poet himself, whom they rescued, recognized and cherished used to carry a piece of bread from the dinner-table to fill the gaps left by the meal and allay subsequent pangs; and he was neither *gourmand* nor *gourmet*. When it came to supervision of the nursery, however, this pencilling mamma was scrupulous in care and tenderness. She made sure that no nurse should neglect, bully or frighten the children.

In the library the long table 'turned white with papers; the little litter of authorship, the great litter of journalism'. Papers were stuffed into book boxes on the shelves, into lockers under the window-seats; some of them, anyhow. Wilfred was a preserver, Alice a destroyer.

Upstairs, in the big drawing-room hung with old Japanese embroideries in gold, she was the most gracious of hostesses. Sunday afternoon was in the fullest sense an At Home Day. Guests began to arrive about half-past three, to depart about midnight, not the same guests all the time, but there was a coming and going, never a complete segregation of the afternoon from the evening party. It was, this daughter remembered, *fun*, for with all her scholarship, her wisdom, her holiness of mind and heart, Alice Meynell was also fun in herself, full of wit and humour, of zest and brilliance. The men of letters of the nineties came about her: Oscar Wilde, Lionel Johnson, Aubrey Beardsley, Richard le Gallienne, and most of all, Francis Thompson the beloved, honoured poet and friend of all their hearts.

The children wove their way in and out of the library and drawing-room, in and out of this literary and adult company, in and out of the intimacy of their parents. They had their own private world as well. They used to write letters to their mother and post them in a book box. Her love for them was deep and tender, but how far she knew one from the other at any moment of speaking might be questioned. 'Child' was her common form of address. But they were not ignored or neglected, and they knew themselves loved, protected, essential to the life of the house.

'Our parents had a glamour for us that is perhaps lost by parents who occupy themselves more with their children's affairs.'

Something of that glamour may have been felt by children in great households whose parents visited them, from time to time, in the nursery or schoolroom, or summoned them on a visit to the splendid adult world.

In the same decade of the nineties, an author now unjustly neglected, whose talent also lay in the essay, in rich, evocative prose, was living very comfortably on the borders of Bohemia: that pleasant and civilized borderland where authors and artists could, at that time and for a few years of the new century, live with ease and dignity. Arthur Machen had come there from the Bohemia of bitter poverty; and beyond that, in his boyhood, from a country of enchantment.

'I shall always esteem it as the greatest piece of fortune that has fallen to me, that I was born in that noble, fallen Caerleon-on-Usk in the heart of Gwent . . . convinced that anything which I may have accomplished in literature is due to the fact that when my eyes were first opened in earliest childhood they had before them the vision of an enchanted land.'

So he recalled the *Far Off Things* of his boyhood in his father's rectory in Wales. The houses looked across woods and valleys to the hills, over the land of a people more ancient than the Celts who came there long ago, a land of saints and others, of legends holy or dreadful, of old cults and worship. Hardly a house could be seen, only hints and tokens of human dwelling and occupation:

the gleam of a whitewashed house, the sight of a gable, the smoke rising from a cottage deep in an orchard. A glimmer of light showed where a farmer was carrying a lantern on his last round of the fields, the barking of a dog came faintly, and the cry of an owl. It was a land by no means barren or deserted, but spacious and very peaceful, old with memories far beyond history.

Within the rectory was that boon of a literary childhood, 'a hugger-mugger of books . . . the most revered stocks mingled with the most frivolous'; Fathers of the Church in Tractarian translations with yellow-backed novels from railway bookstalls, the *Dialogues of Erasmus* with the *Adventures of Mr. Verdant Green*, and such new classics as the works of the Brontës and of George Borrow. This was in the sixties. Arthur Machen learned the art, essentially part of the author's and bookman's mind and habit, of browsing, of looking for one book and finding another. Going to find a copy of *Wuthering Heights* he came upon a Hebrew Grammar and was briefly spellbound, then passed to *The Bible in Spain* and to a book on Brasses; finally subsiding with a bound volume of *Chambers's Journal* or of *The Cornhill* or of a long-forgotten weekly, *The Welcome Guest*. It was, incidentally, one of the glories of the Victorian house that it had room for those bound volumes of magazines. The Edwardian house kept it, in some degree, in the big cupboard or the boxroom, or the bookcase in the morning-room which had a shelf of bound *Chambers's* and *Strand Magazines* and *Leisure Hours*, as well as the novels of Scott, Dickens and Thackeray, various Poetical Works, and a volume or two of unread theology such as *MacKnight on the Epistles*.

Reading these old magazines was a joy, a relaxation from 'reading in the solid block' and often a discovery of odd bypaths of learning. Some classics were absent: *The Arabian Nights* which he bought himself, for a shilling; and De Quincey's *Confessions of An Opium-Eater* which he also bought, at Pontypool station, while waiting for his father to come in the pony-trap, and began reading at once. The magic of that prose was ever afterwards part of the magic of the remembered scene, the drive through green lanes with the mountains in the background to the dear, familiar house and orchard. Another classic, beloved in youth and age, was discovered in a neighbour's drawing-room. The boy taken on an afternoon call by his mother, found a copy of *Don Quixote* in the bookcase, and became so lost in delight that his kind hostess allowed him to borrow and finish it: 'for which benevolence I am ever bound to pray for her.'

There was little wealth of money in this boyhood but there was amplitude with simplicity in the country life. He recalled local dishes: cawl, which was 'a broth made of fat bacon and vegetables, and decorated, oddly enough, with marigold blossoms' which some of the older folk ate for breakfast. One old man despised tea as a drink fit only for women, preferring to drink cider. Most of the farmers breakfasted on bacon and potatoes, cold potatoes fried, then pressed into a dish and browned before the fire, following this with home-made cheese. Most meals began or ended with cheese, of the Caerphilly type, and with it they drank cider: 'And the cider of that land was good . . . greenish yellow with a glint of gold in it . . . as it were a remembrance of the August and September suns . . . of full body and flavour and strength.' Few were so poor as to lack a barrel or two. His mother used to make fermety or frumenty, of new wheat, eggs, milk and sugar, currants, raisins and spices: 'a most ancient and honourable Christian pottage' though perhaps more curious than delectable.

Of country poverty he saw nothing until many years later he lived in an English village where the labourers' houses were poor and squalid, no one grew vegetables or kept bees or fowls and the poor had a rancorous envy of the rich. In this Welsh parish and countryside most of the people held land. It might be a great farm or a mere patch but it was cultivated. A man might work for a farmer by day and attend to his own garden in the evening. The women kept poultry, pigs and bees. There was abundant natural food, and a market for any surplus in Pontypool which was on the borders of the mining country. New bread was eaten thickly spread with butter and cheese or with honey; an apple tart was baked with butter and sugar merging delectably with the fruit.

The memory of this amplitude was to become poignant. This boy might have followed his father's and grandfather's way through college to Holy Orders and a country rectory; but London and literature tempted him: he would write a great book, and win fame and fortune. The London to which he came in the eighties was rich and elegant. Men, from the rank of clerk upwards wore morning or frock coats and shiny top hats, women walked gracefully or drove splendidly in carriages more elegant than any motor-car of later days. There was a concentration of wealth and luxury in the shops of Regent Street, Bond Street, and Piccadilly. The parks were a background for the leisurely strolling, the riders, the carriages.

The boy saw, admired and did not envy although he lived far outside the orbit of wealth or even of comfort. The dream of living and writing in an attic on bread and cheese was only too fully realized; it was not an attic only because there was no sloping ceiling, but it was very small and bare, and most of his belongings were kept in a wooden chest on the landing, his books on the rungs of the fire-escape ladder. He lived mainly on bread and green tea, with an occasional dinner, in an excellent tavern, of a grilled chop and potatoes, bread and beer, for one and twopence. He wandered about London, discovering many odd nooks and corners, read voraciously, wrote hopefully, desperately, and somehow stumbled into literature.

Towards the end of the eighties his parents died, he inherited a little money, he married, and he earned something by his writing, and so passed out of this region of poverty into the most agreeable borderland of Bohemia. With an income of four or five hundred a year, two people could live very comfortably. Food was cheap, and a bottle of very reasonable wine cost little. The pleasure of an occasional dinner in Soho was not spoiled by a heavy bill. Income Tax was slight. People could travel, and spend a month in France every year, very pleasantly.

That little golden age of the vast middle-classes, and in particular, of the authors and artists, of all who loved good food, wine and comfort without luxury or ostentation, lasted through the nineties into the new century; for fourteen years more until the midnight of an August day.

14

Victorian Abbotsford

Scott's Abbotsford was built at the full tide of his fame and fortune, in the high summer of the Romantic Movement. It immured his idea of the Middle Ages, made visible and tangible his conception of the Gothic, and only he could have made it Victorian Abbotsford. Victorian Abbotsford grew during the Second Spring of Catholicism (as Newman called it) in this country. It is hardly surprising if one seems now to walk into more than a kind, historic house, if one breathes the past, neither mustily nor mournfully but as a vital atmosphere, if one is aware of a background of mingled piety and geniality, of old loyalties and new ardours.

The house was mournful indeed after Scott's death, that September day in 1832, in the bay-window of the room that looked to the river, with the 'sound above all others most delicious to his ears, the ripple of Tweed over its pebbles', audible until the last quietness. Then, for a while, the shadows of mortality lay about his family. Anne, his younger daughter, lived for only nine months after her father, exhausted by the long labour of nursing. Within a few years her sister Sophia, Lockhart's wife, followed her, and then their brother Charles. Only Walter, the elder son and second baronet lived into his own forties and those of the century, and died childless. The estate passed to a third Walter, the son of Lockhart and Sophia.

That happy marriage had produced three children: the adored Johnny, Hugh Littlejohn as Scott called him, for whom were written the *Tales of a Grandfather*; Walter; and Charlotte. Johnny was pitifully delicate and he died in his tenth year. Walter had health and great good looks and a lively mind; he seemed a worthy son of his distinguished father, not unworthy of his grandfather, but in young manhood he went astray, became alienated from his father, went into the far country of the prodigal. Lockhart, most loving of fathers to his family when young (his friend Christie said he had never seen such tenderness in a man) was not indulgent to a foolish young man. Of Walter's sins and frailties we have no precise knowledge, only hints and allusions in the family letters. His father could not easily forgive the sins of the flesh; his own had been those of the mind – pride, arrogance, a cruel wit. In Walter, pride deteriorated into vanity, a caricature which his father could not bear. The estrangement ended only in the boy's last fevered illness. He died at peace with his father, but Lockhart did not recover from the blow.

In his daughter Charlotte he found from her childhood a complete comfort and joy. She inherited a large share of the qualities of both parents: much of her father's intellect and habit of intellectual discipline, all of her mother's gentleness. An old great-aunt noted this in her when she was still a child. She was mature, without being dull or priggish. After Sophia's death Lockhart began writing to his little daughter in the schoolroom, when they were separated for any time, almost as to a woman of cultivated mind and knowledge of the world. He gossiped with her about books and people; she was his companion.

Charlotte was educated at home by a governess, Miss Watkins, to whom she was devoted, and who must have been a woman of solid qualifications, for we find Charlotte, aged eleven, writing to her father with a request for an Italian and a German dictionary, being already well taught in French. Victorian schoolroom education at its best could form, enrich and discipline a girl's mind, and Charlotte was the fine flower of this cultivation. Her maturity of mind, as well as her charm of looks and manner, captivated the brilliant young lawyer, James Hope Scott, son of General the Honourable Sir Alexander Hope of Rankeillour and Luffness, and grandson of the Earl of Hopetoun; *jeune homme très sérieux* and highly successful in his profession at the Bar; not so very young, perhaps, being thirty-five to Charlotte's nineteen when they became engaged in 1847. He wrote to his sister, wife of the Reverend Lord Henry Kerr, a letter of decorous rapture about his future wife:

'She is not yet twenty, but has lived much alone; much, also, with people older than herself, and people of high mental cultivation. She has also had the discipline of depending on those habits of her father which are inseparable from a literary, and in some degree, a secluded life. In short, she has had much to form her, and with great simplicity of character and unbounded cheerfulness, she combines far more thought than is usual at her age. Having no mother, and very few connections, she is the more likely to become entirely one of us; which I value not only on my own account but for the sake of my mother, to whom I am sure she will be a very daughter.'

If not among the world's great love letters or expressions of passion, this is a choice piece of Victoriana, and very expressive of the writer, himself mature, serious and high-principled, relieved to find that his heart had not led him astray, that he had fallen in love with no unformed girl whose whole charm lay in her face and figure. Such charm was by no means lacking. Charlotte was graceful, with a very sweet face, large, brilliant brown eyes, and a beautifully shaped head. Her manner was 'a mixture of shyness and diffidence with self-reliance and decisiveness, quite peculiar to herself'.

They had met at the house of Lockhart's old friend, the eccentric and diverting Lady Davy, who chaperoned them on a visit to Lockhart's sister and brother-in-law in their Rectory at Dittisham, near Dartmouth. They were married by that brother-in-law, the Reverend Lord Henry Kerr, in 1848. James Hope was wealthy; he rented Abbotsford from young Walter Lockhart who was then its owner; on Walter's death in 1853 Charlotte inherited house and estate, and she and her husband assumed the name of Scott. Hope-Scott made Victorian Abbotsford.

He had something of the passion for building which had possessed Scott himself and which marked many of the rich gentry of his own day. Abbotsford was already a place of pilgrimage, but it must also be a home with some privacy for its new family. Hope-Scott contrived a new entrance for the tourists, a sunk path between courtyard and garden, leading to the basement floor of the house; from thence, visitors went up to Scott's own rooms, the library and study, drawing-room with its Chinese paper still brilliant, hall and armoury. A new wing was built which is still the private and domestic part of the house; to the left of the new front door are the study and chapel, to the right a corridor leads to a large sitting-room opening on the court, and a bookroom. Beyond that lies the breakfast-room of Scott's own house, leading into the dining-room and so to the historic quarter. Upstairs were the family bedrooms, Charlotte's dressing-room above the front door, with one window looking on the drive, another charmingly and unusually set above the fireplace.

The chapel was the heart of the house, for on Whitsunday 1851, James Hope-Scott was received into the Roman Catholic Church, along with his friend Henry Manning, the former archdeacon and future cardinal. Charlotte followed her husband a few months later. They were both by nature devout; Hope-Scott had been a High Churchman of the Tractarian period and school, a friend of Newman as well as of his antagonist Manning, and of Gladstone whose friendship survived the shock of this conversion. He was one of the founders of Glenalmond, the new public school in Perthshire, intended chiefly for the sons of the Scots Episcopalian clergy and gentry, and developed on Wykehamist lines. This serious energy was transferred to the service of his new Church. Husband and wife took kindly to the sober and profound Catholicism of those who had held to the old religion through penal times, with nothing of the Italian flamboyance about it, no cheerful Latin tincture of paganism. Within a year they were followed by the Henry Kerrs, whose family was to give a daughter to the Society of the Sacred Heart. Lord Henry's sister-in-law, the Marchioness of Lothian, was also a convert and a zealot; two of her daughters entered the Society. Abbotsford became the centre of a little Catholic world on the Borders. The Henry Kerrs rented Huntley Burn, near Abbotsford, from the Hope-Scotts.

The new laird could give his time and energy to this new country and Catholic way of life, having almost retired from the profession in which he had been so successful but to which he had never entirely given his heart. He told Gladstone that it was his kitchen-garden while his work for the Church was his flower-garden; this he now zealously cultivated.

There is a glimpse of the great, secluded Catholic households of the nineteenth century in Archbishop Mathew's *Life* of the young Lord Acton:

'In the eighteenth century their leaders had been familiar with the idea of splendour which was now quite lost to them. In its place they kept up a domestic and staid magnificence. The ladies of the family were, for the most part, at home; they worked at their embroidery by the fireside; they were esteemed and much respected. There went with this quiet life and its tamed and specialized concerns an interest in the religious state. The daughters of the old Catholic families entered in considerable numbers into those grey stone steep-roofed convents that had been built since the Emancipation.'

Charlotte had her embroideries by the fireside. She did quantities of needlework, some for the Church, some for the poor. In addition, she led a disciplined, intellectual life, which had begun in the schoolroom and been developed and fostered by her companionship with her father. She had, of course, her social and domestic life as well; the former not, perhaps, varied or lively, but she did not neglect the obligations of the lady of Abbotsford.

Her husband's biographer, Robert Ornsby, said that she had 'an extraordinary sense of order and method'. It was inborn in her and had been fostered. In all her habits she was punctilious, 'punctual to a minute and never seemed to lose a moment'. Her daily life was ordered by a rule drawn up for her first by Bishop Grant of Southwark, then by Manning, and to this she adhered in spite of delicate health and frequent child-bearing. She was as scrupulous as a nun. In the morning she saw to her household, dealt with her correspondence, acted amanuensis to her husband.

'If she lay on her sofa in the afternoon to read Dante or Tasso, every note would have been answered, every account set down.' And this was her form of relaxation; not novel-reading, in a decade which produced many masterpieces of fiction as well as some entertaining frivolities.

There was never 'a sudden choice of recreation'. A time was set for social calls, for driving out, and those drives had their own ordered stateliness. Charlotte, although she had gone about a good deal in London, with her father, did not much enjoy society; she performed her duties gracefully, but she preferred to be at home with her husband and their small daughter, Mary Monica, Mamo as she was always called, from childhood days. Other babies came but did not survive.

Lockhart came to Abbotsford to die, older than his sixty year through work and grief. He lay in the little breakfast-room nex the dining-room, with its window upon Tweed. Charlotte was hi devoted nurse and companion until the end. The shadows mus have deepened about the house, that November of 1854. Wit much gentleness and loving kindness there can have been little cheerfulness. And in her habits Charlotte was almost austere, with something of conventual discipline. She kept a seemly degree of state, but one without extravagance or any hint of frivolity. A jewel, given her by her husband, and said to have belonged to the Empress Josephine, was sold and the price given, partly to the new church in Galashiels, for the altar, partly to her favourite charity, the orphanage kept by the Sisters at Norwood. Her husband encouraged this devout generosity. He himself built the church in Galashiels and those in Kelso and Selkirk. A visitor to Abbotsford in the 1850's described it as 'the most perfect type of a really Christian household. A religious atmosphere pervades the whole house'; and with it all 'so much geniality, everyone made to feel completely at home'.

In the winter of 1852–3 the house welcomed its most illustrious guest in Newman, then at the nadir, or nearly so, of his career since his conversion seven years before. It was the year of the Achilli trial in which that apostate priest sued Newman for libel. Newman had uttered the truth, but he was a Papist, a convert at that, and therefore suspect; likely, in popular opinion, to be a liar. Judgement had been given against him. Even in his own Church he was being thwarted and frustrated. Hope-Scott, who had the same Anglican background of scholarship and disciplined piety in Tractarian Oxford, was a loyal friend and disciple. He invited Newman to come on a long visit:

'We have a chapel in the house but no chaplain. You may say Mass at your own hours, observe your own ways in everything, and feel, I hope, perfectly at home.'

Newman, in expressing the pleasure it would give him to spend some time at Abbotsford, added: 'I have ever had the extremest sympathy for Sir Walter Scott. It would delight me to see his place. When he was dying, I was saying prayers (whatever they were worth) for him continually.'

He arrived in December, and wrote to one of his Oratorians in Birmingham, Joseph Gordon, who also loved Scott and had begged for details about his home:

'The house itself is dark and the rooms low,' the corridor on the first floor outside his room being so narrow that I could shake hands with the nursery-maids in the room opposite without leaving my room'. This was in the old part of the house. The weather was foul, with rain and high winds, and his fire would not light. When he tried using a newspaper as blower he nearly set himself on fire. And for all the unstinted and reverent kindness of his hosts, their devotion and that of their other guests, he did not feel wholly at ease:

'Quite saints, I do not know which of them is in chapel most' – but he did not want such obvious though sincere sanctity all the time on the part of everyone; he longed for a breath of worldliness, even a gleam of levity. The formality amused him, but he must not show his amusement. Like Sir Thomas More he could find ease of spirit in a jest, but here he felt uncertain whether a jest would be commendable.

'Never was a party which got on so well together. Yet even here there is considerable cause for anxiety, and I am not at my ease. The very absoluteness with which I feel at home is certainly dangerous, and I have to be ever on my guard lest I go too far. I am in danger of arguing too much, and laughing too much . . . The thought of giving scandal comes before me and annoys me.'

It would be interesting if this passage (from Meriel Trevor's *Pillar of the Cloud*) were quoted during the cause for Newman's Beatification. The Church rightly demands joyfulness of her saints, and with this Newman has rarely been credited. This letter might be held to prove its presence in him by describing his frustration in an atmosphere of solemnity.

That is perhaps too stern a word; it was a gentle reverence, a subdued devotion which pervaded the house. Hope-Scott was the builder of Victorian Abbotsford; it grew by his planning his energy, his wealth; but Charlotte made the atmosphere. The Second Spring of Catholicism in both Scotland and England flourished under the care of feminine converts, as well as of priests and religious. Archbishop Mathew, writing again of the period, in his *Catholicism in England*, pictures the 'stream of converts' headed by 'the dons and learned clergy of the Oakeley-Faber period', and continued through the serious laity like Hope-Scott and 'the aristocratic, rather *mondain* incumbents' of Anglican parishes to the final female confluence:

'Behind them, almost snuffing out the intellectual aspects of the

movement in their crinolines, stretched the long line of the convert peeresses', including 'the saintly, impetuous Lady Lothian',
most of them unaccompanied by their husbands. These ladies
brought an immense charity, a fervent piety, a devout culture.
Among them was Lady Georgiana Fullerton, daughter of Lord
Granville, grand-daughter of a Duke of Devonshire. Her novels
give glimpses of this high Catholic world, but her talent, though
genuine, was limited. The great lack in this new Catholic society
was of a really popular, vivid and influential novelist such as was
given to the Anglican Church in Charlotte Yonge. In her novels
the Anglican background of vicarage and country house, of
middle- to upper-class life is held as in a crystal. Archbishop
Mathew has appreciated it:

'. . . That protected Christian life, with its decorous, chaste
sentiment, faintly romantic which had grown up in the enclosed
gardens of the vicarages of England. The shadow of Mr. Keble's
principles fell on those lawns. Thus, in the rectory of Dittisham,
looking down through the plum-blossom to the Dart by the
horse-ferry above the Anchor Stone, Hope-Scott's sister Dorothea
lived with her husband, Lord Henry Kerr. There the rector and
his wife ministered with a practical charity, their days as easy as a
Devon summer.'

They seem to belong to a Charlotte Yonge novel. Their Devon
life she could delightfully have presented. With their conversion
they walk out of her range. To her, the Roman Catholic was
indeed a sister-Church to be respected, regarded with admiration
and sympathy, so long as it stayed abroad or in history. That any
instructed Anglican could desire to pass from his own, the true
Catholic Church in England, to this other, she could not comprehend. Of the agony and the rapture of the convert she knew
nothing. Among the tantalizing dreams of literature is the vision
of what Charlotte Hope-Scott might have written for her Church
had she inherited even a touch of the creative genius of her
grandfather.

Her reign as *châtelaine* of Abbotsford was brief. She died in
1858, closely followed by two tiny children, a girl and a boy,
leaving only the six-year old Mamo to continue Scott's name and
line. A little more than two years later, early in 1861 her husband
married again, this time into the old Catholic nobility. His wife

was the Lady Victoria Howard, sister of the Duke of Norfolk. Of this marriage were born five children. One son died in infancy, a second, the youngest child, lived into our own day. (He was Lord Rankeillour.) There were three daughters; the middle one, Josephine, became Mrs. Wilfred Ward, and through her memories, cherished and recorded by her daughter Maisie Ward, we continue to see Victorian Abbotsford, in the sixties and seventies. These little girls brought new life, gaiety, even hilarity to the house. They were – it goes without saying – brought up in strict devotion, and one of them was to become a nun, but this put no curb on their high spirits:

'*Des diablotins,*' one governess called them, adding:

'There is, decidedly, in all English girls, a strain of madness.' Their favourite lunacy was to put out the light, and in a given space of time do the oddest thing possible.

'The first Miss Hope started her influence over me,' Josephine remembered, 'by sitting on my head when I was lying in bed, and on another occasion she is said to have thrown me into a bath.'

Josephine used to say that she *saw* her life in houses: at Abbotsford first, later on at Arundel where, after the death of both parents, the girls were brought up by their grandmother, the Dowager Duchess of Norfolk.

'She [Josephine] has told,' Maisie Ward writes, 'how at Abbotsford she passed between the suits of armour, shivering, on her lonely way to bed. But I am certain the shiver was of excitement as well as fear. Child as she was, the romance that Sir Walter had built up was already with her, feeding her rich and delicate imagination.'

It was she who recalled Newman's second visit in 1872, and long drives with him and her father, the latter making one pun after another, while Newman looked grave and pained; he could not bear puns. She was too small, at the time of Queen Victoria's visit in 1867, to remember any details; her mother, Lady Victoria, was from home, and the Queen, coming over from Floors Castle with the Duke and Duchess of Roxburghe, was received by Hope-Scott and Mamo. The Queen made an interested tour of Scott's rooms, and in the dining-room was offered a collation of cake, fruit and wine; being of simple tastes, she preferred a cup of tea and a slice of Selkirk bannock.

Three years later, Cousin Anne Scott came to Abbotsford and wrote to her brother Walter:

'Nothing could be kinder than they [Hope-Scott and Mamo] were, and the place looked lovely, all in perfect taste and order. The improvements are really great improvements.'

Unhappily for a delightful source of memories, this Victorian childhood at Abbotsford ended in 1873. Lady Victoria died in 1870, at the birth of her second son, Hope-Scott in 1873. In those last years he was often ill, and much shadowed by grief. He used to read aloud to his daughters, melancholy poems like Mrs. Hemans's 'Graves of the Household'. The atmosphere was like that of many a Victorian home, making something of a cult of death and sadness.

The three younger girls at least escaped it. Josephine could not recall any bitter grief at the deaths of her parents. They had both been somewhat remote, especially the delicate mother, and Josephine was only eight when her father died.

'She was absorbed in a sort of melancholy pride at being that very interesting person, "an orphan". She examined her heavy crape with infinite satisfaction.' Children's books of the period made much of orphans; this might breed in some natures a hint of morbidity, in others, like Josephine's, more robust, it produced an objective pride and interest in bereavement.

She and her sisters spent the rest of their girlhood in England. The tide again receded from Abbotsford. Mamo married, in 1874, the Honourable Joseph Constable-Maxwell, son of Lord Herries, again an alliance with an old Catholic family. They took the surname of Maxwell-Scott, still borne by their grandchildren. Circumstances kept them away, much of the time, from Abbotsford, but the tradition, begun by Charlotte, of devout culture was not broken. Mamo had much of her mother in her and there was a resurgence of the literary habit. She wrote an account of *The Making of Abbotsford*, and some brief histories and biographies: *The Tragedy of Fotheringay*, *Joan of Arc*, and others, scrupulously written in a manner which would have pleased Lockhart, and Scott too. They might, however, have found more entertainment in the books of the girl, not of their blood, who recalled a childhood at Abbotsford. Josephine Ward wrote several Catholic novels, historical and contemporary, with a religious *motif* but without religiosity. She could create background, a little world, and prove the reality of religious beliefs, scruples or difficulties in human life. She had the knack of story-telling, and it would seem as if The Wizard in passing had swept a fold of his cloak over her, or lightly touched her with his staff.

15

Royal Household

The pattern of the home life of the Queen and its visible background were formed not so much by Victoria as by Albert. In the early days of their marriage he might complain that he was 'only the husband and not the master in the house', and find small comfort in the rejoinder of Uncle Leopold of Belgium that he, in a similar marriage, had been 'much more the master of the house than is generally the case in private life'. This inferiority lasted briefly, for Prince Albert had the same power over Queen Victoria that Prince Leopold had held over the Princess Charlotte; both bridegrooms were adored by their strong-willed young brides.

'The Queen' announced an imperious voice outside the locked door of the Prince's study, but to that, and a repeated announcement there was no reply; only when a meek and tearful voice called: 'Your wife, Albert' was the door opened and the applicant embraced and welcomed. He was now, and continued to be to the end of his life and beyond it, master of the house. His rule was effective and practical, his remarkable intelligence was shown in details of domestic economy as it was later to be in affairs of state. Only in one aspect of life did he suffer frustration: in the purely intellectual, the academic, the scholarly matters for which he longed.

He began by having the Baroness Lehzen deposed from her autocracy, and sent home, with the utmost friendliness and amiability, to Germany. Then, with his chief counsellor the Baron Stockmar he investigated the affairs of Buckingham Palace and Windsor Castle. These were, to borrow Sean O'Casey's immortal phrase, 'in a state of chassis', lit by flashes of Gilbertian comic light. Four great officers of state conflicted or overlapped in their domestic duties: the laying of fires was in the department of the Lord Steward, the lighting of them in that of the Lord Chamberlain; on the other hand the Lord Steward or his minions cleaned and lit the lamps provided by the Lord Chamberlain. The Master of Woods and Forests was responsible for cleaning the outside of the windows, the Lord Chamberlain the inside. Whether or not the two cleanings coincided was nobody's business. Housemaids were in the Lord Chamberlain's department, cooks in the Lord Steward's, footmen under the Master of Horse. The temptation to imagine a Gilbert and Sullivan chorus and dance is irresistible, with lyrical and tuneful backchat between the respective Lords. There were forty housemaids at Windsor, forty in Buckingham Palace, each having £45 a year in wages for what amounted to half a year's work, as the Court moved from Palace to Castle. At Windsor, whether or not the Court were in residence, some fifteen to twenty joints were roasted every day. Then there were the candles. These were replaced every day in multitudes of candlesticks and candlelabra, whether they had burned down or been lit for a few minutes or not lit at all; yet by a perverse economy guests were allowed only two candles in their bedrooms.

The Prince changed all that. He reduced both staff and wages, he stopped payment for obsolete duties, he looked into everything including the sanitation which was poisonous, and he united all the exalted household offices in one, that of the Master of the Household.

From the money thus saved to the Queen's private purse, they were able, in 1845, to buy Osborne estate and house, on the Isle of Wight, and to build a new mansion of adequate size planned by the Prince himself and the architect of many West-end London houses, Mr. Thomas Cubitt. The Prince showed himself a creator as well as a reformer, full of zeal as well as of thoroughness. He had ideas and he saw them take shape. Windsor and Buckingham Palace, however reformed and refurnished, must always be Royal Courts. Windsor, certainly offered a little more privacy and relaxation, with much of the sweetness of country life which the Queen was coming more and more to enjoy. Nothing, however, could make them homely, and these two united German minds longed for a touch of *Gemütlichkeit*. They found it at Osborne. It was their own place, not an inheritance. Stately it must be, as a Royal residence, but a certain homeliness, even cosiness was not incompatible with grandeur and they had things of their own choosing: many things for the Victorian love of quantity was at its most intense in the Queen herself.

The rooms were full, and so were the corridors, and the alcoves painted in Garter blue; full of tables laden with *bibelots* of all kinds, and as the new art of photography was cultivated, of photographs of innumerable relations. There were busts in bronze and in marble, models of the hands and the feet of the royal children, and frescoes. The Prince loved frescoes which could be allegorical, instructive and edifying. There was a huge one of Neptune, surrounded by minor deities, giving the empire of the sea to Britannia and in Albert's own dressing-room and bathroom one of the marriage of Hercules and Omphale which might not appear to be altogether well chosen. There were two chairs hewn out of coal to indicate the royal interest in mining and industry and other chairs with staghorn legs, as trophies of the chase. Pictures by Winterhalter and Landseer hung thickly on the walls, and everywhere were statuettes of Highland ghillies and of dogs, and the fashionable 'porcelain views', which were favourite scenes painted under glaze on plates and teapots. Here, indeed, was richness with refinement.

It was noted by a clear-sighted observer, Mrs. Ward the artist, that the Prince was a much more tender parent than the Queen. To his eldest son he was misguidedly, even tragically harsh, but to the younger children he was fond and caressing. It was he, not their mother who held and cherished and sang to them. And it was he who planned for them a miniature Swiss chalet in the grounds of Osborne. There was a model kitchen where the little Princesses might learn to bake and cook, and with their produce regale their parents at tea; there was a carpenter's shop for the young princes. Osborne was loved, as only one other house would be – and that one indeed even more. In the late forties the Queen and Prince began visiting Scotland, staying first at Dalkeith with the Duke and Duchess of Buccleugh, falling in love with Edinburgh and with the Scottish landscape; then going north to Deeside which held the Queen's heart till the end of her life. They found the country ways they loved, the simplicity, the romance; it reminded the Prince of Thuringia. After a lease of the small Balmoral Castle they bought that estate, and, as at Osborne, began to build a new home, in true Scots baronial or pepperpot style, of gleaming granite, a complete expression of the Prince's taste and his multitudinous ideas.

'This dear Paradise . . . my dear Albert's own creation . . . his great taste and the impress of his dear hand have been stamped everywhere,' the Queen wrote of it. Lady Augusta Bruce, who came to the Queen's Household from that of the Duchess of Kent, admired it with slight reservations. The new Castle was finished and furnished in 1855. 'There are beautiful things,' Lady Augusta told her sister: 'Chandeliers of Parian; Highlanders, beautifully designed figures holding the light . . . table ornaments in the same style, and loads of curiously devised and tasteful, as well as elaborately executed articles; the only want is a certain absence of harmony of the whole – in such matters as the papering of the rooms', which, many of them displayed gold thistles on a blue background. Add to that the effects of carpets, curtains and chair-covers in tartan, Royal Stuart, hunting Stuart, dress Stuart and Balmoral, some chintzes with a pattern of thistles, and we may accept Lady Augusta's temperate comment: 'all highly characteristic and appropriate, but not equally *flatteux* to the eye'.

To the Queen's eyes it was flawless, as Albert's own creation and as the background and setting for the happiest months of every year. She liked simplicity and here, more even than at Osborne, she could enjoy it with no diminution of dignity. She was always the Queen, but she was also a woman, mistress of a house, lady of an estate. Her duties as monarch were never laid aside; ministers must come to her, bearing dispatches, and she worked diligently over her papers; but her work done, she could drive out on a picnic, visit the cottages, gossip with the people. On Sunday she went to the parish church to worship with the people in the austere Presbyterian mode she preferred, to listen to a sermon from the parish minister or from a visiting chaplain like the much-loved Dr. Norman Macleod.

'We were always in the habit of conversing with the Highlanders,' the Queen noted in her Journal, 'with whom one comes so much in contact in the Highlands' – perhaps the most brilliant glimpse of the obvious ever given.

Balmoral was truly Paradise for both Queen and Prince; for him the only one he had known, perhaps, for by this time he had weathered the storms of misunderstanding, suspicion, criticism and dislike which had beset him since his marriage. He was increasingly respected by ministers and statesmen, more and more popular with the vast middle-class. The aristocrats had not taken kindly to him, with his solemn pedantic ways, his primness, his lack of geniality, and the vulgar populace in this as in many matters agreed with their uppermost rather than with their immediate betters. But Albert had gone steadily on, however hard might be the path of duty. He had resolved to serve the Queen, not necessarily according to her desires but according to her best interests, and to serve his adopted country. Hie patience, industry and statesmanship were now fully recognized and fully exercised; he spent hours at his writing-table over state papers. The delights of outdoor life in the Highlands were exactly the relaxation he needed and enjoyed. He was at last living a full life.

It had not been so in those early days at Windsor, and still less at Buckingham Palace. The young Queen was reluctant to delegate authority; ministers were even more so, to the point, at times, of suspicion and hostility. And although Albert conceded the need for Royal dignity and splendour, the excessive ceremonial of Court was tedious. He disliked London. Windsor was better, he could ride in the Park, he could play his beloved organ by the hour; but at the end of the day there was the almost unendurable evening.

The Queen let it be known that she disapproved of the long masculine potations after dinner, enriched by bawdy talk, which had been taken for granted in Regency and Georgian society. The men must join her and her ladies in the drawing-room very soon indeed. Albert had no thirst for port, and no liking or talent for bawdiness, but he longed, with all his austere, intellectual being for good, masculine talk about public and world affairs, about books, science and philosophy. He loved academic discussions, he would have welcomed scholars to his table, men of letters and of science, to hear from them what was being thought and said, done and written in the world, and Victoria cared for none of these things. With plenty of common sense and a capacity for practical wisdom which deepened with the years, she had nothing at all of intellectual appetite or curiosity. She liked gossip, jokes of the simplest kind, personal and factual conversation. Feeling herself quickly out of her depth among the intellectual she avoided them or approved only of those who had the tact to cloak their brilliance in her company. After dinner, one indulged in small talk, one looked at albums, one enjoyed a little music. This became a pattern of domestic life throughout the century, in every grade of the middle-class, although in a great many families the intellectual zest was keener than in the royal house. Books were abundant in many of the country houses and vicarages, old books and new, with periodicals and reviews. Albert would have been very happy to read aloud to the Queen and her ladies as they sat with their netting or embroidery; but reading, like discussion, did not amuse her.

The tedium must have been almost intolerable. Music probably saved the Prince from the last agony of boredom. The Queen had a pretty voice, an ear and liking for pleasant tunes; they played and sang together. Albert composed Chorales, he spent hours at the organ. They entertained musicians; Mendelssohn came, listened, played, pleased and was pleased. Music and home-making consoled the Prince for his loss of freedom, his frustration; it would seem rather a feminine solace and way of fulfilment, but he put all his mental energy into these arts, his emotions into organ music, his dreams into stone or granite, furniture, carvings, every kind of adornment. Osborne and Balmoral were more than private Royal residences, they were the local habitation of a vision, an ideal, and they were the most exalted and splendid exposition of Victorian taste. The majority of the Queen's subjects would have shared Lady Augusta's admiration of Balmoral without the reservations; they would not have worried about the lack of harmony. The more of everything the better was a general if implicit rule of decoration: plenty of colours, of carving, of ornaments and draperies, no empty spaces or uncovered surfaces. Countless drawing-rooms and parlours in varying degrees of richness reflected Osborne and Balmoral.

The Prince truly became master, having asserted himself in the incident of the locked study door, and in one still more disciplinary. When he attended, with enjoyment, a dinner of the Royal Academy he received a note from the Queen, at half-past ten, bidding him return; this he ignored. Another, more peremptory, followed at eleven o'clock. The Prince summoning his carriage had himself driven – not to Buckingham Palace and the Queen but to Windsor where he spent the night. Having sufficiently established his authority he expressed himself in his creation of homes. He made considerable progress in shaping the Queen's character and career. If she could not sympathize with his intellectual demands, he made somewhat inadequate response to her natural gaiety, almost an exuberance of spirit.

He made the Victorian house, and in many ways he made the Victorian ethos. Albertian might almost seem the more accurate epithet. The new decorum came from him, the new high seriousness, and the new sentimentality, that very German quality was fostered by him. If, however, he subdued the Queen's gaiety he by no means banished a proper courtly splendour. There were balls and banquets, the Palace was the apex of society, the Queen appeared in state. Had he lived there would have been no gloom though there might have been dullness; a proper degree of pageantry would have been maintained.

But all the happiness, the *gemütlichkeit* and the splendour were quenched by his death, that terrible day in December 1861. The sequel is well known: the almost demented agony of the Queen, her cult of death, of the beloved memory, the morbid and pagan treasuring of visible and tangible tokens and possessions of the dead. His rooms were kept precisely as he had left them; every night his dressing-room was prepared in a ghastly remembrance, almost a recall of his living presence. His clothes were laid out, candles were lit, hot water brought in. Nothing that he had designed or placed in any of the royal homes must be removed. So it continued to her life's end. Lord Rosebery saw it when summoned to the royal presence. Albert was still master of the house.

The pattern of regality interwoven with simplicity was maintained in the houses he had created. More and more the Queen lived in one or other of those beloved homes. The Court spent a fair part of the year at Windsor, but Buckingham Palace saw as little as the Queen could contrive of her household and herself. One vivid modern memory shows us the pattern. Dame Ethel Smyth, while staying at Birkhall, which had been lent to the Empress Eugénie, was bidden to accompany her imperial hostess to Balmoral. She dined at the household table about which hung 'an air of distinguished boredom'; ate off silver and gold plate which was impressive though irritating, when knife and fork scraped on the precious metal. As the only lady guest at that table she headed the procession to the drawing-room when summoned by the

Queen, and there saw a human avenue leading up to the hearth. On the rug stood the Queen and the Empress in animated talk; nearest them, but not on the rug, stood other royalties, the highest nearest the rug, the minor farther away, declining into ladies and gentlemen in waiting, finally dwindling to mere maids of honour. The friendly and uninhibited Miss Smyth (her Damehood far in the future) advanced up the aisle, prepared to greet the Queen. At once she was aware of a stillness, an atmosphere such as might surround a dog trotting up the aisle in church. The Queen turned her head and looked, turned away in a repudiation deeper and more dreadful than any anger. Then kind Princess Christian stepped forward to shake hands and murmur a word of greeting, and somehow the shocking and shocked intruder backed away from the near Presence.

Afterwards the Queen spoke to her graciously without the faintest hint of allusion to the semi-sacrilege, and asked her to play something from her Mass. It was a stupendous performance on the piano, with orchestral effects, and the calm of the audience was also stupendous in its acceptance of this. The Queen appeared to listen with pleasure. At the end, Queen and Empress left the room together, by the special royal door. Pausing on the threshold each offered the other precedence with exquisite gestures of courtesy, then together shoulder to shoulder walked out of the room, incomparably majestic.

The Queen's son and heir, like his father, made his own private home, at Sandringham which was as Edwardian as Osborne was Victorian – or Albertian, and was neither a model nor a reflection of middle-class domesticity. When *his* son, the Duke of York, in turn married, he and his bride, Princess May of Teck, were given as country house, York Cottage on the Sandringham estate, within far too easy distance of the Big House. Alexandra Princess of Wales was a loving and possessive mother, and a jealous and interfering mother-in-law. The young Duchess of York found the house already furnished, and must have known something of the frustration of the Prince Consort more than half a century before. Like him she waited, moved and acted slowly, with her own feminine tact and gentleness. She had to face much criticism, less crude and public than that directed at him, but subtle and sometimes spiteful; like him she had both defence and weapons in the devotion of her husband. Behind him stood another defender, the old Queen herself.

From the first she had approved, admired and loved this Royal bride who was not, in the eyes of some of her critics, in the first rank of royalty, her maternal grandmother being non-royal in blood. The Queen recognized in her the qualities of enduring queenliness: honour, integrity, a sense of duty that was of her very being, respect for the throne, for tradition. She recorded her delight in the marriage in her journal and her letters; showed it by many acts of favour. When the Duke and Duchess of York stayed with her at Osborne she noted the grace and courtesy of the Duchess, her good looks, her simplicity with dignity.

Something of the old antagonism she had felt for her heir, the Prince of Wales had died beside what had so nearly been his death-bed, and she had always felt a kind, indulgent affection for the lovely Princess. But in the next generation she saw the spirit and ideals of the Prince Consort revived. The young Duke and Duchess spoke her own language, with a larger vocabulary, a new accent, a livelier tone, but it was her language, one she understood.

It was indeed a picking up of the pattern, even in the character and background of the bride. The Duchess, like the Prince Consort, had known something of life outside a royal court. Her home indeed had had at least one window open towards Bohemia, through the cheerful and incurable extravagance of her mother, the Duchess of Teck. At one period, this family had gone into an agreeable exile in Florence, in order to make retrenchments and pay off debts. This had given Princess May a knowledge and love of art, an opportunity for study, a sense of history unknown to her husband. From her father she had inherited artistic taste and interest. She was endowed with an excellent brain which found scope, later, in her management of the royal palaces; only the purely intellectual part of her mind was, most of her life, frustrated, as the Prince's had been. Like him she could have enjoyed intellectual company. She read seriously, and in one detail was more fortunate than the Prince. At the beginning of her married life she discovered that the Duke, her husband, liked reading aloud, and this was encouraged to their mutual pleasure.

As Queen Mary she renewed the royal background, maintaining

the inheritance, adding, or often unearthing new or forgotten treasures. Her achievement is beyond the scope of this chronicle, but those who remember the reign of King George and Queen Mary have known a living continuance of the Victorian tradition. The Victorian house at its grandest, at its regal height endured in the neo-Georgian years.

Bibliography

Victorian Furniture, R. W. Symonds & B. B. Whinneray, (Country Life).

The Englishman's Castle, John Gloag, (Eyre & Spottiswoode).

Hints on Household Taste, Charles L. Eastlake, (Longmans).

Decoration and Furniture of Town Houses, Robert Edis, (Kegan Paul).

The Complete Servant, Samuel and Sarah Adams, (Knight & Lacey).

What the Butler Saw, E. S. Turner, (Michael Joseph).

The Book of Household Management, Mrs. Isabella Beeton, (Ward Lock).

Records of a Later Life, Fanny Kemble, (Bentley).

The Letters of the Hon. Mrs. Edward Twistleton, Written to her Family, 1852-62, John Murray.

Hospitable England in the 1870's, Richard Henry Dana, (John Murray).

The Diary of an Oxford Lady, Edited by Margaret Jeune Clifford, (Basil Blackwell).

With Dearest Love to All, Life & Letters of Lady Jebb, Edited by Mary Reed Bobbitt, (Faber).

Period Piece, Gwen Raverat, (Faber).

Gathering Up the Threads, Florence Keynes, (Cambridge, Heffer).

What I Remember, Mary Paley Marshall, (Cambridge University Press).

Recollections and Impressions, E. M. Sellar, (Blackwood).

Early Reminiscences, and *Later Reminiscences*, Mrs. (Janet) Story, (Maclehose).

Notes on a Cellar Book, George Saintsbury, (Macmillan).

An Unfinished Autobiography, H. A. L. Fisher, (Oxford University Press).

Life and Letters of Mandell Creighton, By His Wife [Louise Creighton], (Longmans).

Life of Charlotte Brontë, Mrs. Gaskell, (John Murray).

Mrs. Gatty and Mrs. Ewing, Christabel Maxwell, (Constable).

A Hundred Wonderful Years, Mrs. (Dorothy) Peel, (John Lane).

Looking Forward, Harold Anson, (Heinemann).

Glimpses of the Past, Elizabeth Wordsworth, (Mowbray).

Edward White Benson, A. C. Benson, (Macmillan).

Our Family Affairs, E. F. Benson, (Cassell).

Home For the Holidays, Winifred Peck, (Faber).

Bibliography

Vicarage in the Slums, Cannon Barnett, By His Wife, [Dame Henrietta Barnett], (John Murray).

Randall Davidson, G. K. A. Bell, (Oxford University Press).

History of the Working Classes in Scotland, Thomas Johnston, (Forward Publishing Co., Glasgow).

From Pit to Parliament, Keir Hardie, David Lowe, (Glasgow Labour Publishing Co.).

Not I But the Wind, Frieda Lawrence, (Heinemann).

Life and Works of D. H. Lawrence, Henry T. Moore, (Allen & Unwin).

Memoir of Dr. Norman Macleod, D.D., Donald Macleod, (Isbister).

The Bettesworth Book, George Bourne, (Duckworth).

The Furrow Behind Me, Angus McLellan. Translated from the Gaelic by John Lorne Campbell, (Routledge & Kegan Paul).

The Age of the Chartists, J. L. & Barbara Hammond, (Longmans).

Miss Clare Remembers, 'Miss Read', (Michael Joseph).

A London Family, 1870–1900, M. Vivian Hughes, (Oxford University Press).

Drawn From Memory, Drawn From Life, Ernest Shepard, (Methuen).

Over the Bridge, Richard Church, (Heinemann).

Memorials of Edward Burne-Jones, G. B. J. [Lady Burne-Jones], (Macmillan).

Life of William Morris, J. W. Mackail, (Longmans).

Three Houses, Angela Thirkell, (Oxford University Press).

Jane Welsh Carlyle, Letters to Her Family, ed. Leonard Huxley, (John Murray).

Jane Welsh Carlyle's Letters, ed. Trudy Bliss, (Gollancz).

Alice Meynell, Viola Meynell, (Cape).

Far Off Things, Things Near and Far, Arthur Machen, (Secker).

Memoir of James Robert Hope-Scott, Robert Ornsby, (John Murray).

The Wilfred Wards and the Transition, Maisie Ward, (Sheed & Ward).

Queen Victoria, E. F. Benson, (Longmans).

Letters of Queen Victoria, ed. Buckle, (John Murray).

Leaves From the Journal of Our Life in the Highlands, Queen Victoria.

Letters of Lady Augusta Stanley, 1849–63, ed. The Dean of Windsor and Hector Bolitho, (Gerald Howe).

Streaks of Life, Ethel Smyth, (Longmans).

Index

Index